ULTIMATE
IRON MAN II

ULTIMATE IRON MAN II. Contains material originally published in magazine form as ULTIMATE IRON MAN II #1-5. First printing 2008. ISBN# 978-0-7851-2995-0. Published by MARVEL PUBLISHING, INC., a subsidiary of MARVEL ENTERTAINMENT, INC. OFFICE OF PUBLICATION: 417 5th Avenue, New York, NY 10016. Copyright © 2007 and 2008 Marvel Characters, Inc. All rights reserved. $19.99 per copy in the U.S. and $21.00 in Canada (GST #R127032852); Canadian Agreement #40668537. All characters featured in this issue and the distinctive names and likenesses thereof, and all related indicia are trademarks of Marvel Characters, Inc. No similarity between any of the names, characters, persons, and/or institutions in this magazine with those of any living or dead person or institution is intended, and any such similarity which may exist is purely coincidental. **Printed in the U.S.A.** ALAN FINE, CEO Marvel Toys & Publishing Divisions and CMO Marvel Entertainment, Inc.; DAVID GABRIEL, SVP of Publishing Sales & Circulation; DAVID BOGART, SVP of Business Affairs & Talent Management; MICHAEL PASCIULLO, VP of Merchandising & Communications; JIM O'KEEFE, VP of Operations & Logistics; DAN CARR, Executive Director of Publishing Technology; JUSTIN F. GABRIE, Director of Editorial Operations; SUSAN CRESPI, Editorial Operations Manager; OMAR OTIEKU, Production Manager; STAN LEE, Chairman Emeritus. For information regarding advertising in Marvel Comics or on Marvel.com, please contact Mitch Dane, Advertising Director, at mdane@marvel.com. For Marvel subscription inquiries, please call 800-217-9158.

10 9 8 7 6 5 4 3 2 1

ULTIMATE IRON MAN II

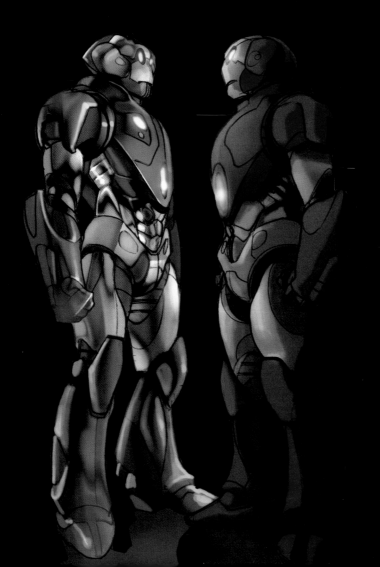

Writer
ORSON SCOTT CARD

Artist
PASQUAL FERRY
with Leonardo Manco (Issue #5, pages 10-23)

Colorist
Dean White with Laura Martin, Dave McCaig,
Paul Mounts & Larry Molinar

Letterer
Virtual Calligraphy's Cory Petit

Assistant Editor
Lauren Sankovitch

Editor
Bill Rosemann

Senior Editor
Ralph Macchio

Special Thanks to Nick Lowe

Collection Editor Cory Levine • Editorial Assistant Alex Starbuck • Assistant Editor John Denning •
Editors, Special Projects Jennifer Grünwald & Mark D. Beazley • Senior Editor, Special Projects Jeff Youngquist •
Senior Vice President of Sales David Gabriel • Production Jerry Kalinowski •
Book Designer Spring Hoteling

PREVIOUSLY IN ULTIMATE IRON MAN...

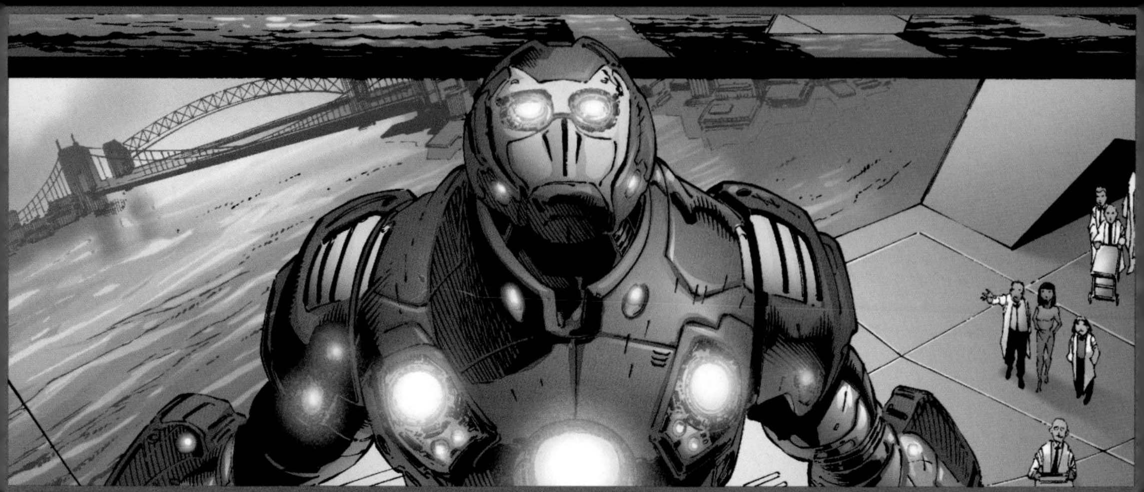

Tony Stark wasn't a normal boy. His mother, Maria, was a geneticist working on a regeneration process through which a virus turns every body cell into a neural cell capable of new growth. The problem with the process is that each cell becomes hypersensitive, causing the infected person great pain. Maria accidentally infected herself and Tony (who was in her womb at the time) with the virus. The pain caused Maria's death during Tony's birth. Tony's father, Howard, developed a revolutionary nanotech armor that saved Tony from this pain. The armor is a thin layer on the wearer's skin that absorbs shock and eats any metal that comes into contact with it.

Zebediah Stane, Howard Stark's main competitor in the world of defense technology, stole Howard's company and first wife, Loni, but couldn't get what he wanted most — the nanotech armor technology. So he started playing dirty. He kidnapped Tony and tortured him to get information on the armor. Zebediah was caught, sent to prison and his company went to Loni and their son — Obadiah. The fate of his father and his mother's instability led Obadiah to serious sociopathic behavior. Obadiah became a student at the Baxter Building, a U.S. government-run think tank, along with Tony's best friends, James Rhodes (aka "Rhodey") and Nifara.

When Tony and Howard paid a recent visit to the Baxter Building, they noticed Obadiah taking a loose hair off of Howard's jacket. As Tony tested his new prototype suit for his father, Zebediah was kidnapped from prison and killed by persons claiming to be hired by Howard Stark. Later, at a benefit gala, Howard discovered that Stane had been murdered and DNA evidence at the scene pointed to himself as the prime suspect! After taking the reins of Stark Enterprises in the wake of his father's incarceration, Tony encountered his own set of troubles: his increasing taste for alcohol and a ferry full of explosives barreling headlong into the Stark building! Tony leapt into action inside the prototype armor — saving the building, but getting caught in the explosion.

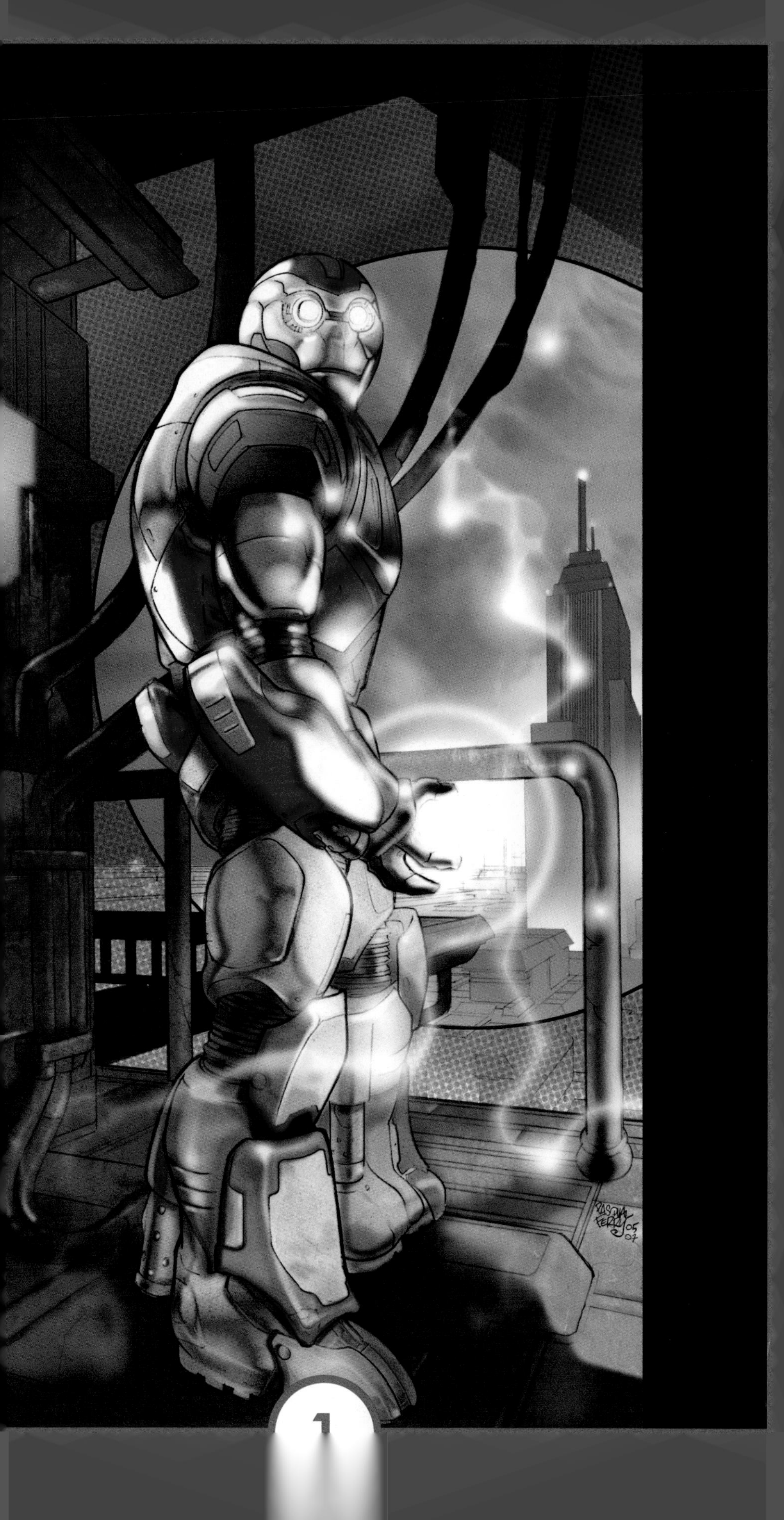

1

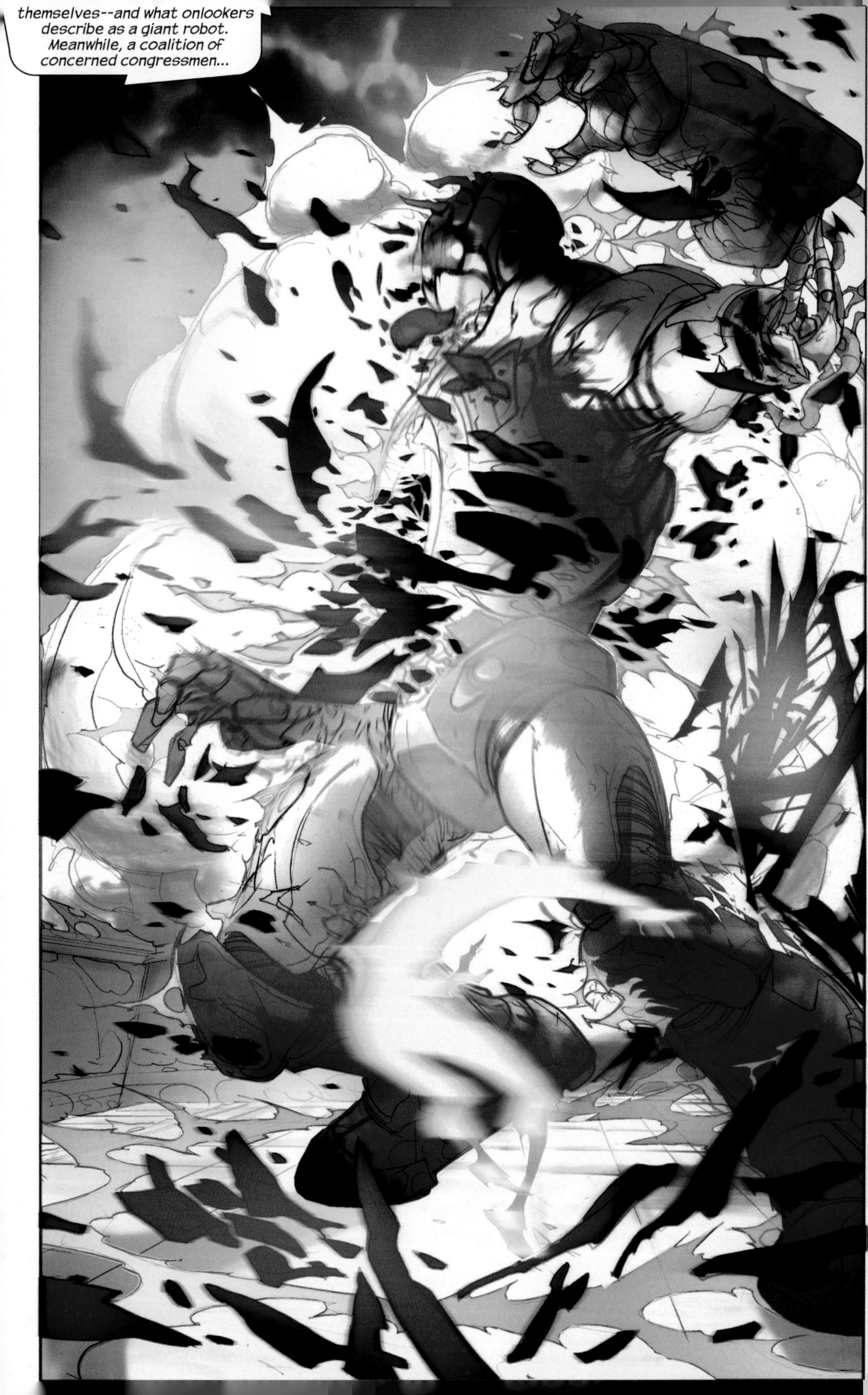
themselves--and what onlookers describe as a giant robot. Meanwhile, a coalition of concerned congressmen...

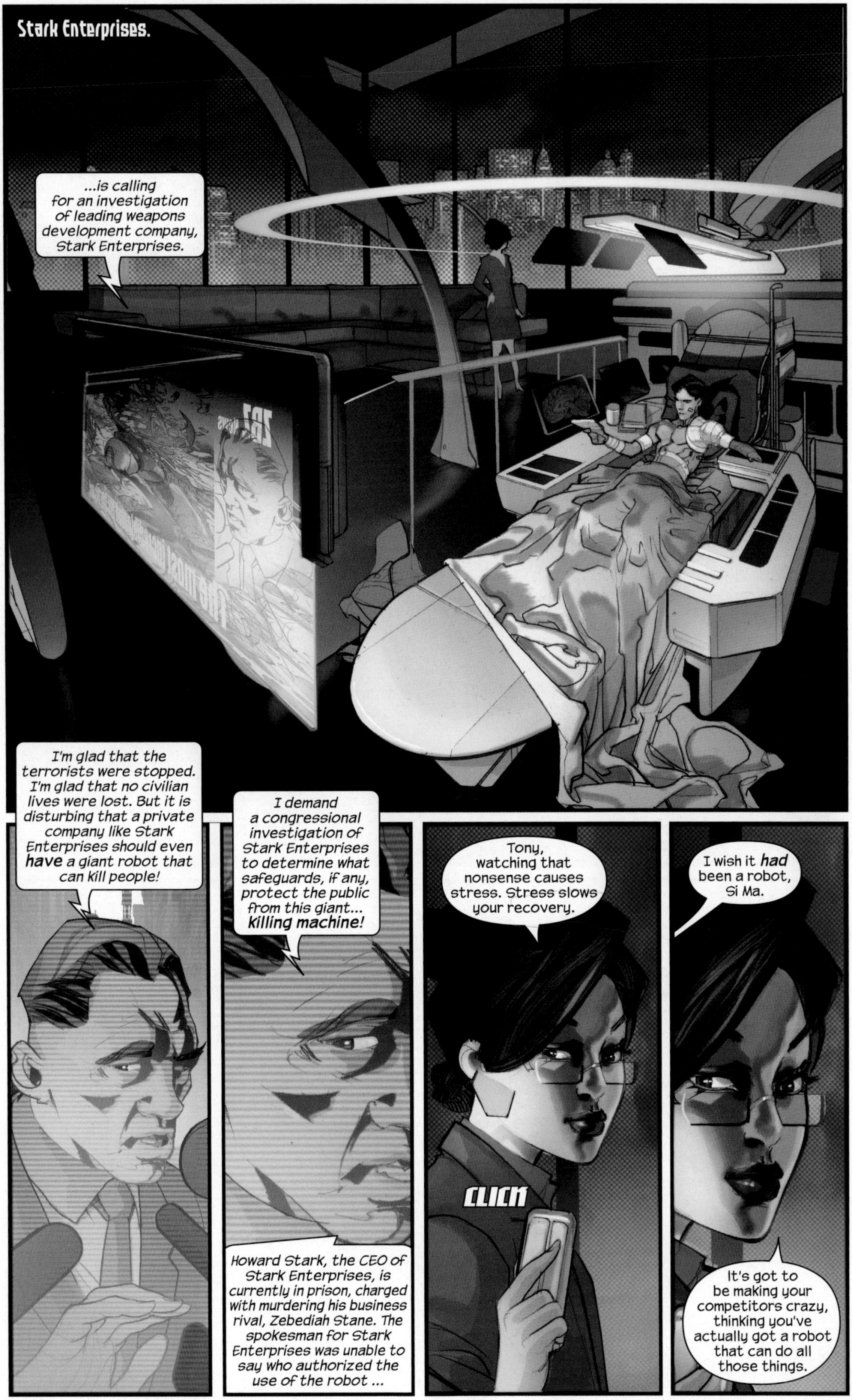
Stark Enterprises.
...is calling for an investigation of leading weapons development company, Stark Enterprises.
I'm glad that the terrorists were stopped. I'm glad that no civilian lives were lost. But it is disturbing that a private company like Stark Enterprises should even **have** a giant robot that can kill people!
I demand a congressional investigation of Stark Enterprises to determine what safeguards, if any, protect the public from this giant... **killing machine!**
Howard Stark, the CEO of Stark Enterprises, is currently in prison, charged with murdering his business rival, Zebediah Stane. The spokesman for Stark Enterprises was unable to say who authorized the use of the robot ...
Tony, watching that nonsense causes stress. Stress slows your recovery.
CLICK
I wish it *had* been a robot, Si Ma.
It's got to be making your competitors crazy, thinking you've actually got a robot that can do all those things.

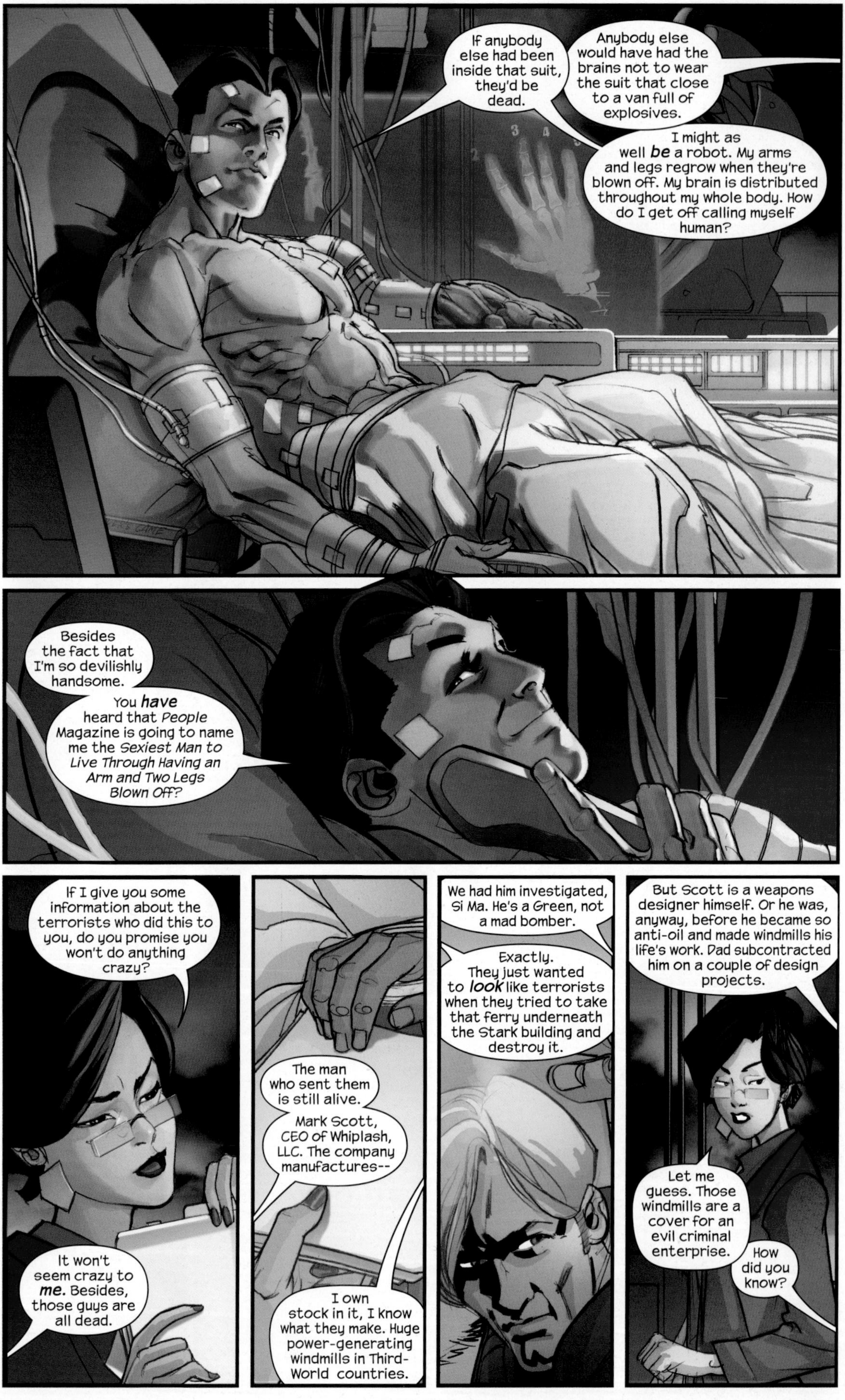

If anybody else had been inside that suit, they'd be dead.
Anybody else would have had the brains not to wear the suit that close to a van full of explosives.
I might as well *be* a robot. My arms and legs regrow when they're blown off. My brain is distributed throughout my whole body. How do I get off calling myself human?
Besides the fact that I'm so devilishly handsome.
You *have* heard that *People* Magazine is going to name me the *Sexiest Man to Live Through Having an Arm and Two Legs Blown Off?*
If I give you some information about the terrorists who did this to you, do you promise you won't do anything crazy?
It won't seem crazy to *me.* Besides, those guys are all dead.
The man who sent them is still alive.
Mark Scott, CEO of Whiplash, LLC. The company manufactures--
I own stock in it, I know what they make. Huge power-generating windmills in Third-World countries.
We had him investigated, Si Ma. He's a Green, not a mad bomber.
Exactly. They just wanted to *look* like terrorists when they tried to take that ferry underneath the Stark building and destroy it.
But Scott is a weapons designer himself. Or he was, anyway, before he became so anti-oil and made windmills his life's work. Dad subcontracted him on a couple of design projects.
Let me guess. Those windmills are a cover for an evil criminal enterprise.
How did you know?

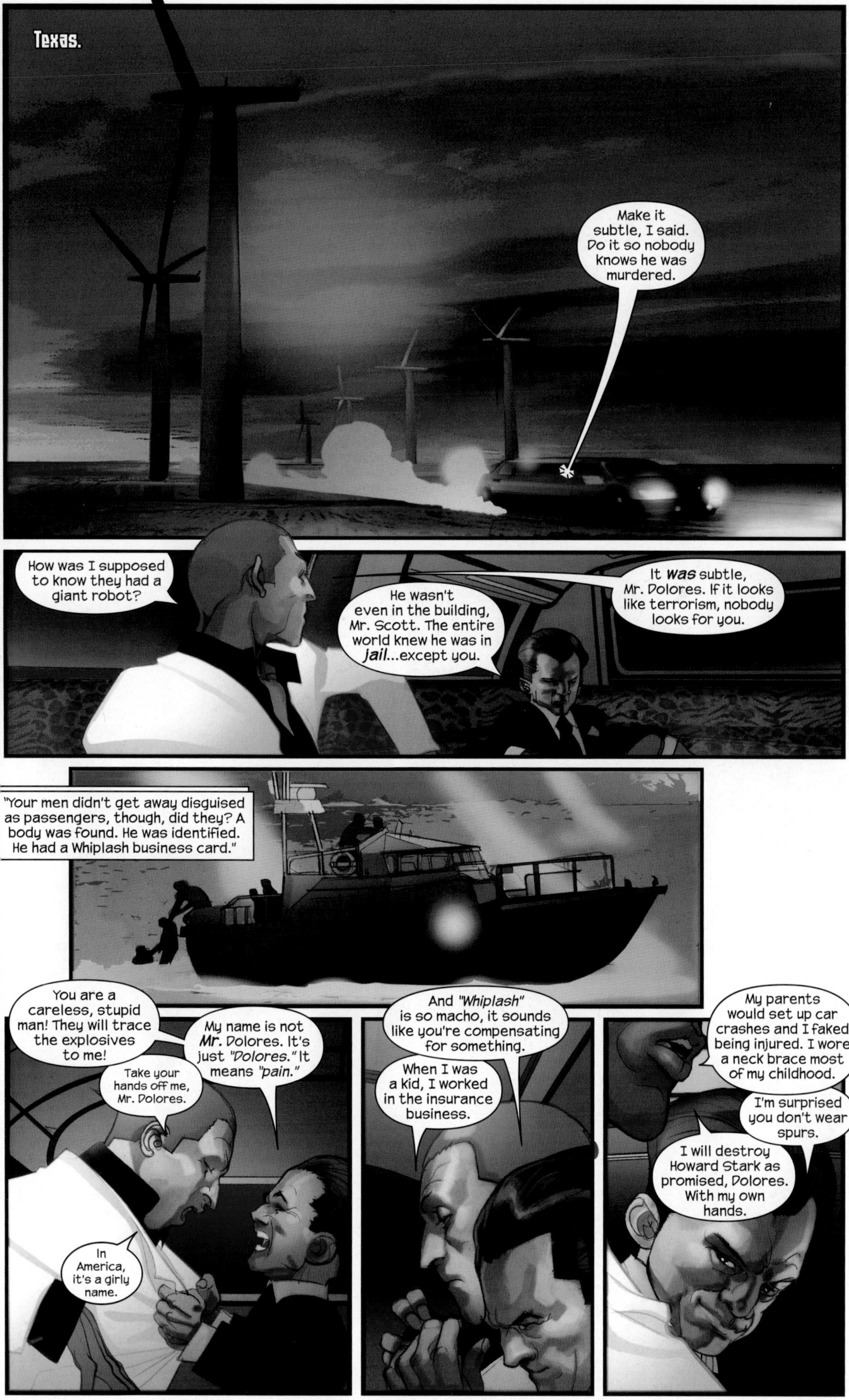
Texas.
Make it subtle, I said. Do it so nobody knows he was murdered.
How was I supposed to know they had a giant robot?
He wasn't even in the building, Mr. Scott. The entire world knew he was in jail...except you.
It was subtle, Mr. Dolores. If it looks like terrorism, nobody looks for you.
"Your men didn't get away disguised as passengers, though, did they? A body was found. He was identified. He had a Whiplash business card."
You are a careless, stupid man! They will trace the explosives to me!
My name is not Mr. Dolores. It's just "Dolores." It means "pain."
Take your hands off me, Mr. Dolores.
In America, it's a girly name.
And "Whiplash" is so macho, it sounds like you're compensating for something.
When I was a kid, I worked in the insurance business.
My parents would set up car crashes and I faked being injured. I wore a neck brace most of my childhood.
I'm surprised you don't wear spurs.
I will destroy Howard Stark as promised, Dolores. With my own hands.

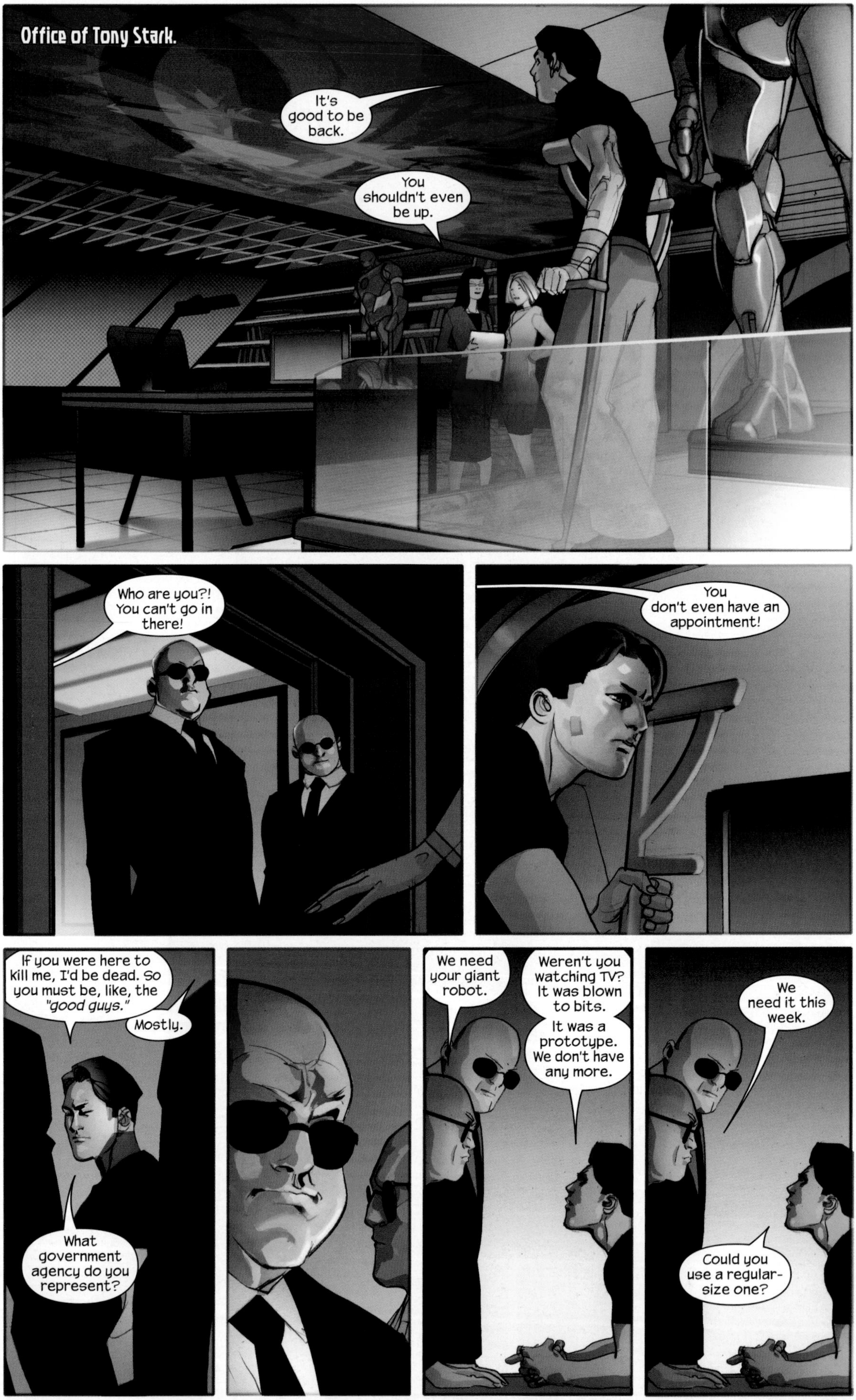

Office of Tony Stark.
It's good to be back.
You shouldn't even be up.
Who are you?! You can't go in there!
You don't even have an appointment!
If you were here to kill me, I'd be dead. So you must be, like, the *"good guys."*
Mostly.
What government agency do you represent?
We need your giant robot.
Weren't you watching TV? It was blown to bits.
It was a prototype. We don't have any more.
We need it this week.
Could you use a regular-size one?

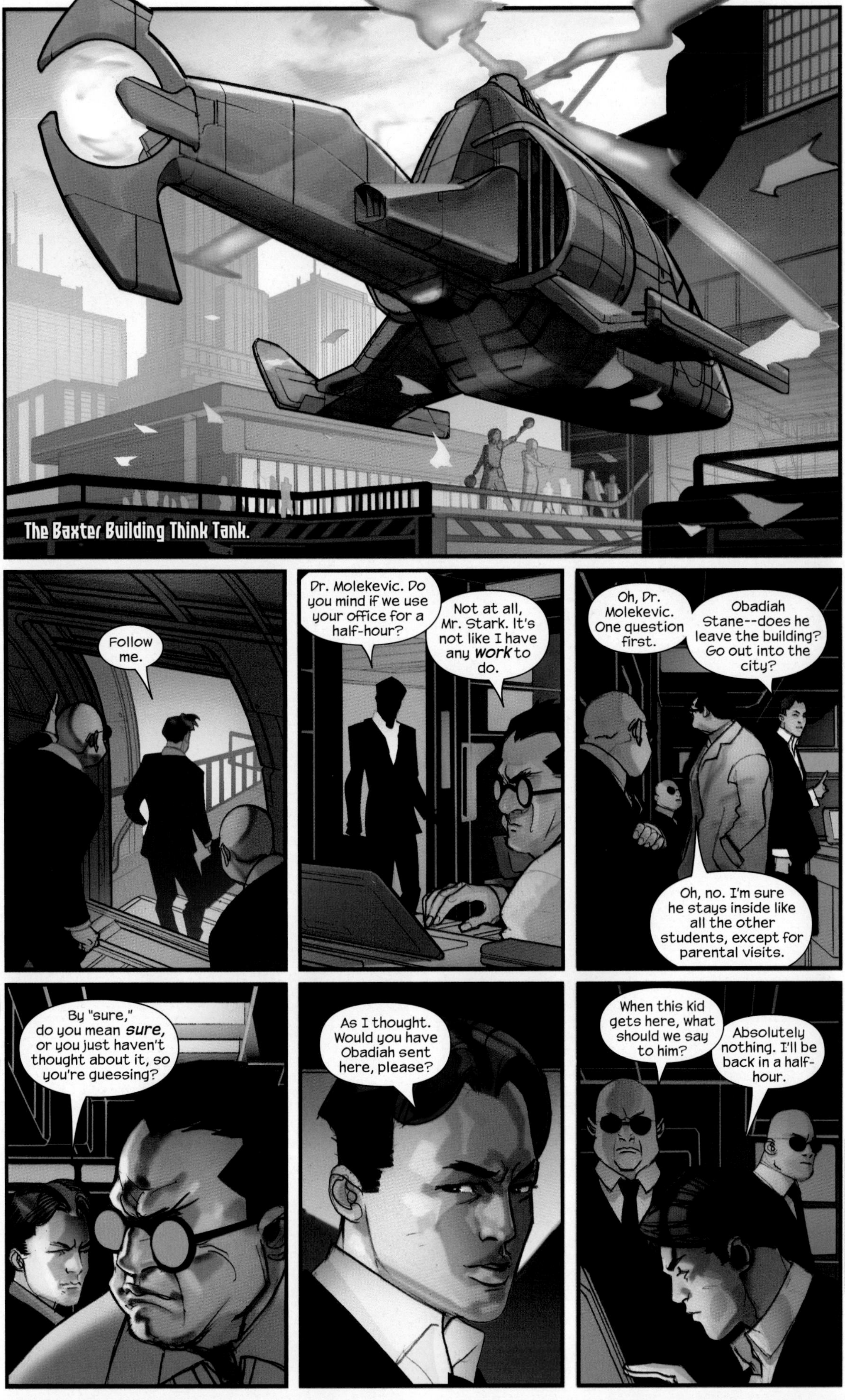
The Baxter Building Think Tank.
Follow me.
Dr. Molekevic. Do you mind if we use your office for a half-hour?
Not at all, Mr. Stark. It's not like I have any work to do.
Oh, Dr. Molekevic. One question first.
Obadiah Stane--does he leave the building? Go out into the city?
Oh, no. I'm sure he stays inside like all the other students, except for parental visits.
By "sure," do you mean sure, or you just haven't thought about it, so you're guessing?
As I thought. Would you have Obadiah sent here, please?
When this kid gets here, what should we say to him?
Absolutely nothing. I'll be back in a half-hour.

Okay, Rhodey, what have you got?

I think you'll like this.

Oh, Nifara, you're so strong.

But it's not just strength. Let's show him the blades.

Hi. Dr. Molekevic said somebody wanted to see me?

Is that a gun in your armpit or did you forget to take out the deodorant when you were done with it?

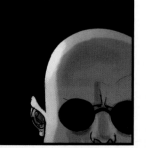

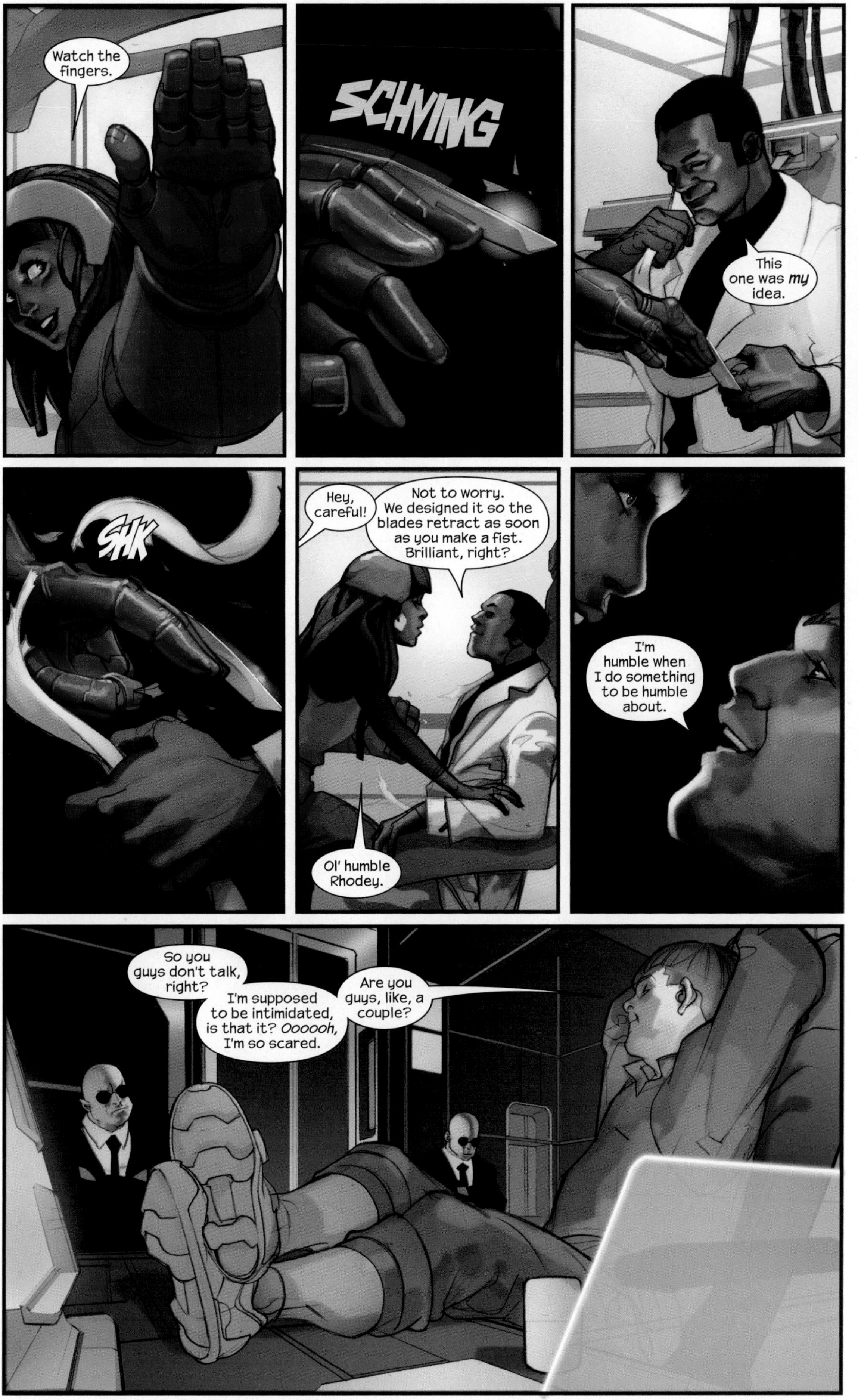

Watch the fingers.
SCHVING
This one was *my* idea.
SHK
Hey, careful!
Not to worry. We designed it so the blades retract as soon as you make a fist. Brilliant, right?
Ol' humble Rhodey.
I'm humble when I do something to be humble about.
So you guys don't talk, right?
I'm supposed to be intimidated, is that it? *Oooooh,* I'm so scared.
Are you guys, like, a couple?

The kid left.

If you were trying to frighten him, I don't think it worked.

Did he talk constantly? Make bad jokes? Try to offend you?

Yes.

That means he was scared out of his mind.

I'm not sending the prototype of the small robot unless I know where it's going and what you expect it to do.

That's classified, Mr. Stark. If we told you--

You'd have to buy me lunch?

It's a prototype. I have to program it for the mission.

All it has to do is kill anything that moves.

Starting when? The moment I turn it over to you? That could be hard on your transport team.

We need your robot to wipe out a terrorist training camp.

In a country we're not currently at war with.

Sit down. We'll show you the maps and pictures.

And we're *not* buying you lunch.

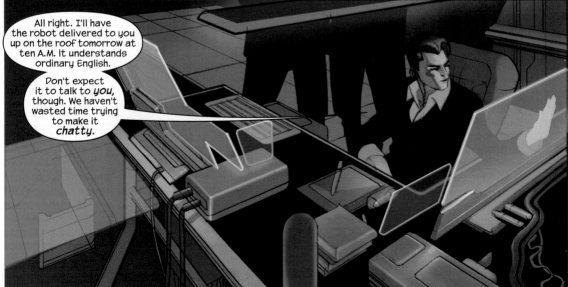

All right. I'll have the robot delivered to you up on the roof tomorrow at ten A.M. It understands ordinary English.

Don't expect it to talk to *you*, though. We haven't wasted time trying to make it *chatty*.

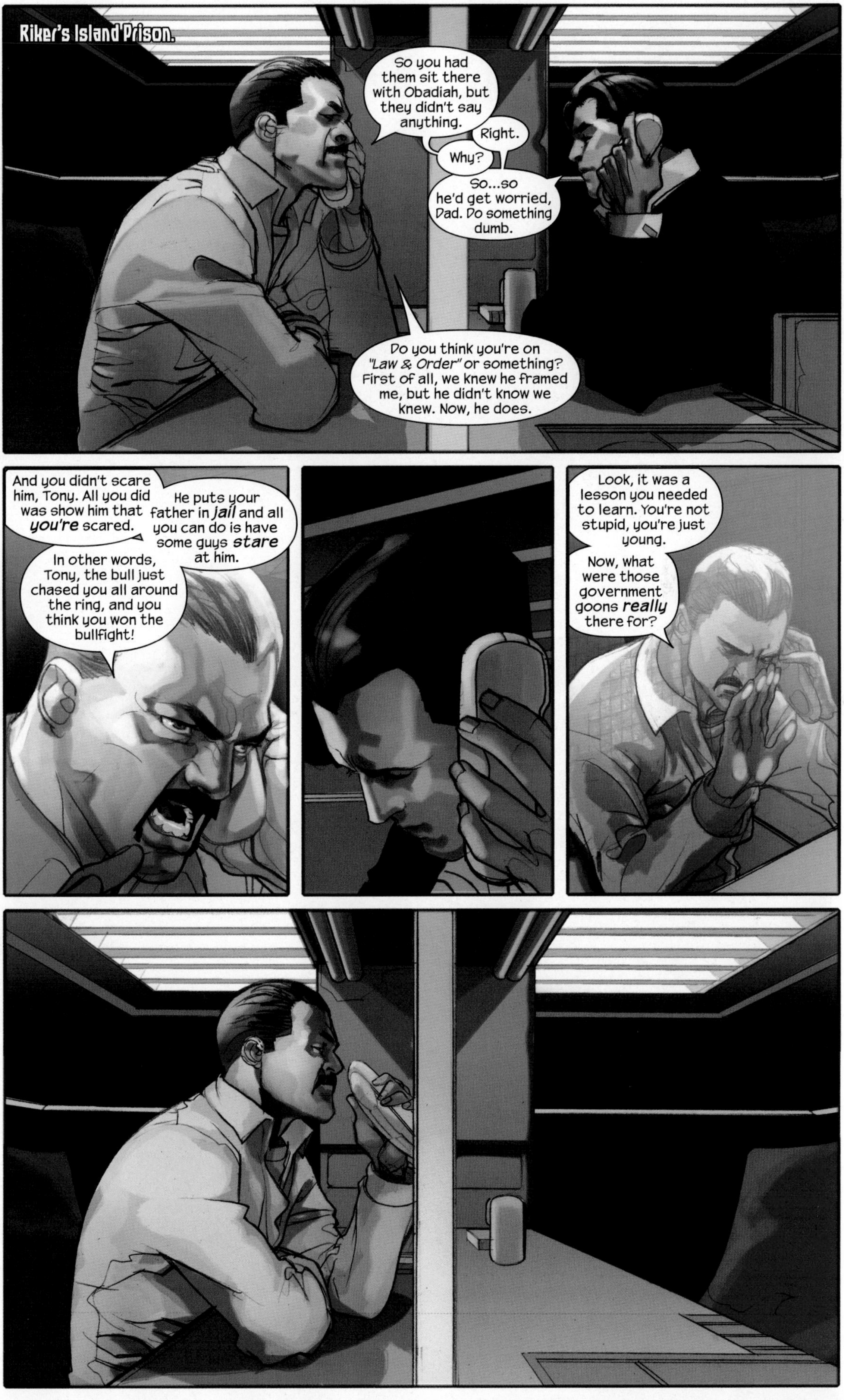
Riker's Island Prison.
So you had them sit there with Obadiah, but they didn't say anything.
Right.
Why?
So...so he'd get worried, Dad. Do something dumb.
Do you think you're on "Law & Order" or something? First of all, we knew he framed me, but he didn't know we knew. Now, he does.
And you didn't scare him, Tony. All you did was show him that *you're* scared.
He puts your father in *jail* and all you can do is have some guys *stare* at him.
In other words, Tony, the bull just chased you all around the ring, and you think you won the bullfight!
Look, it was a lesson you needed to learn. You're not stupid, you're just young.
Now, what were those government goons *really* there for?

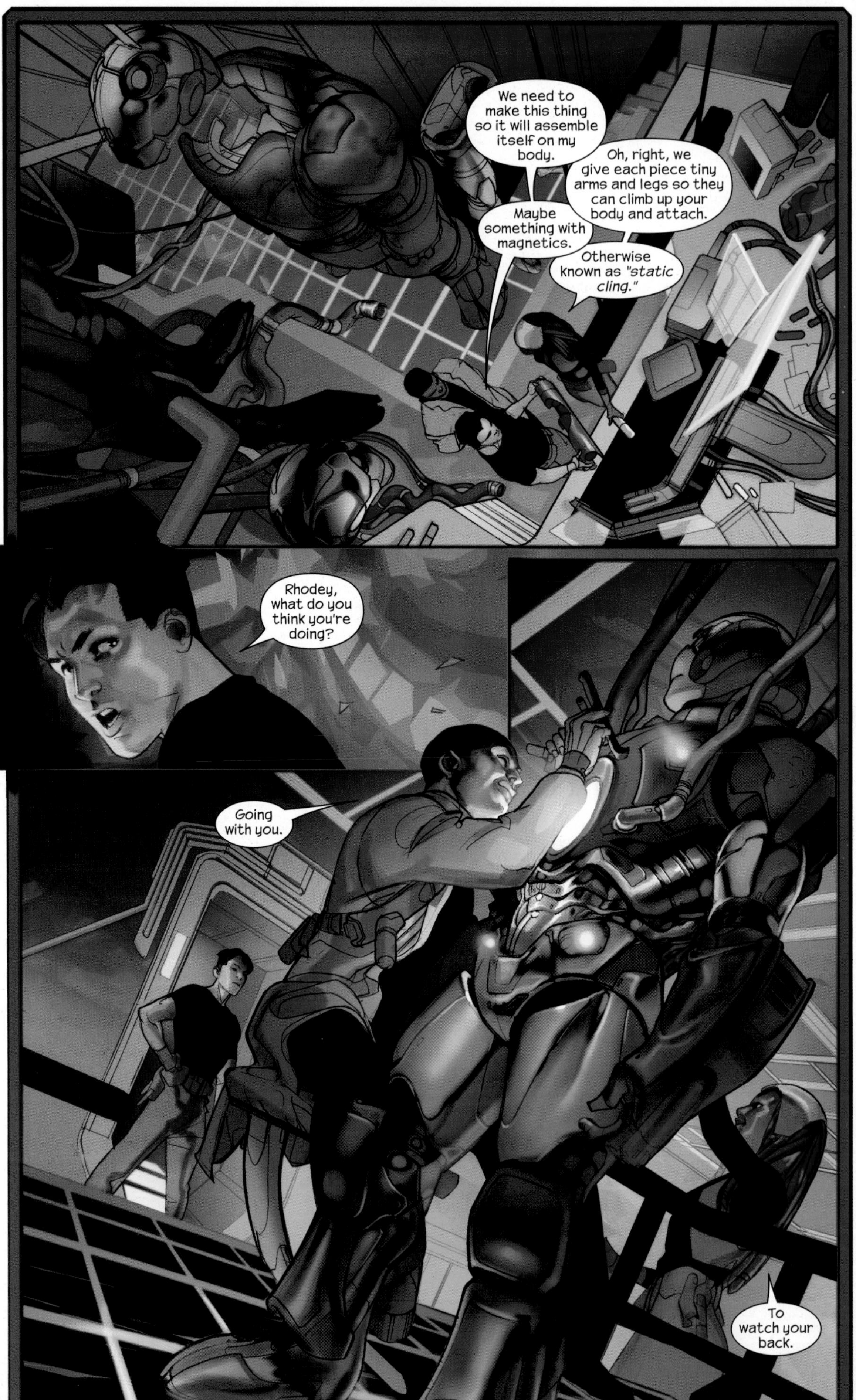
We need to make this thing so it will assemble itself on my body.
Maybe something with magnetics.
Oh, right, we give each piece tiny arms and legs so they can climb up your body and attach.
Otherwise known as "static cling."
Rhodey, what do you think you're doing?
Going with you.
To watch your back.

These suits are still prototypes. If something goes wrong, I can live through it. *YOU* can't.

Besides, they think it's a robot.

So...what makes you think they plan to bring this *"robot"* back again?

They just tell you that it unfortunately got destroyed. So sorry.

Except they can't take them apart to figure out how they work, because there'll be a really irritable guy inside.

What really worries me is this mission they're sending us on. Just go somewhere and start killing people. That doesn't sit right with me.

Everybody at that camp is either a suicide bomber or someone who trains suicide bombers.

Once they leave the camp and melt into the population, it's a thousand times harder to find them.

We're going to the factory where they manufacture suicide bombers and **stopping** them from "going somewhere and killing people."

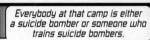

So we're, like, a way-more-accurate cruise missile.

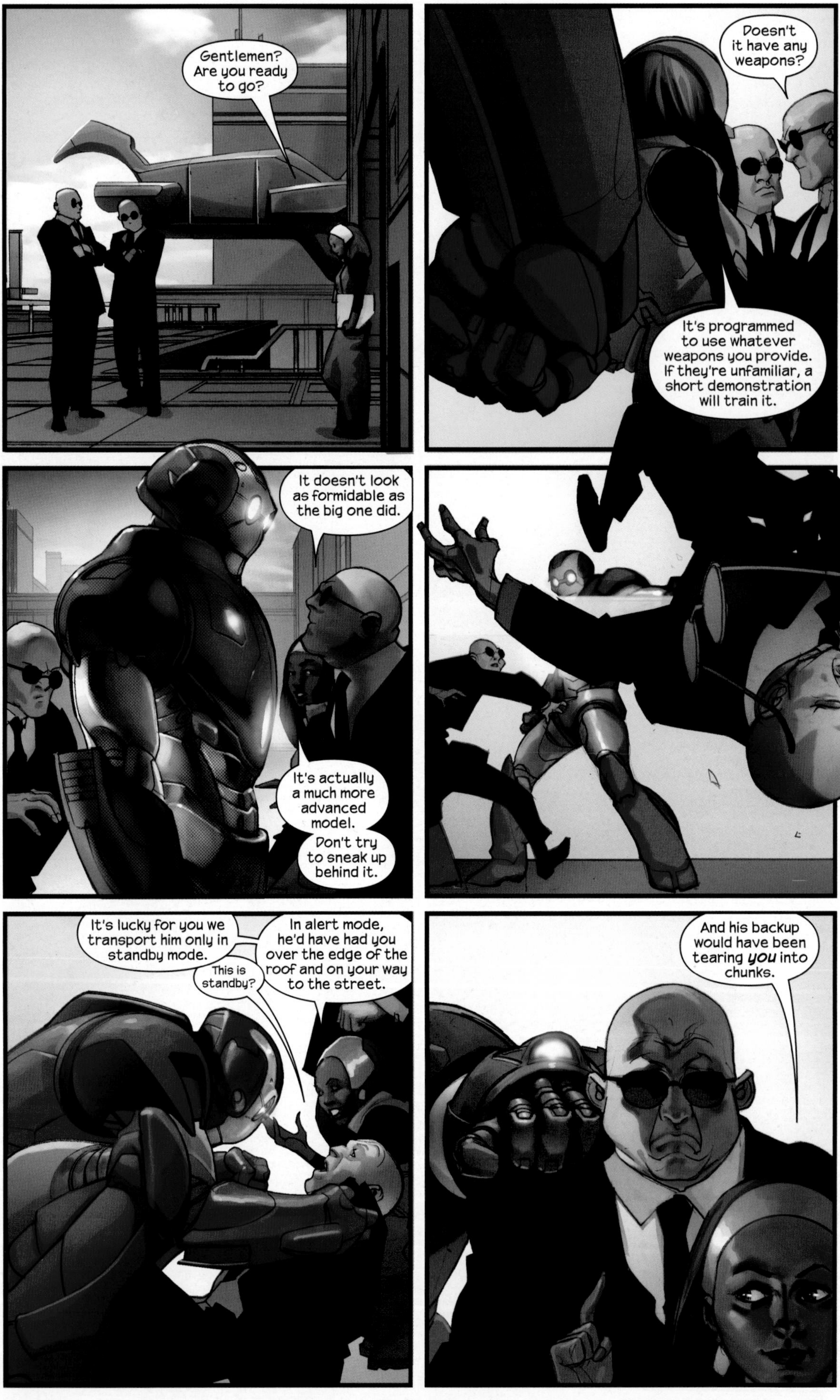
Gentlemen? Are you ready to go?
Doesn't it have any weapons?
It's programmed to use whatever weapons you provide. If they're unfamiliar, a short demonstration will train it.
It doesn't look as formidable as the big one did.
It's actually a much more advanced model.
Don't try to sneak up behind it.
It's lucky for you we transport him only in standby mode.
In alert mode, he'd have had you over the edge of the roof and on your way to the street.
This is standby?
And his backup would have been tearing *you* into chunks.

We want **one** robot.

Either two or zero. Your choice.

Unless you think you can **make** one of them get on the chopper and leave the other one behind.

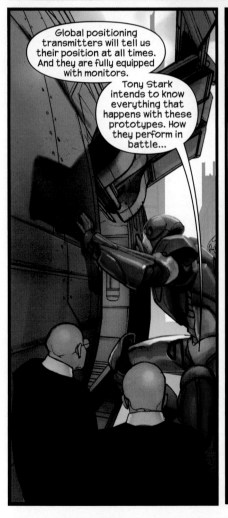

Global positioning transmitters will tell us their position at all times. And they are fully equipped with monitors.

Tony Stark intends to know everything that happens with these prototypes. How they perform in battle...

...and everything **you** do with them.

If you try to disassemble either of them, they **will** kill you. And if you don't bring them out safely, we'll send in our own team to do it. Are we clear on that?

How old are you? Aren't you still in high school?

We made the robots. You didn't.

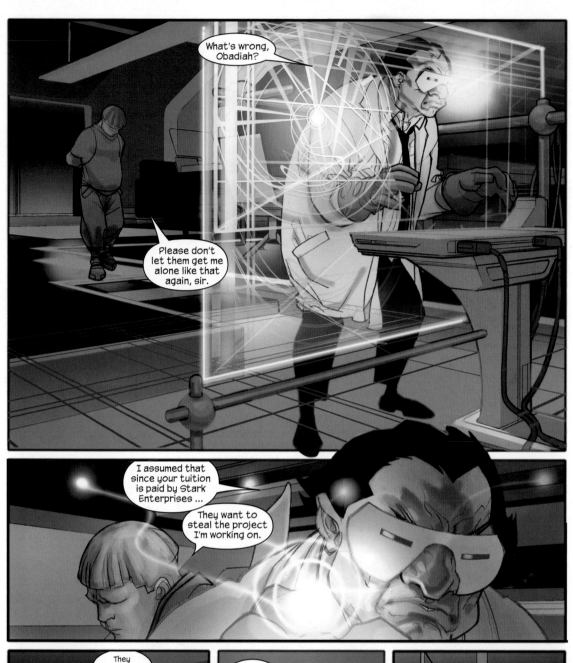

What's wrong, Obadiah?

Please don't let them get me alone like that again, sir.

I assumed that since your tuition is paid by Stark Enterprises ...

They want to steal the project I'm working on.

They hurt me. I'm scared.

I will speak to Mr. Stark at once about this.

No, no, I beg you, don't!

They said they'd do to me... what they did to my father.

I'll make sure no one ever bothers you in your work, Obadiah.

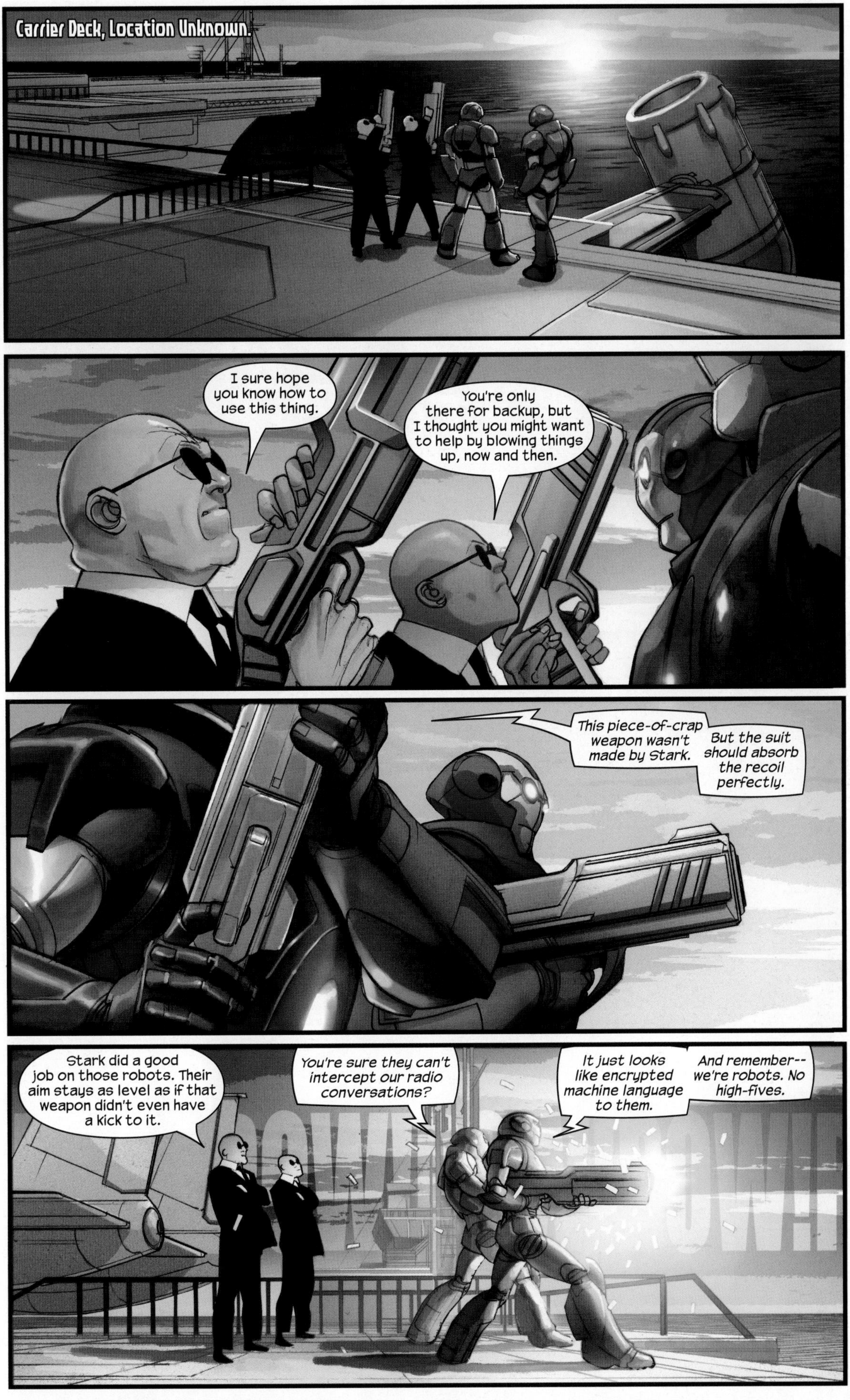
Carrier Deck, Location Unknown.
I sure hope you know how to use this thing.
You're only there for backup, but I thought you might want to help by blowing things up, now and then.
This piece-of-crap weapon wasn't made by Stark.
But the suit should absorb the recoil perfectly.
Stark did a good job on those robots. Their aim stays as level as if that weapon didn't even have a kick to it.
You're sure they can't intercept our radio conversations?
It just looks like encrypted machine language to them.
And remember-- we're robots. No high-fives.

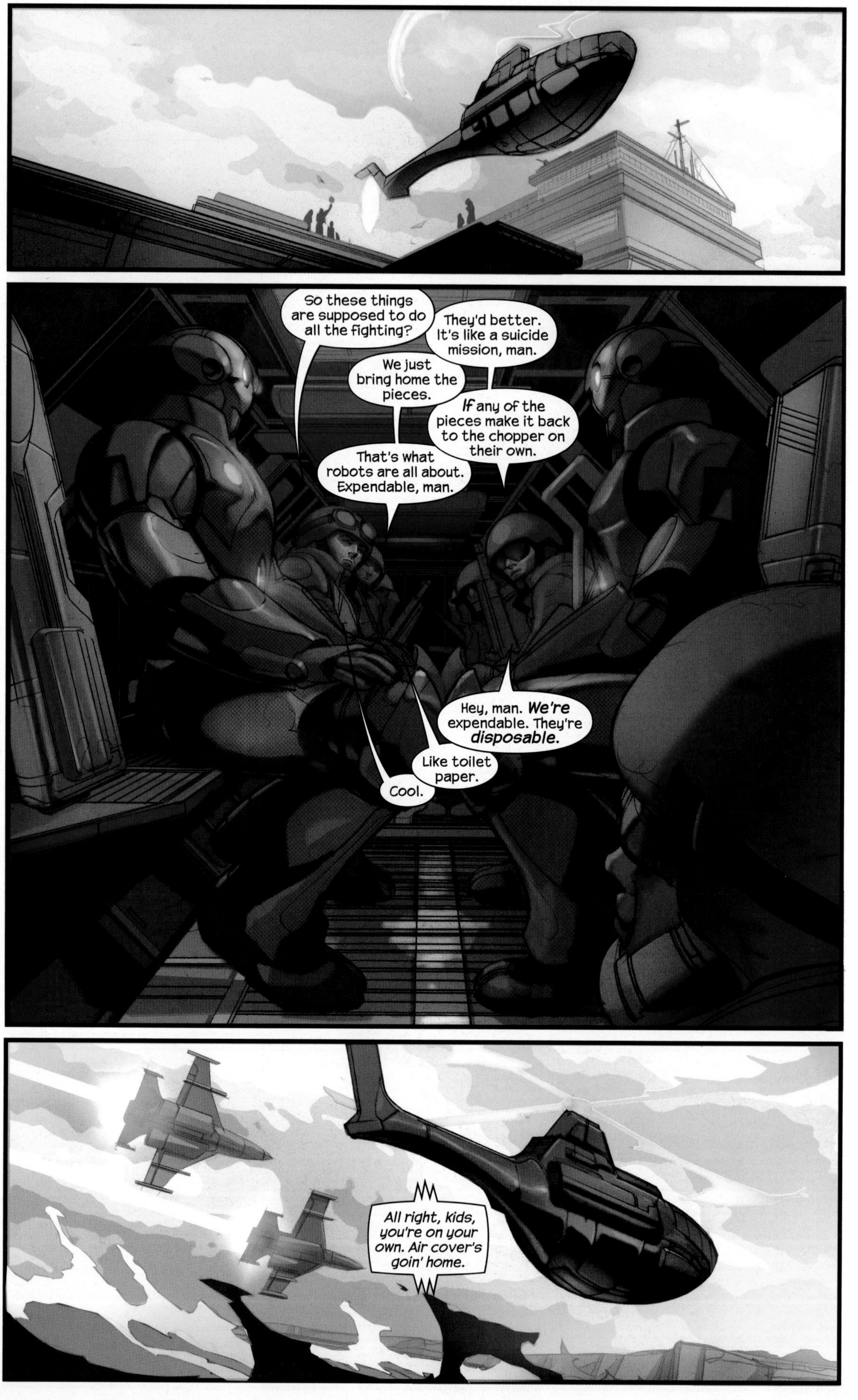
So these things are supposed to do all the fighting?
They'd better. It's like a suicide mission, man.
We just bring home the pieces.
If any of the pieces make it back to the chopper on their own.
That's what robots are all about. Expendable, man.
Hey, man. We're expendable. They're disposable.
Like toilet paper.
Cool.
All right, kids, you're on your own. Air cover's goin' home.

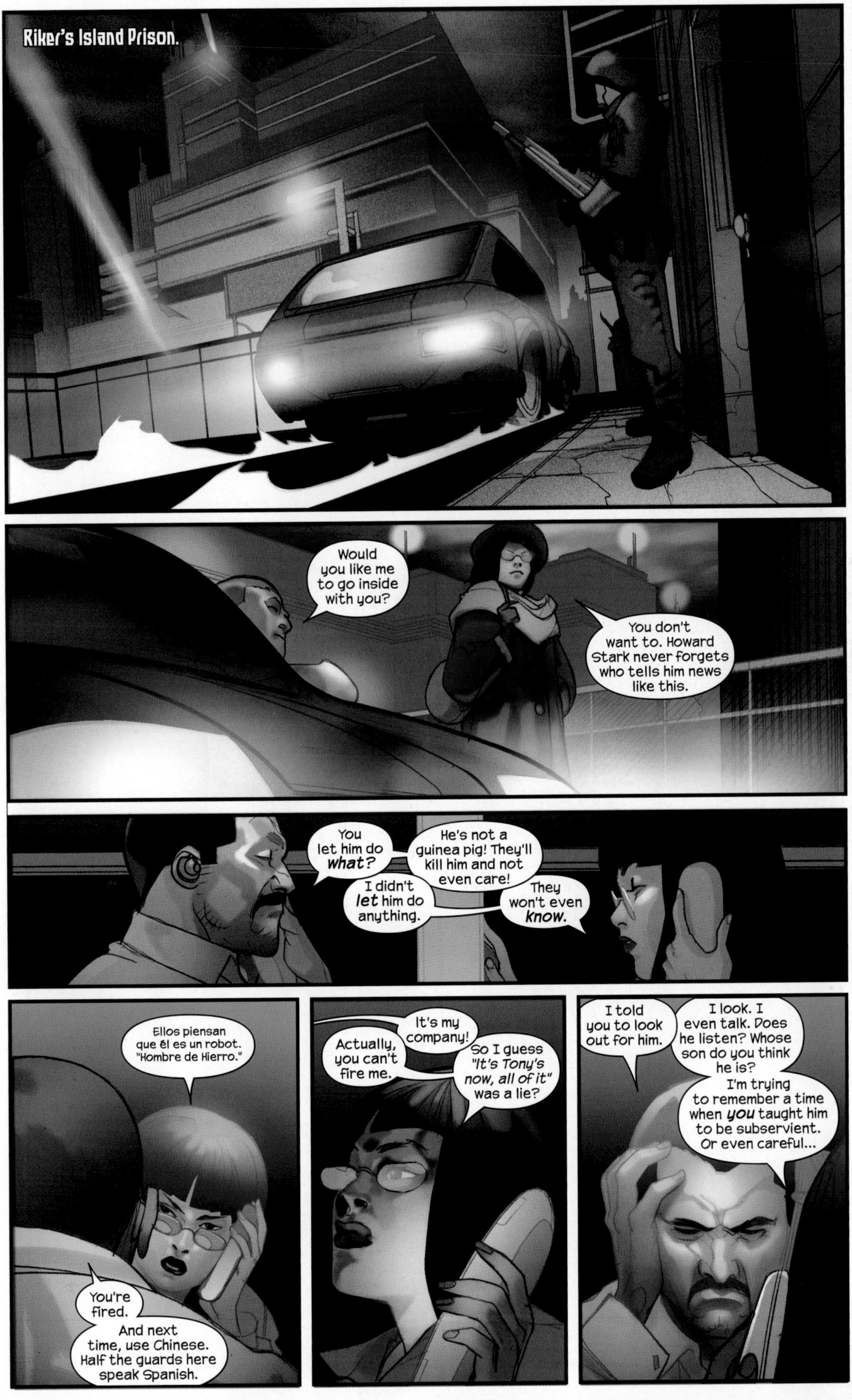

Riker's Island Prison.
Would you like me to go inside with you?
You don't want to. Howard Stark never forgets who tells him news like this.
You let him do *what?*
I didn't *let* him do anything.
He's not a guinea pig! They'll kill him and not even care!
They won't even *know.*
Ellos piensan que él es un robot. "Hombre de Hierro."
You're fired.
And next time, use Chinese. Half the guards here speak Spanish.
It's my company!
Actually, you can't fire me.
So I guess *"It's Tony's now, all of it"* was a lie?
I told you to look out for him.
I look. I even talk. Does he listen? Whose son do you think he is?
I'm trying to remember a time when *you* taught him to be subservient. Or even careful...

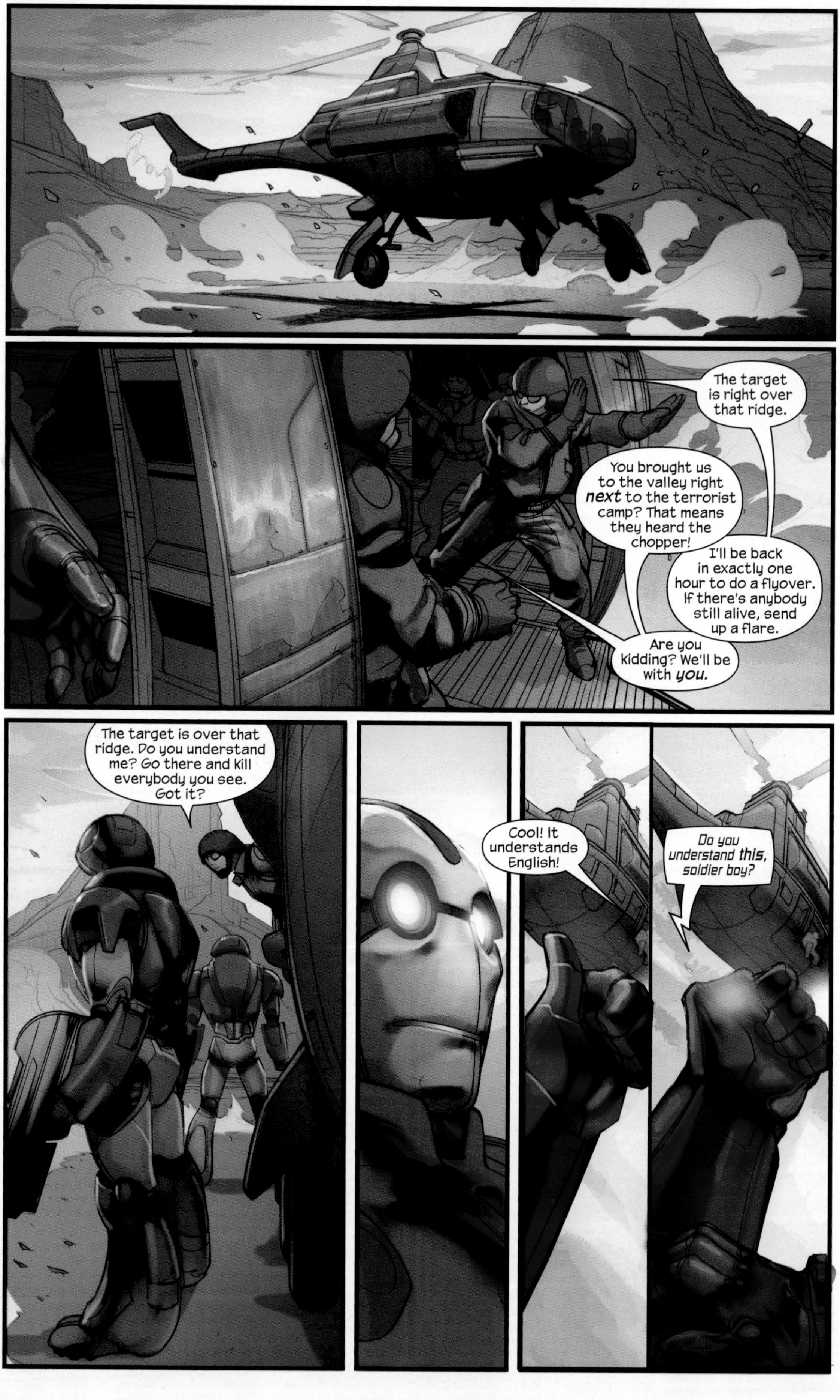
The target is right over that ridge.
You brought us to the valley right next to the terrorist camp? That means they heard the chopper!
I'll be back in exactly one hour to do a flyover. If there's anybody still alive, send up a flare.
Are you kidding? We'll be with you.
The target is over that ridge. Do you understand me? Go there and kill everybody you see. Got it?
Cool! It understands English!
Do you understand this, soldier boy?

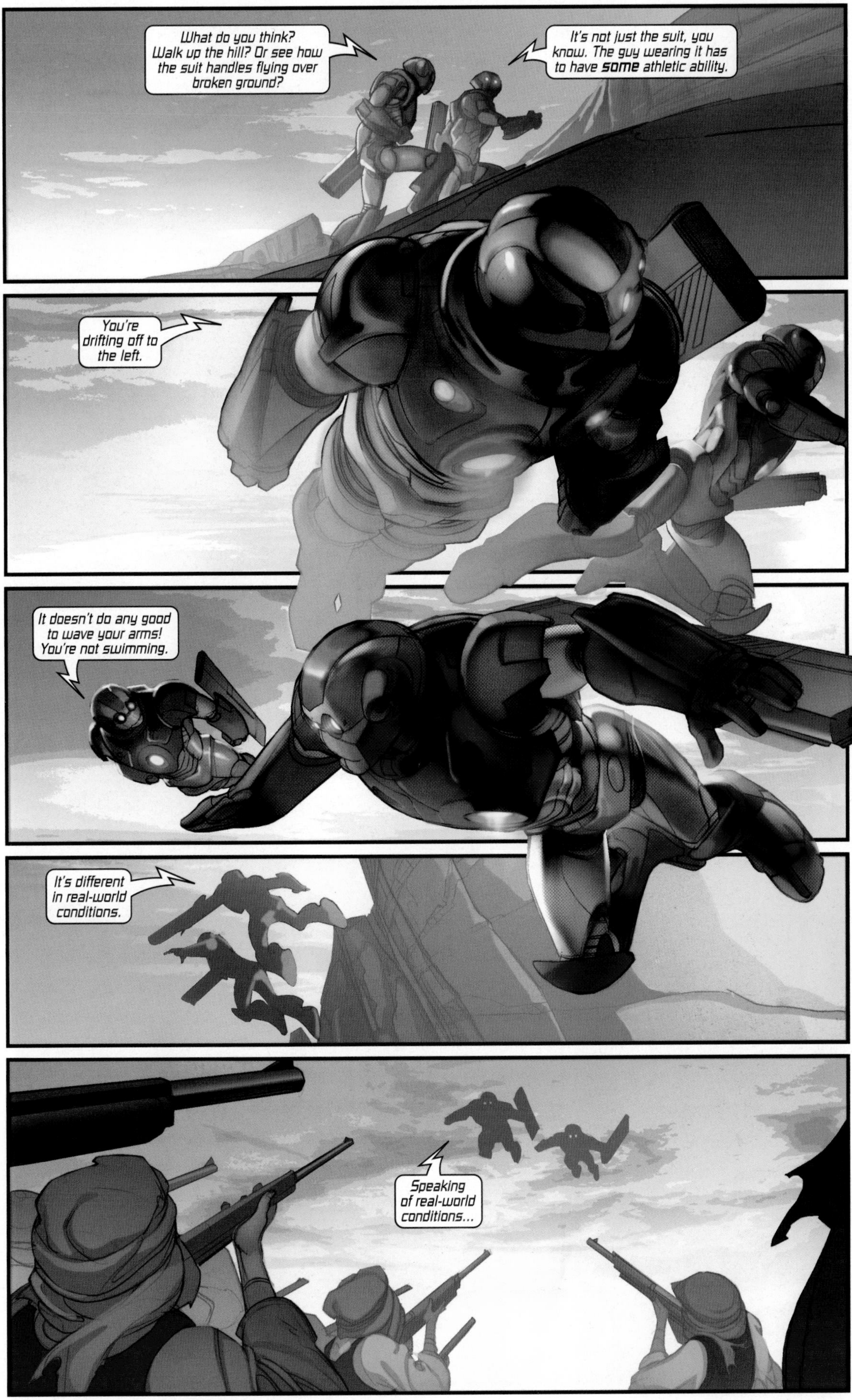
What do you think? Walk up the hill? Or see how the suit handles flying over broken ground?
It's not just the suit, you know. The guy wearing it has to have SOME athletic ability.
You're drifting off to the left.
It doesn't do any good to wave your arms! You're not swimming.
It's different in real-world conditions.
Speaking of real-world conditions...

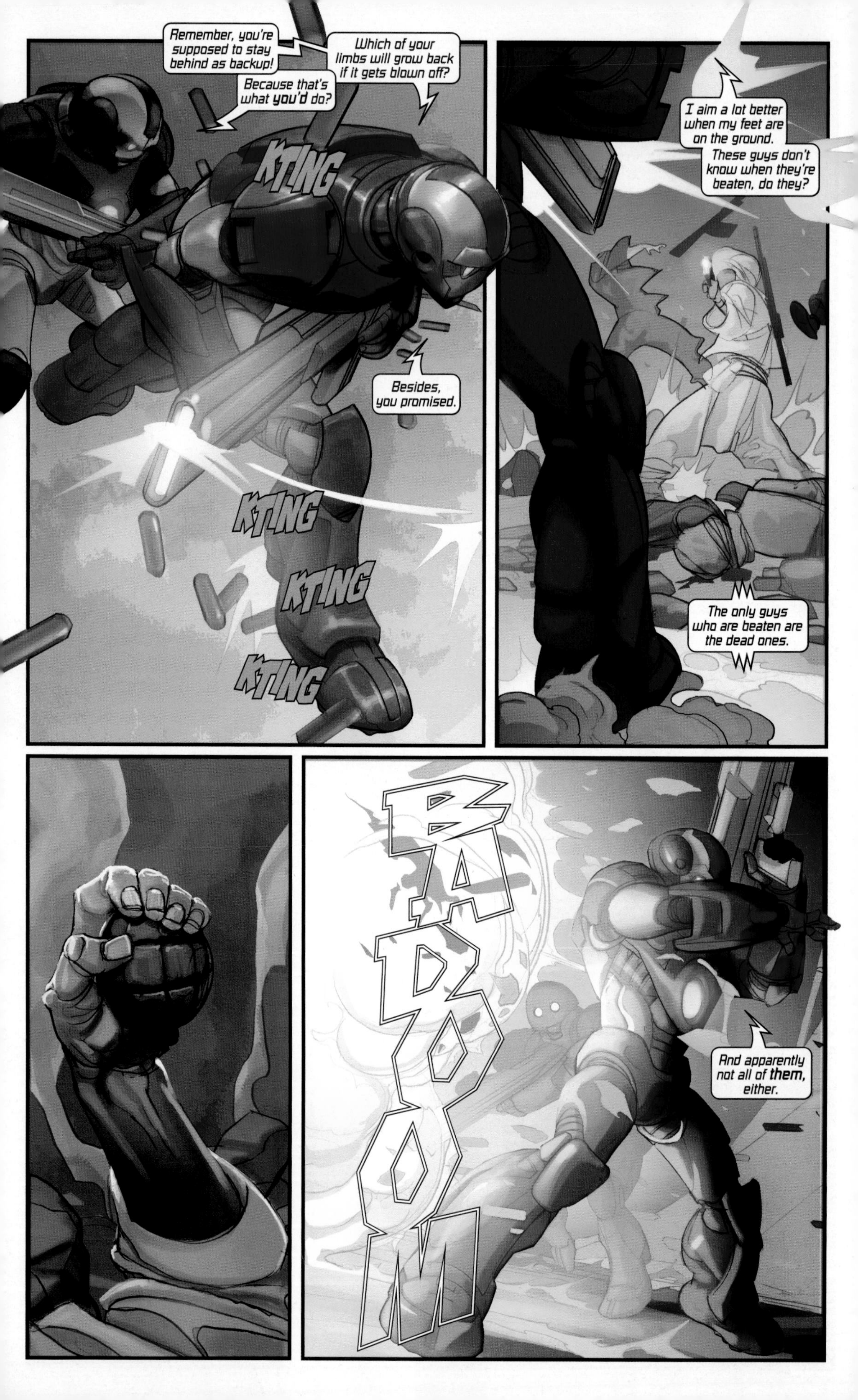
Remember, you're supposed to stay behind as backup!
Which of your limbs will grow back if it gets blown off?
Because that's what you'd do?
KTING
Besides, you promised.
KTING
KTING
KTING
I aim a lot better when my feet are on the ground.
These guys don't know when they're beaten, do they?
The only guys who are beaten are the dead ones.
BADOOM
And apparently not all of them, either.

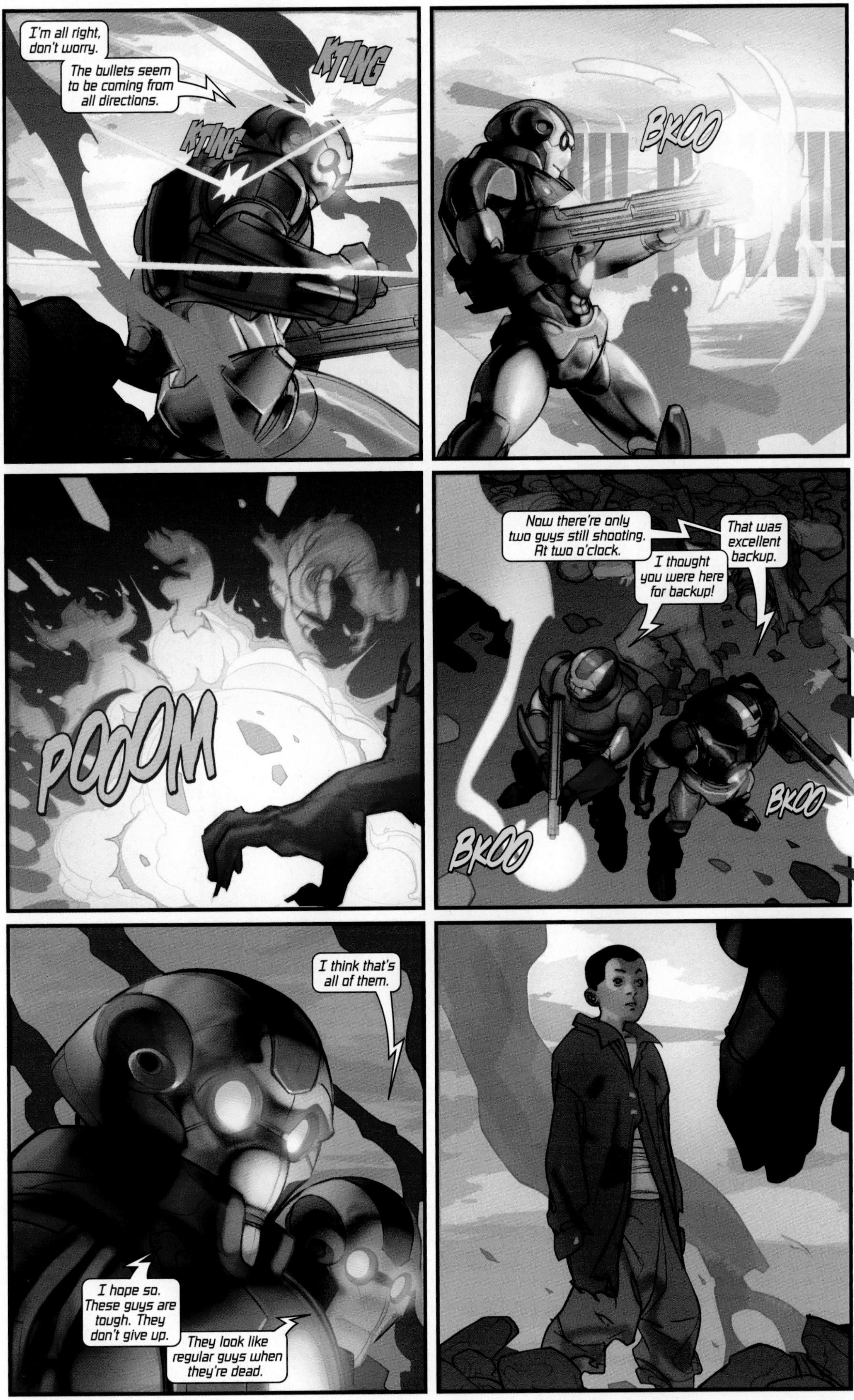

I'm all right, don't worry.
The bullets seem to be coming from all directions.
KTING
KTING
BKOO
POOOM
Now there're only two guys still shooting. At two o'clock.
I thought you were here for backup!
That was excellent backup.
BKOO
BKOO
I think that's all of them.
I hope so. These guys are tough. They don't give up.
They look like regular guys when they're dead.

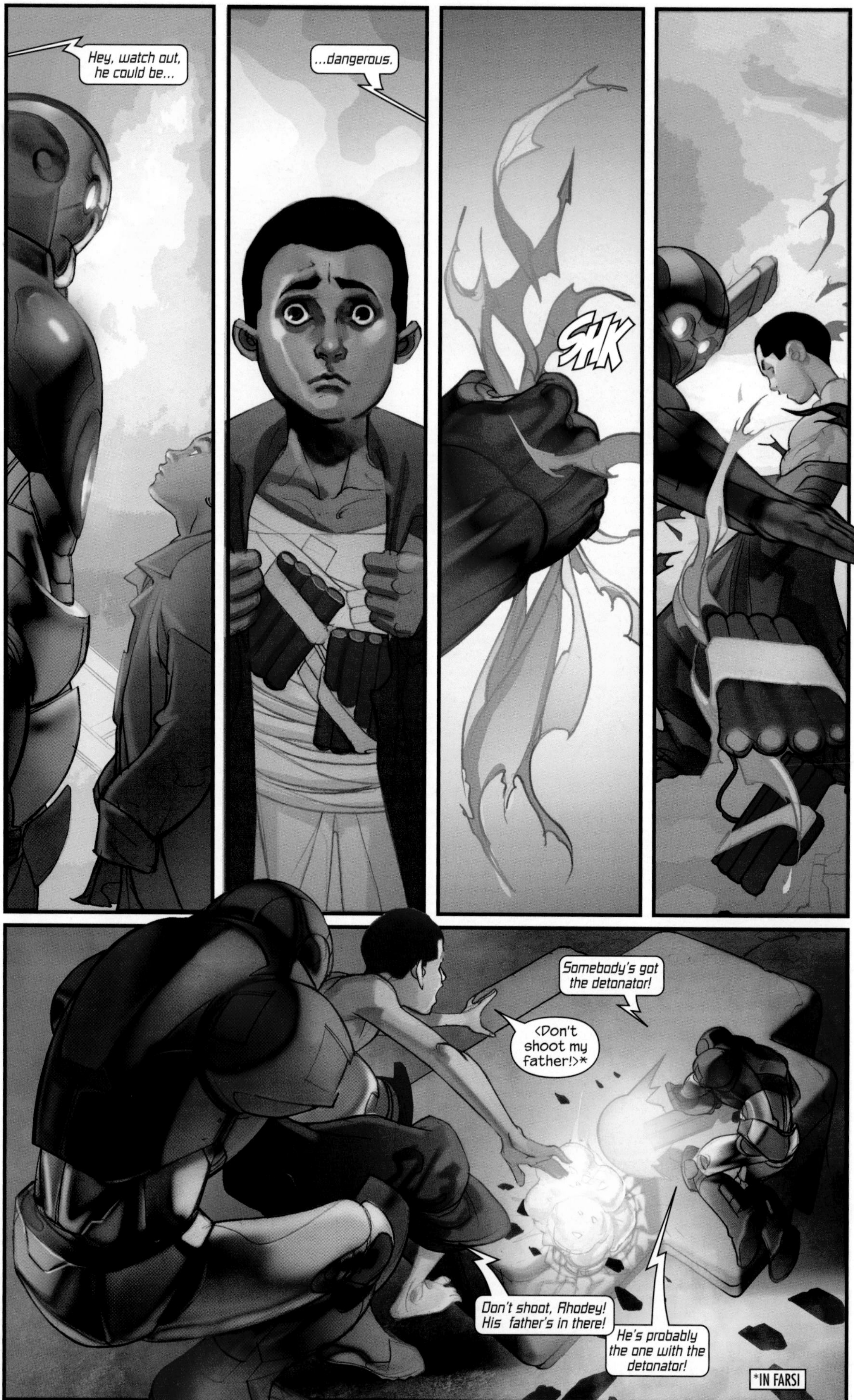
Hey, watch out, he could be...
...dangerous.
SHK
Somebody's got the detonator!
<Don't shoot my father!>*
Don't shoot, Rhodey! His father's in there!
He's probably the one with the detonator!
*IN FARSI

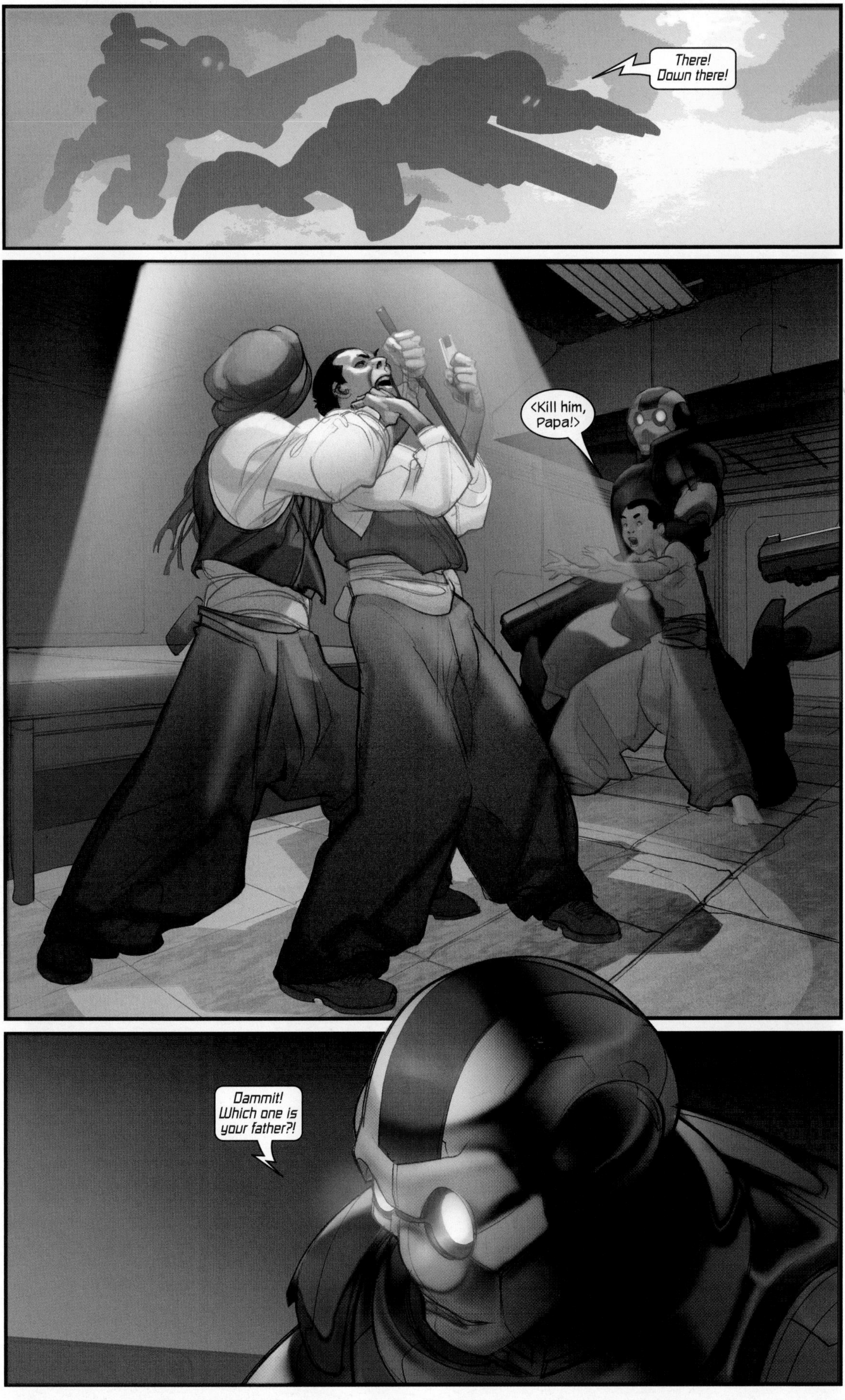
There! Down there!
<Kill him, Papa!>
Dammit! Which one is your father?!

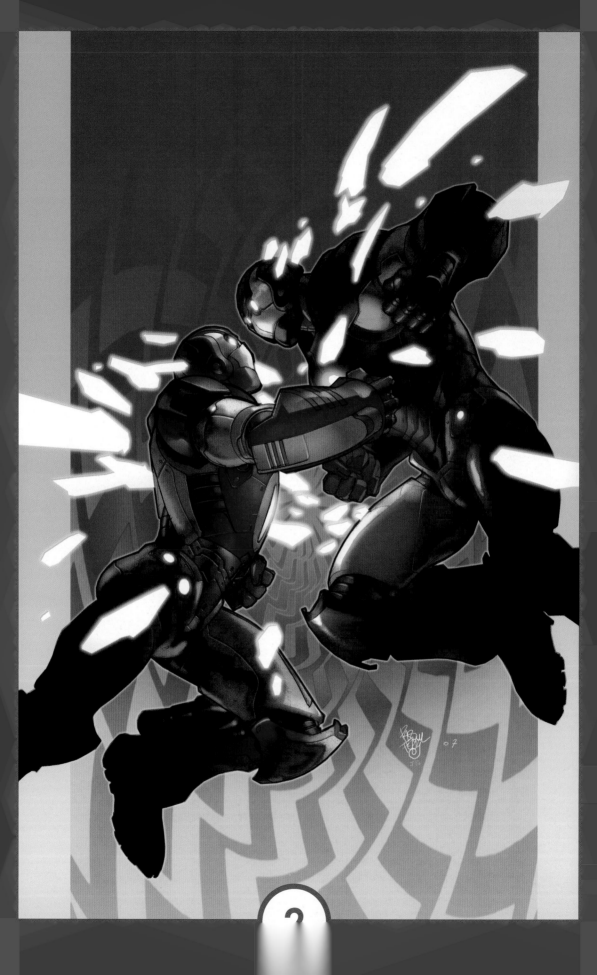

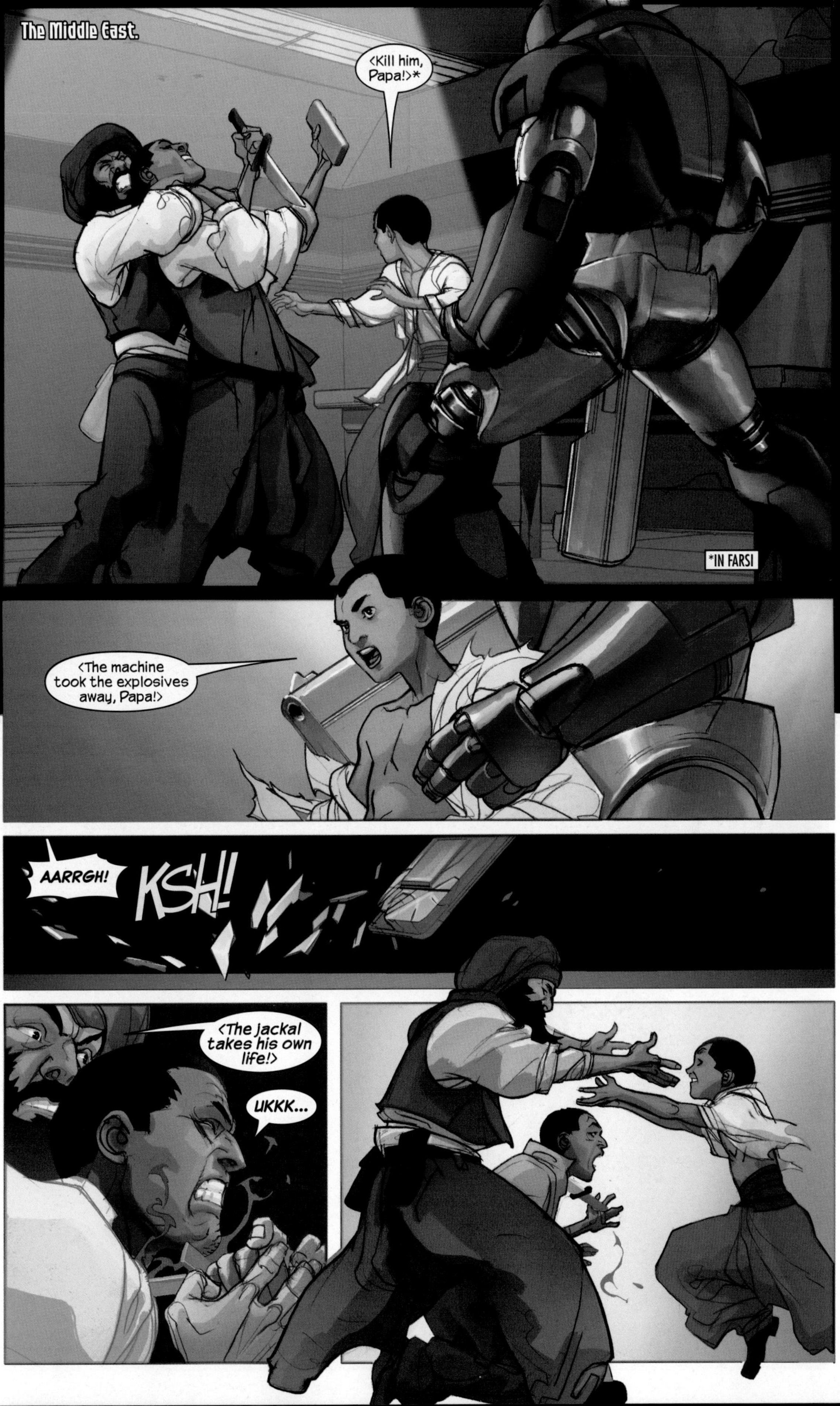
The Middle East.
<Kill him, Papa!>*
*IN FARSI
<The machine took the explosives away, Papa!>
AARRGH!
KSH!
<The jackal takes his own life!>
UKKK...

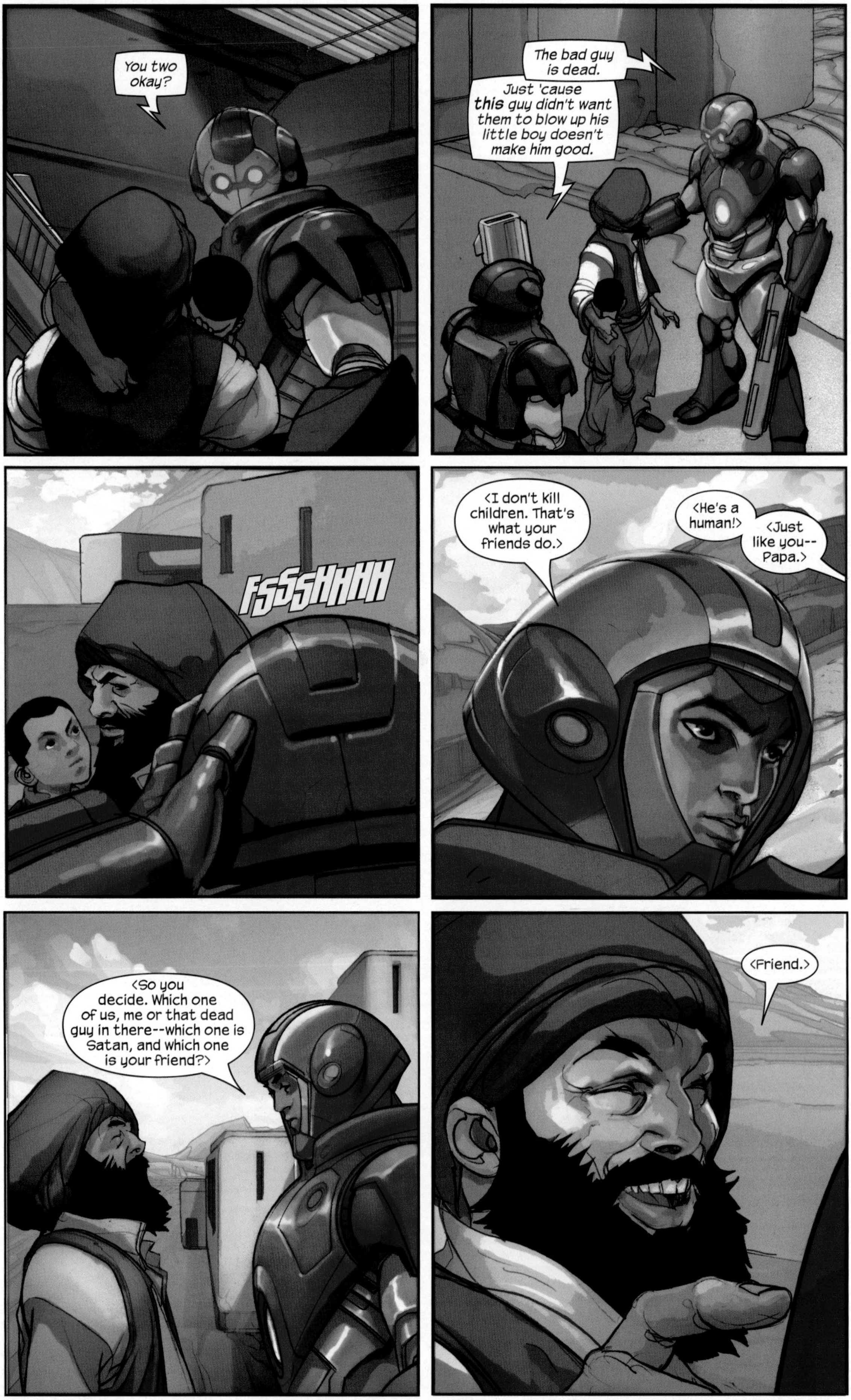
You two okay?
The bad guy is dead.
Just 'cause **this** guy didn't want them to blow up his little boy doesn't make him good.
FSSSHHHH
<I don't kill children. That's what your friends do.>
<He's a human!>
<Just like you-- Papa.>
<So you decide. Which one of us, me or that dead guy in there--which one is Satan, and which one is your friend?>
<Friend.>

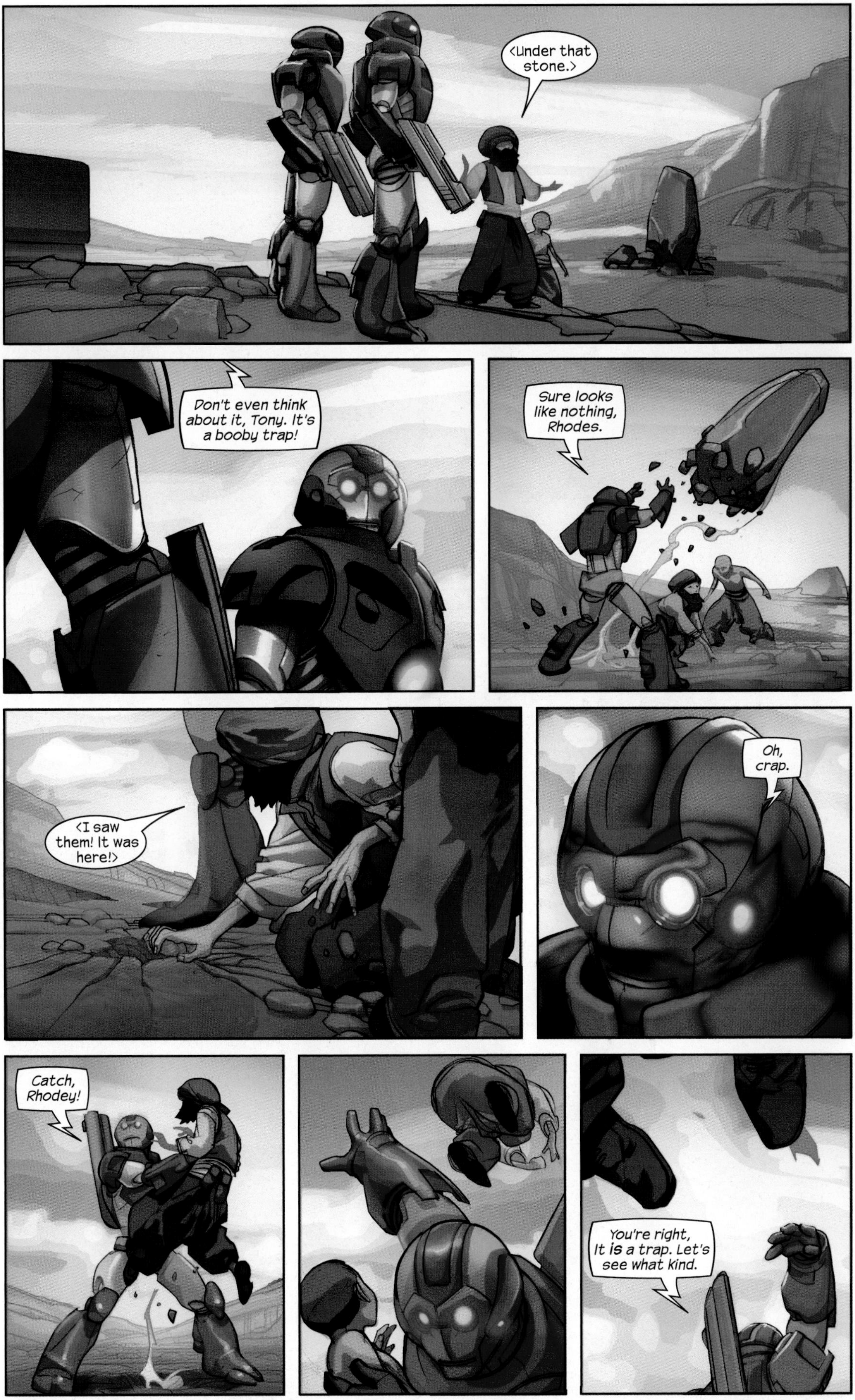

<Under that stone.>
Don't even think about it, Tony. It's a booby trap!
Sure looks like nothing, Rhodes.
<I saw them! It was here!>
Oh, crap.
Catch, Rhodey!
You're right, It is a trap. Let's see what kind.

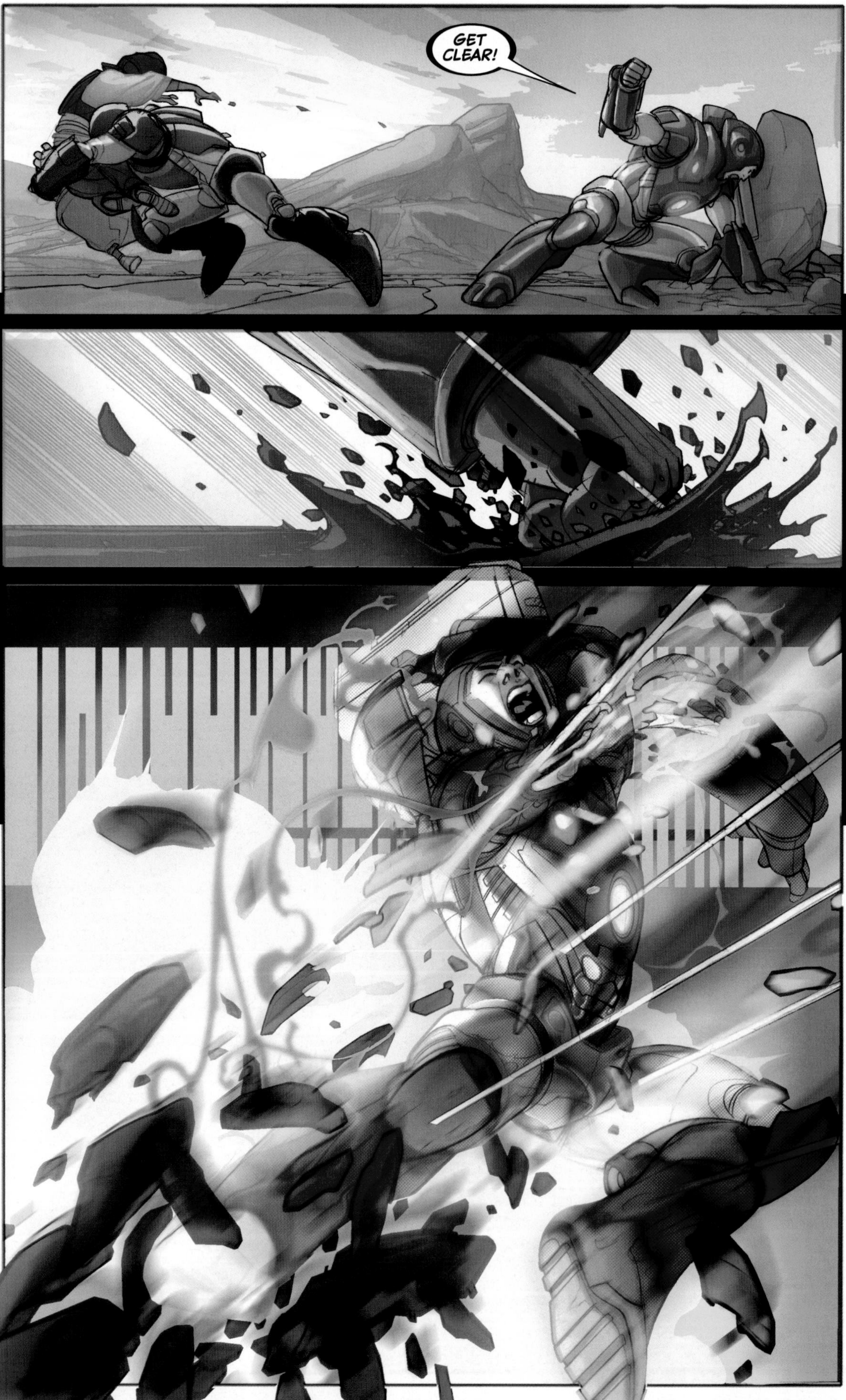
GET CLEAR!

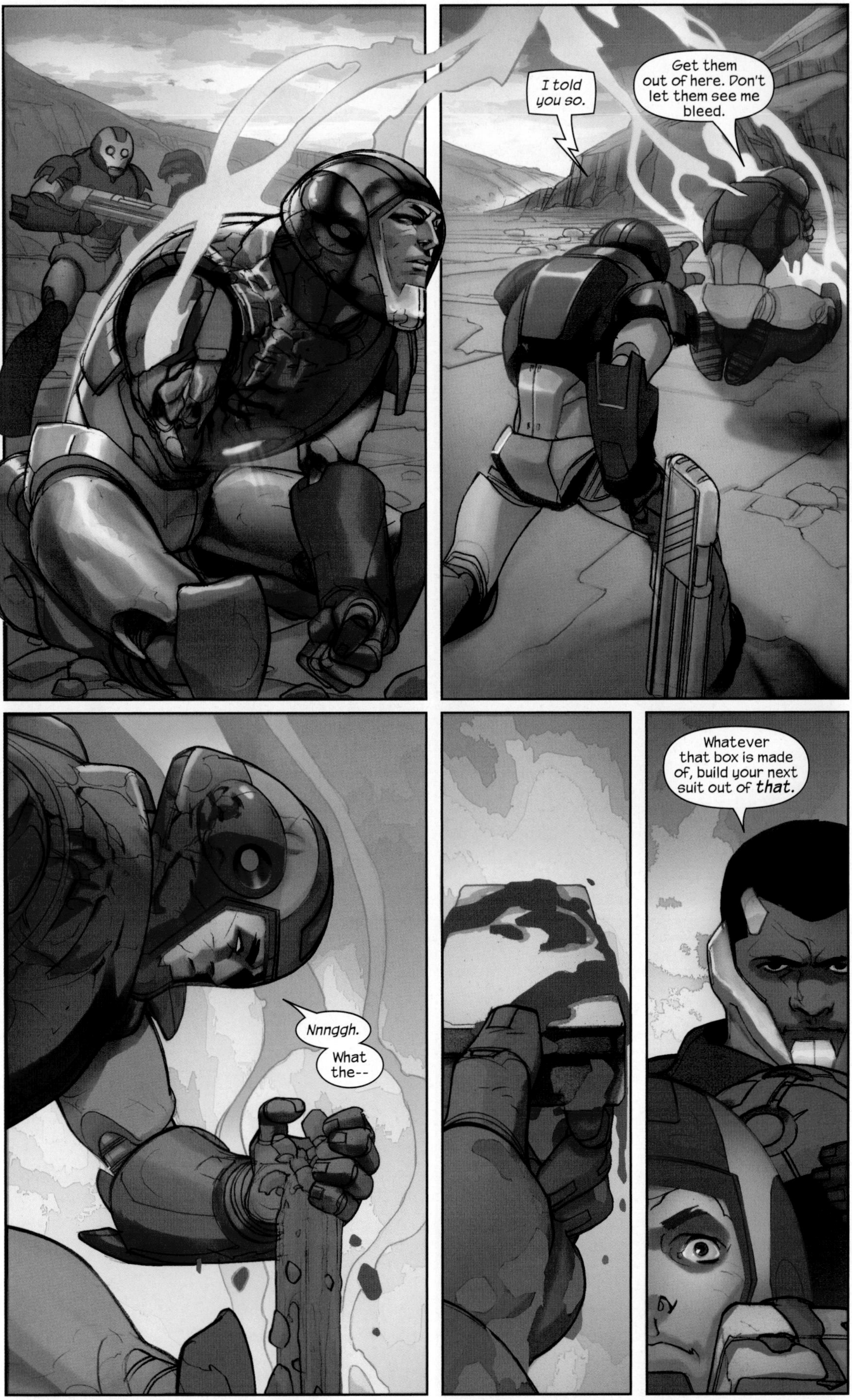
I told you so.
Get them out of here. Don't let them see me bleed.
Nnnggh.
What the--
Whatever that box is made of, build your next suit out of *that.*

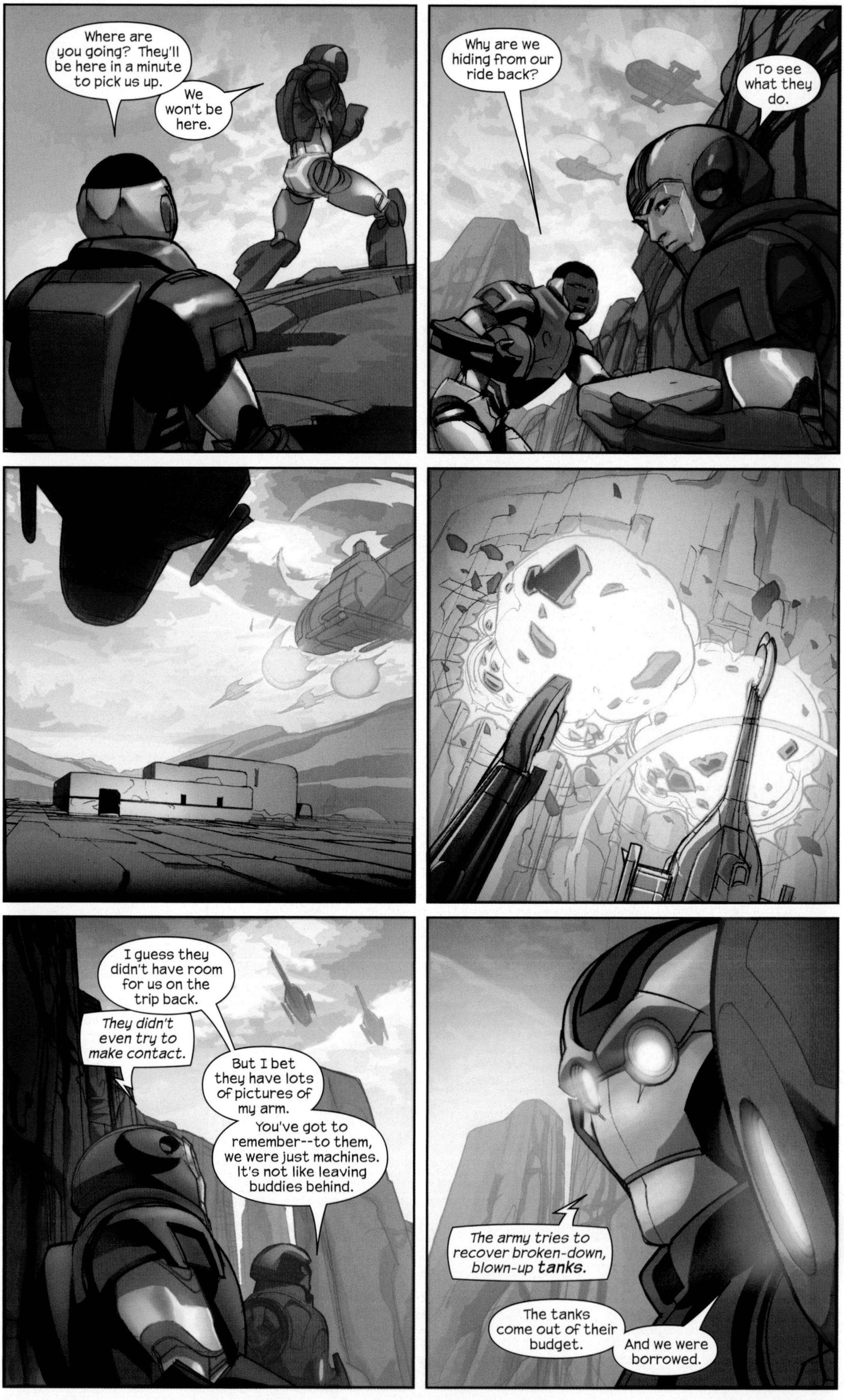
Where are you going? They'll be here in a minute to pick us up.
We won't be here.
Why are we hiding from our ride back?
To see what they do.
I guess they didn't have room for us on the trip back.
They didn't even try to make contact.
But I bet they have lots of pictures of my arm.
You've got to remember--to them, we were just machines. It's not like leaving buddies behind.
*The army tries to recover broken-down, blown-up **tanks.***
The tanks come out of their budget.
And we were borrowed.

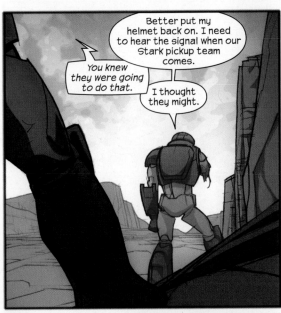

Better put my helmet back on. I need to hear the signal when our Stark pickup team comes.

You knew they were going to do that.

I thought they might.

And you left your arm for anybody to find?

Our guys will pick it up.

We came in person to apologize for not being able to recover your robots.

Stark Enterprises. 24 Hours Later.

Mr. Stark asked me to tell you that your apology is not accepted.

Why not?

Because your apology is insincere.

You made no effort to recover the robots. Your military detail blew up the building they were in.

That's a lie.

We had our own recovery team. And satellite observation. And, of course, the black boxes in the robots.

So why did you even let us come here?

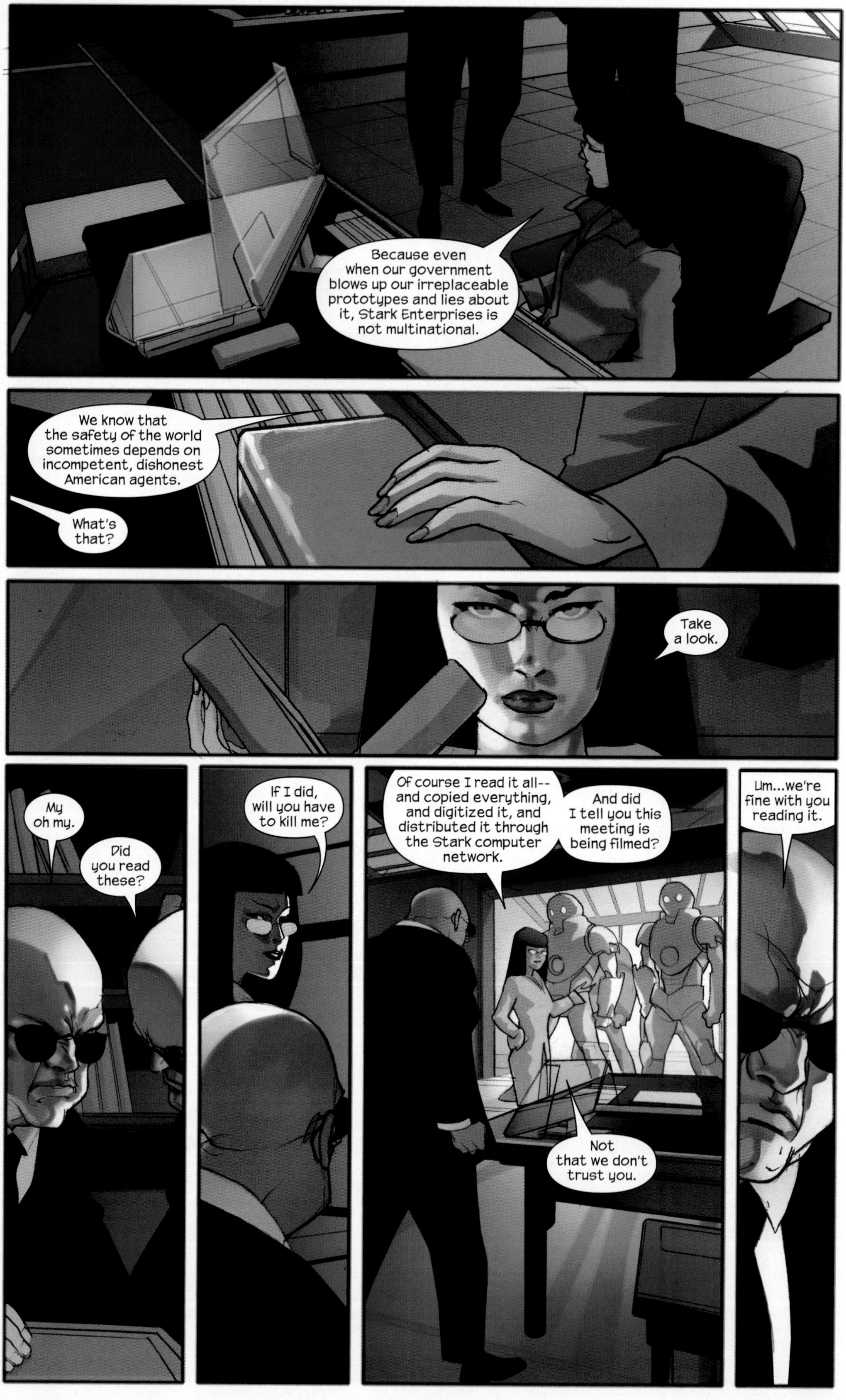
Because even when our government blows up our irreplaceable prototypes and lies about it, Stark Enterprises is not multinational.
We know that the safety of the world sometimes depends on incompetent, dishonest American agents.
What's that?
Take a look.
My oh my.
Did you read these?
If I did, will you have to kill me?
Of course I read it all-- and copied everything, and digitized it, and distributed it through the Stark computer network.
And did I tell you this meeting is being filmed?
Not that we don't trust you.
Um...we're fine with you reading it.

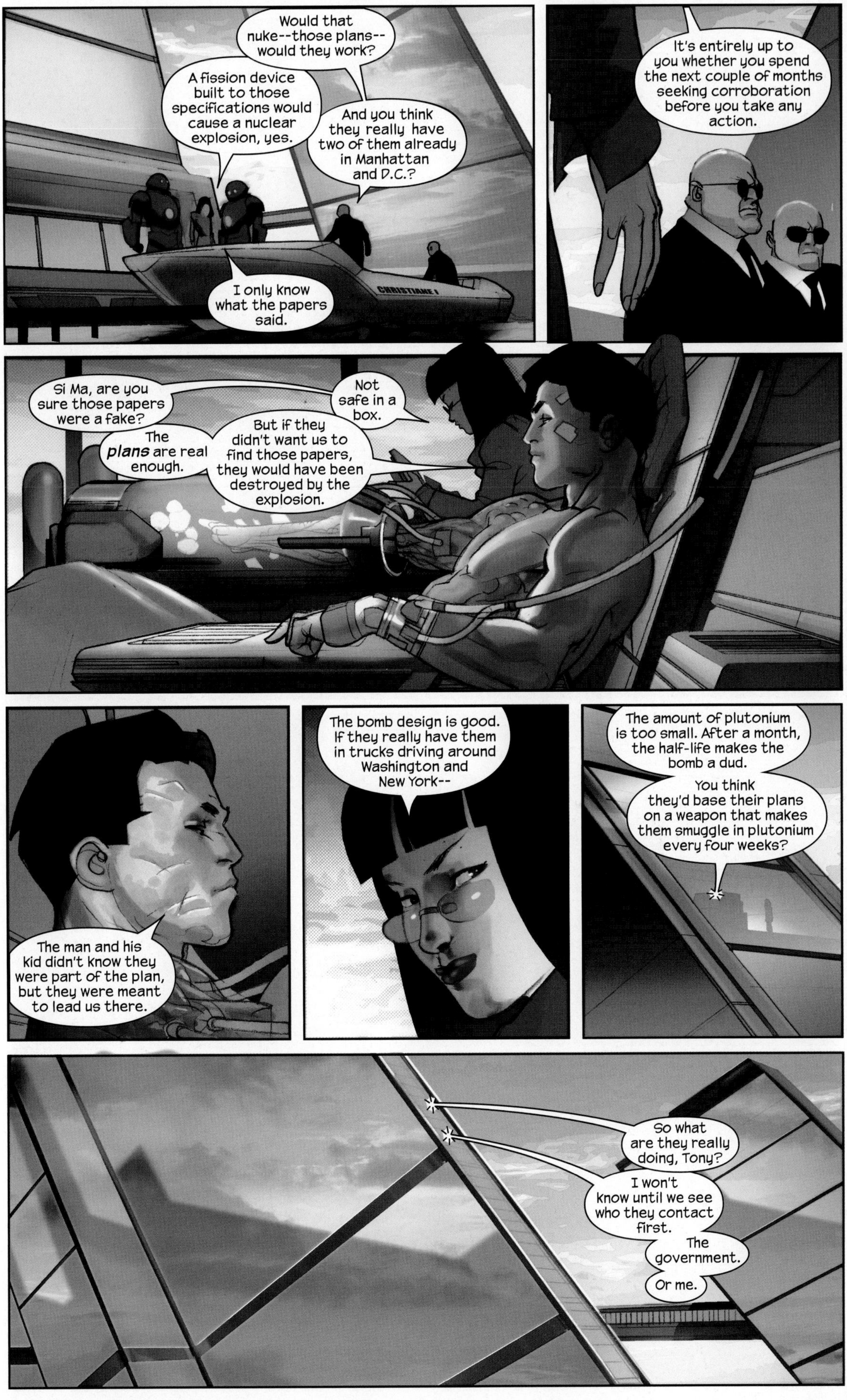
Would that nuke--those plans--would they work?
A fission device built to those specifications would cause a nuclear explosion, yes.
And you think they really have two of them already in Manhattan and D.C.?
I only know what the papers said.
CHRISTIANE I
It's entirely up to you whether you spend the next couple of months seeking corroboration before you take any action.
Si Ma, are you sure those papers were a fake?
Not safe in a box.
The *plans* are real enough.
But if they didn't want us to find those papers, they would have been destroyed by the explosion.
The man and his kid didn't know they were part of the plan, but they were meant to lead us there.
The bomb design is good. If they really have them in trucks driving around Washington and New York--
The amount of plutonium is too small. After a month, the half-life makes the bomb a dud.
You think they'd base their plans on a weapon that makes them smuggle in plutonium every four weeks?
So what are they really doing, Tony?
I won't know until we see who they contact first.
The government.
Or me.

Riker's Island Prison.

Visitor, Mr. Stark. Says it's urgent.

Who?

Teenage kid. Obadiah Stane. Calls you "Mommy's ex-husband."

How well did you search him?

What the hell do *you* want?

They've really upped security since you broke in here and murdered my dad.

Only not well enough, I guess.

I've filled my abdomen with explosives, and when they go off, they'll blast right through this wall and kill you.

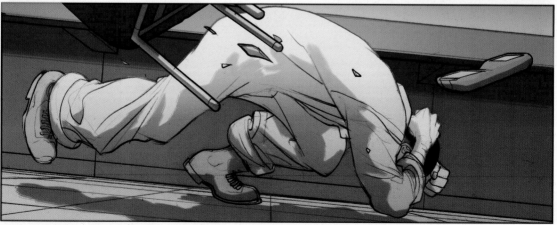

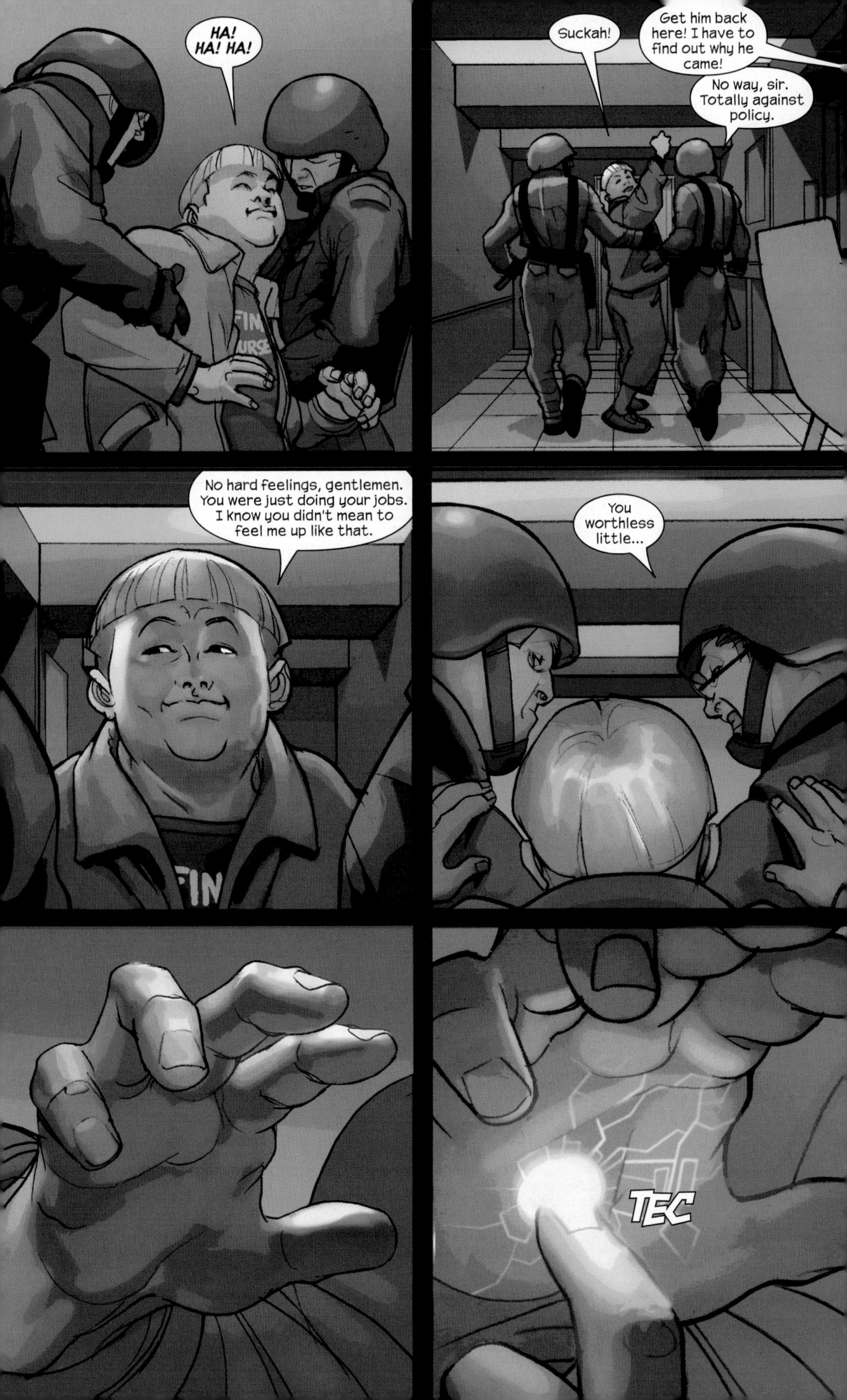
HA! HA! HA!
Suckah!
Get him back here! I have to find out why he came!
No way, sir. Totally against policy.
No hard feelings, gentlemen. You were just doing your jobs. I know you didn't mean to feel me up like that.
You worthless little...
TEC

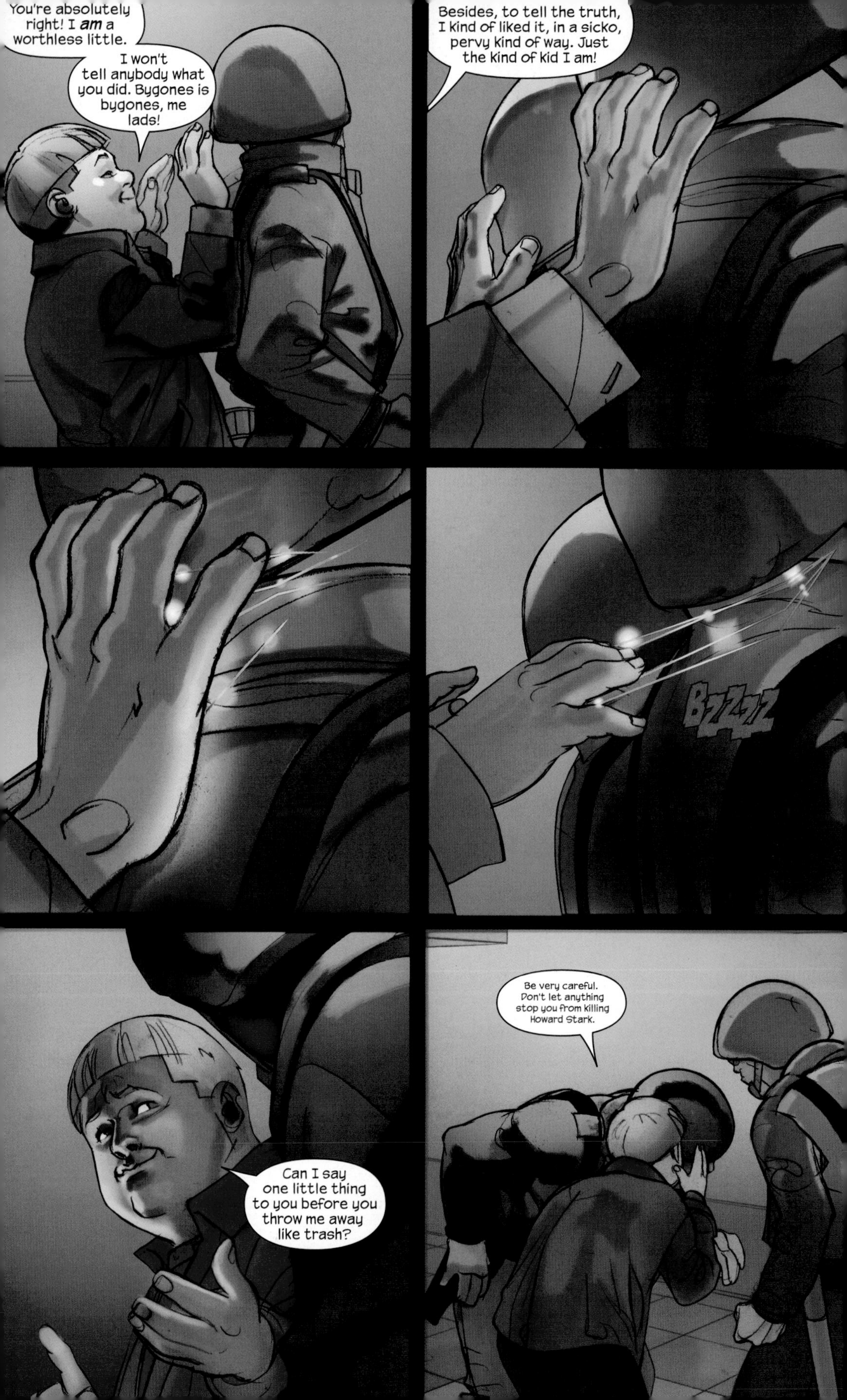
You're absolutely right! I *am* a worthless little.
I won't tell anybody what you did. Bygones is bygones, me lads!
Besides, to tell the truth, I kind of liked it, in a sicko, pervy kind of way. Just the kind of kid I am!
BZZZZ
Can I say one little thing to you before you throw me away like trash?
Be very careful. Don't let anything stop you from killing Howard Stark.

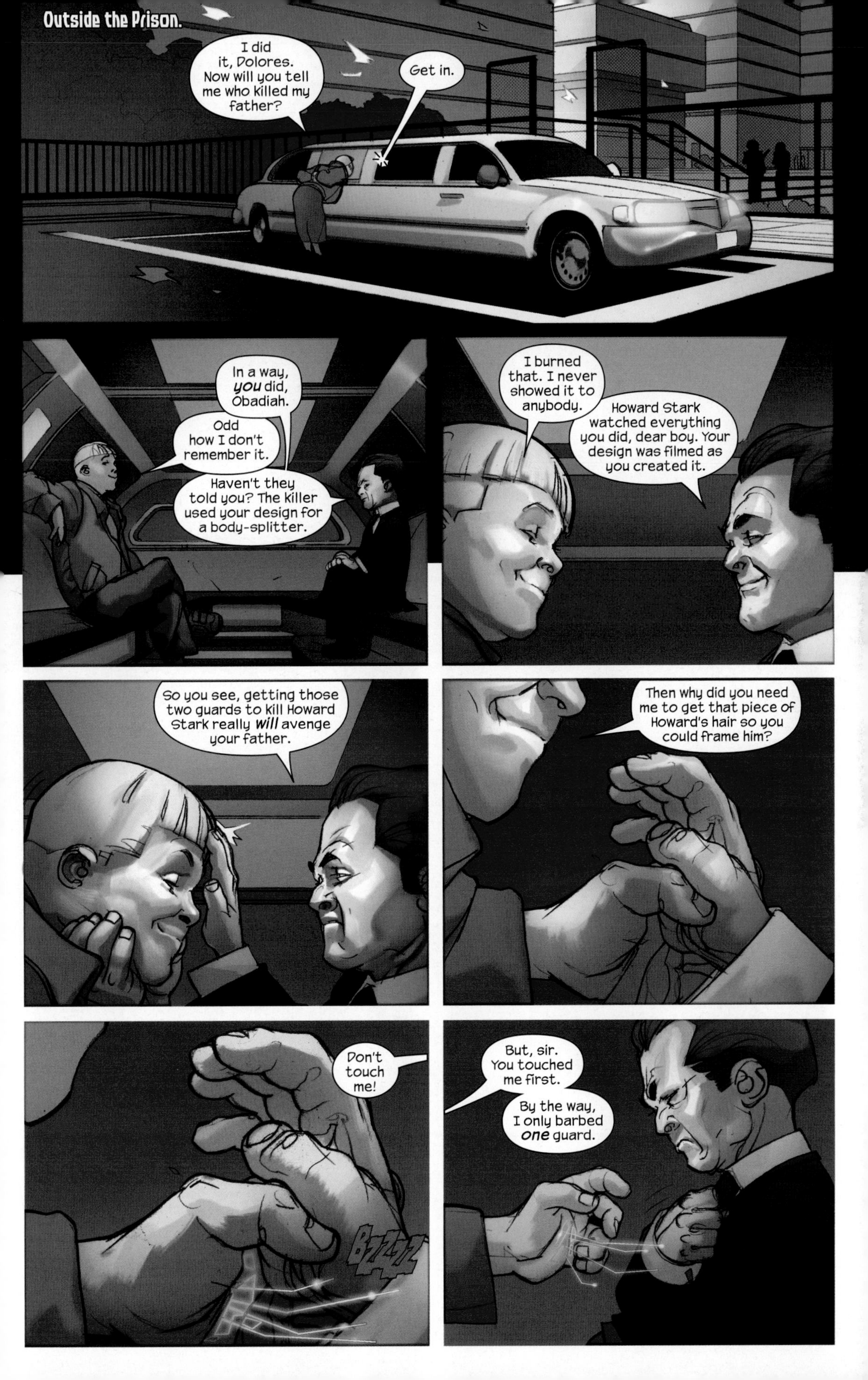
Outside the Prison.
I did it, Dolores. Now will you tell me who killed my father?
Get in.
In a way, you did, Obadiah.
Odd how I don't remember it.
Haven't they told you? The killer used your design for a body-splitter.
I burned that. I never showed it to anybody.
Howard Stark watched everything you did, dear boy. Your design was filmed as you created it.
So you see, getting those two guards to kill Howard Stark really will avenge your father.
Then why did you need me to get that piece of Howard's hair so you could frame him?
Don't touch me!
BZZZZ
But, sir. You touched me first.
By the way, I only barbed one guard.

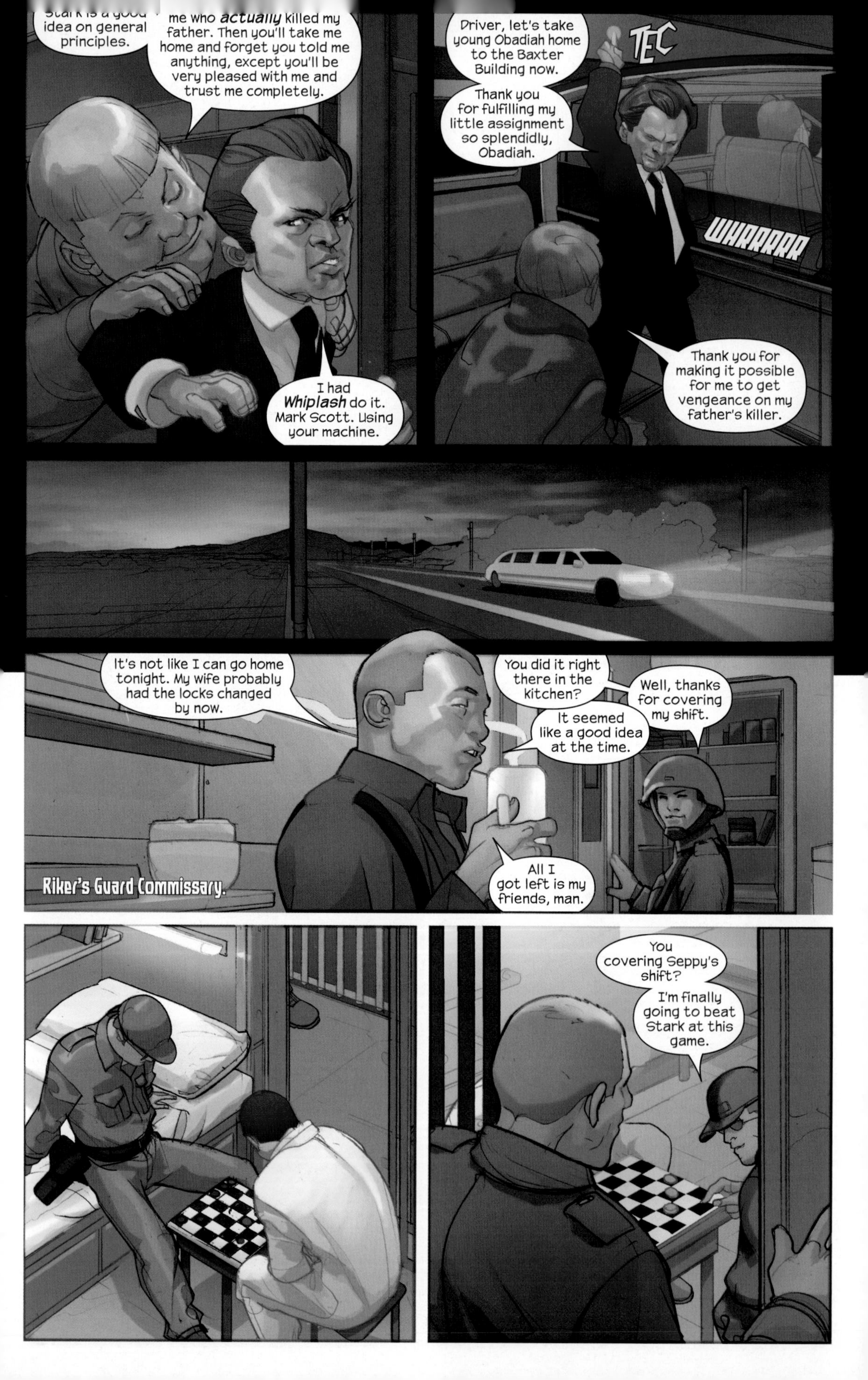

idea on general principles.
me who *actually* killed my father. Then you'll take me home and forget you told me anything, except you'll be very pleased with me and trust me completely.
I had *Whiplash* do it. Mark Scott. Using your machine.
Driver, let's take young Obadiah home to the Baxter Building now.
Thank you for fulfilling my little assignment so splendidly, Obadiah.
TEC
WHRRRRR
Thank you for making it possible for me to get vengeance on my father's killer.
It's not like I can go home tonight. My wife probably had the locks changed by now.
You did it right there in the kitchen?
It seemed like a good idea at the time.
Well, thanks for covering my shift.
All I got left is my friends, man.
Riker's Guard Commissary.
You covering Seppy's shift?
I'm finally going to beat Stark at this game.

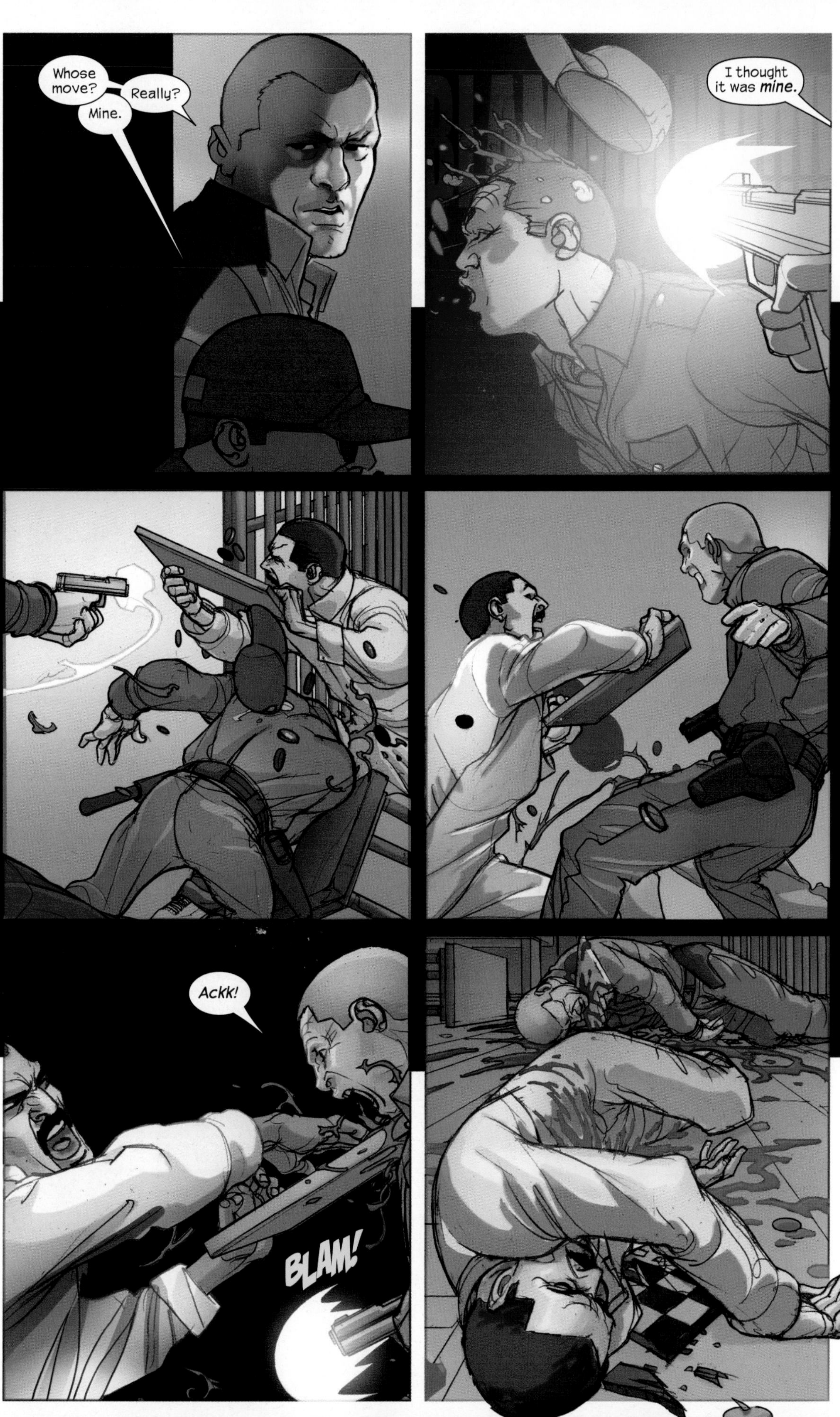
Whose move?
Mine.
Really?
I thought it was *mine.*
Ackk!
BLAM!

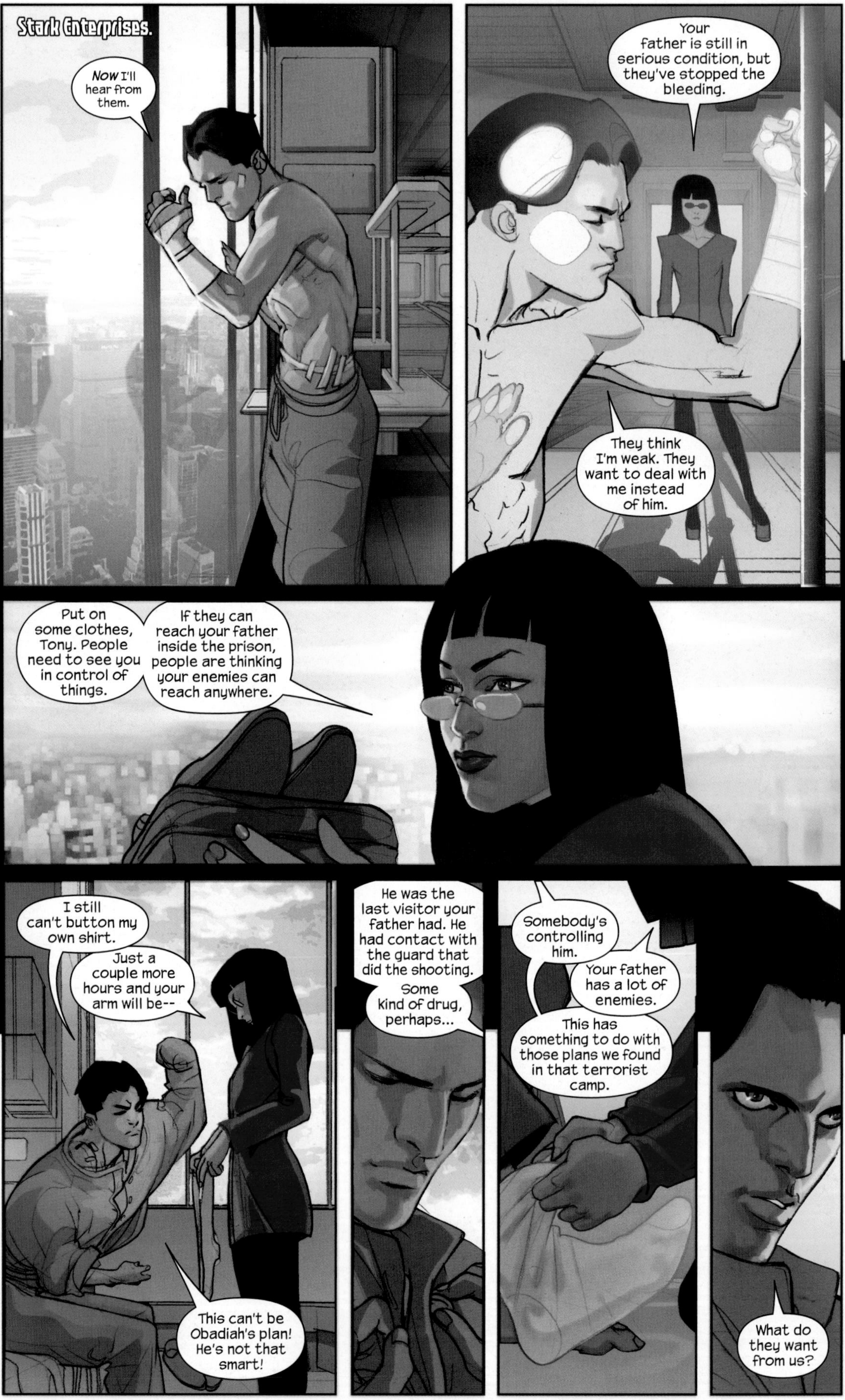
Stark Enterprises.
NOW I'll hear from them.
Your father is still in serious condition, but they've stopped the bleeding.
They think I'm weak. They want to deal with me instead of him.
Put on some clothes, Tony. People need to see you in control of things.
If they can reach your father inside the prison, people are thinking your enemies can reach anywhere.
I still can't button my own shirt.
Just a couple more hours and your arm will be--
This can't be Obadiah's plan! He's not that smart!
He was the last visitor your father had. He had contact with the guard that did the shooting.
Some kind of drug, perhaps...
Somebody's controlling him.
Your father has a lot of enemies.
This has something to do with those plans we found in that terrorist camp.
What do they want from us?

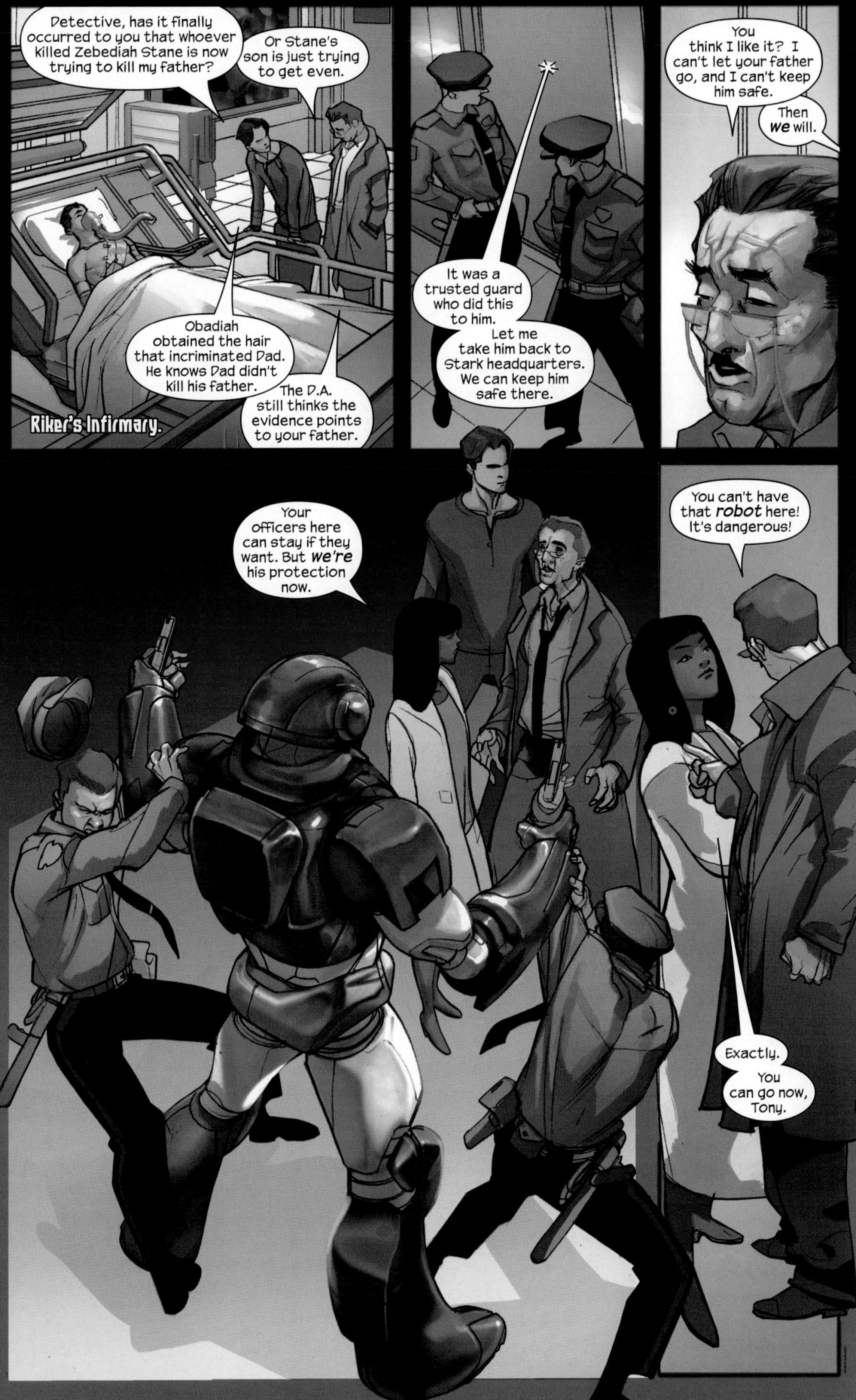
Detective, has it finally occurred to you that whoever killed Zebediah Stane is now trying to kill my father?
Or Stane's son is just trying to get even.
Obadiah obtained the hair that incriminated Dad. He knows Dad didn't kill his father.
The D.A. still thinks the evidence points to your father.
Riker's Infirmary.
It was a trusted guard who did this to him.
Let me take him back to Stark headquarters. We can keep him safe there.
You think I like it? I can't let your father go, and I can't keep him safe.
Then **we** will.
Your officers here can stay if they want. But **we're** his protection now.
You can't have that **robot** here! It's dangerous!
Exactly.
You can go now, Tony.

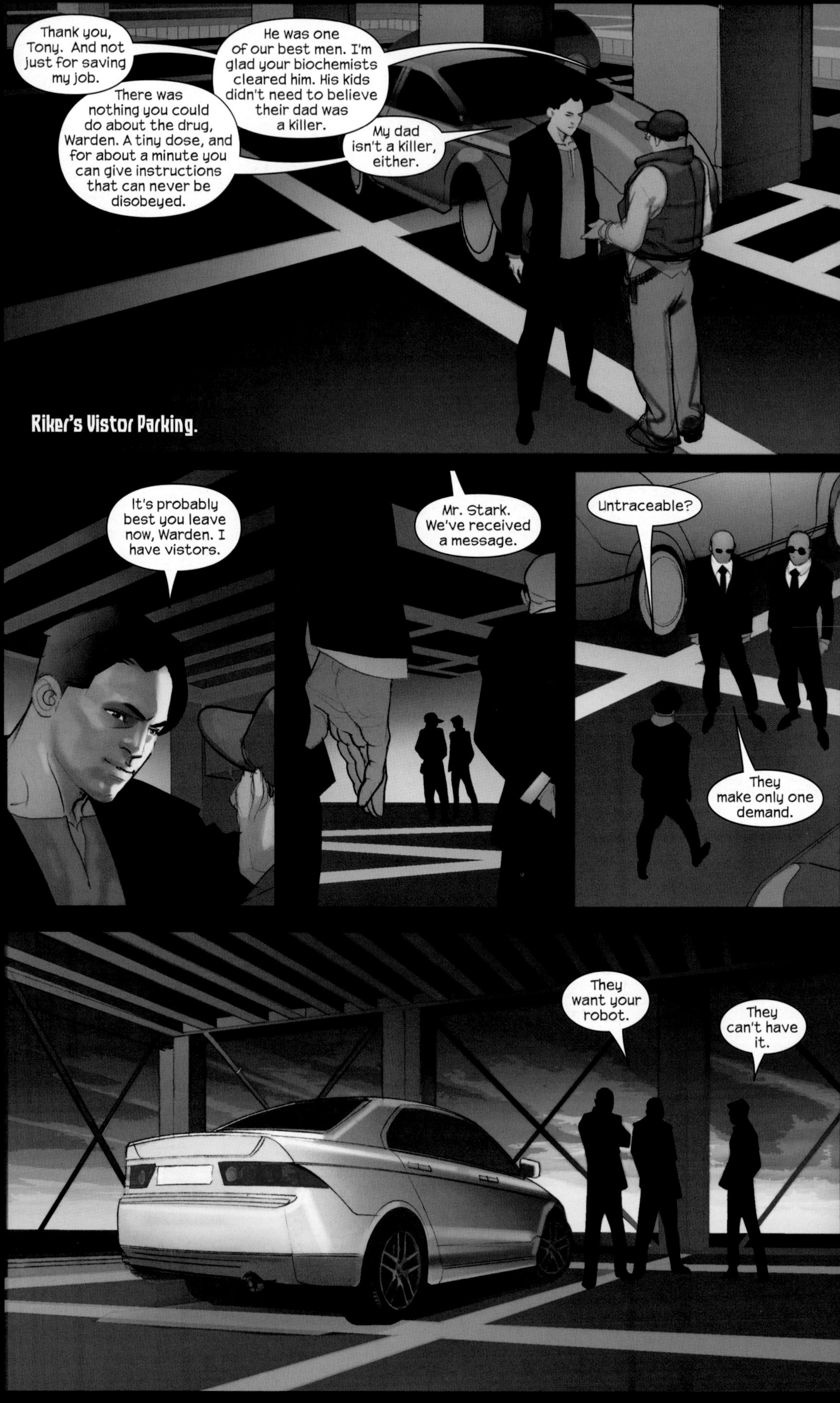
Thank you, Tony. And not just for saving my job.
He was one of our best men. I'm glad your biochemists cleared him. His kids didn't need to believe their dad was a killer.
There was nothing you could do about the drug, Warden. A tiny dose, and for about a minute you can give instructions that can never be disobeyed.
My dad isn't a killer, either.
Riker's Vistor Parking.
It's probably best you leave now, Warden. I have vistors.
Mr. Stark. We've received a message.
Untraceable?
They make only one demand.
They want your robot.
They can't have it.

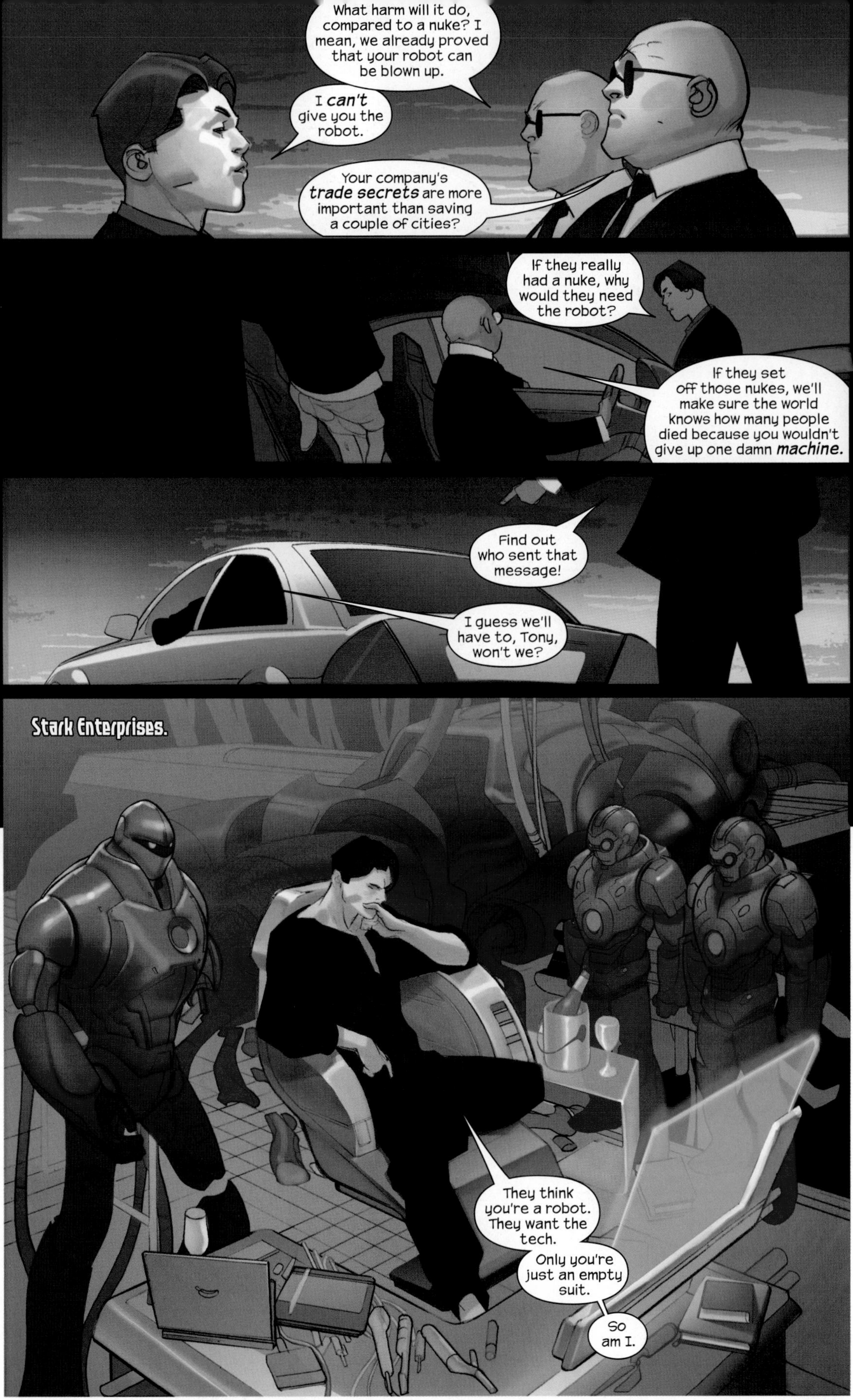
What harm will it do, compared to a nuke? I mean, we already proved that your robot can be blown up.
I *can't* give you the robot.
Your company's *trade secrets* are more important than saving a couple of cities?
If they really had a nuke, why would they need the robot?
If they set off those nukes, we'll make sure the world knows how many people died because you wouldn't give up one damn *machine.*
Find out who sent that message!
I guess we'll have to, Tony, won't we?
Stark Enterprises.
They think you're a robot. They want the tech.
Only you're just an empty suit.
So am I.

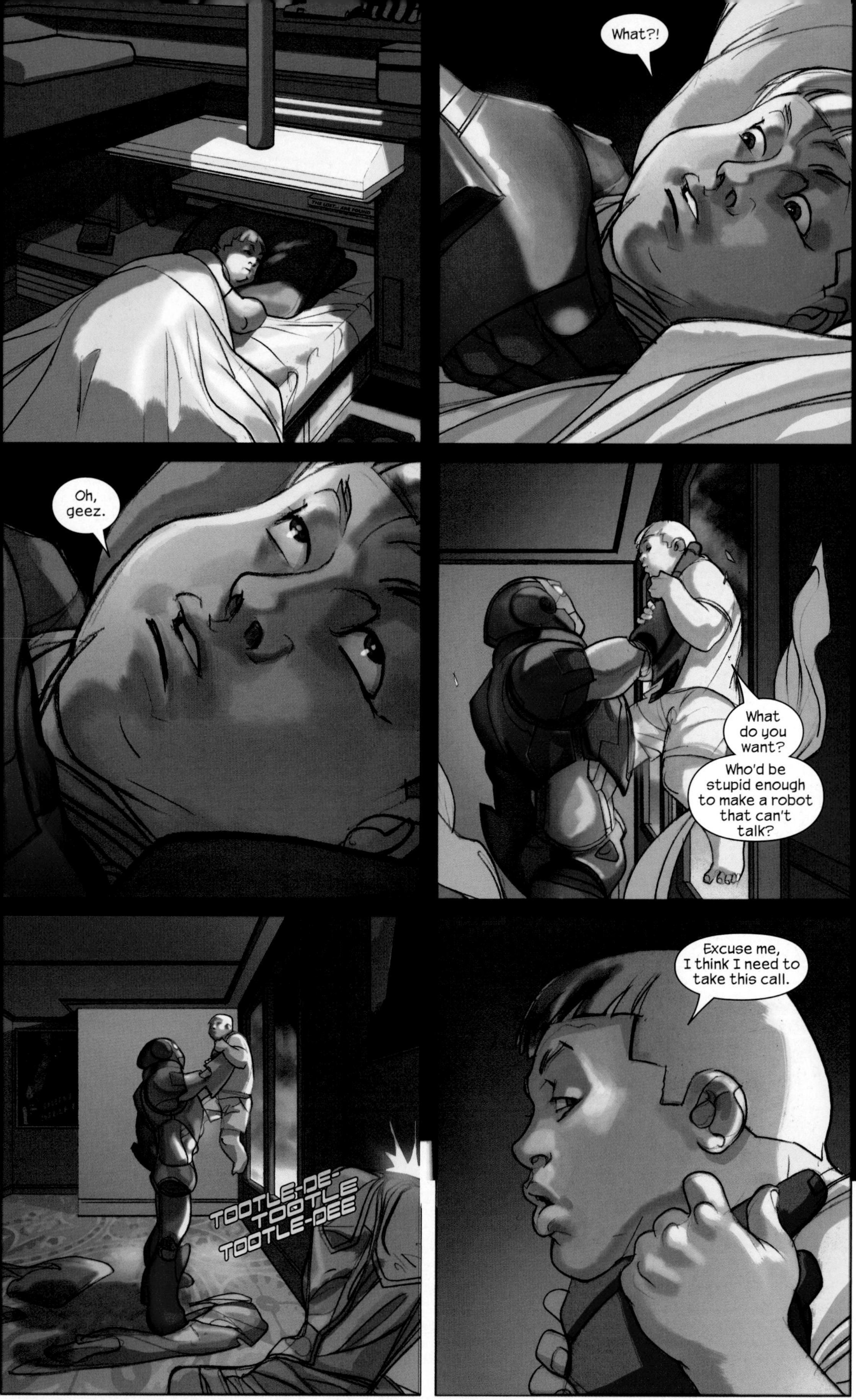
What?!
Oh, geez.
What do you want?
Who'd be stupid enough to make a robot that can't talk?
TOOTLE-DE-TOOTLE TOOTLE-DEE
Excuse me, I think I need to take this call.

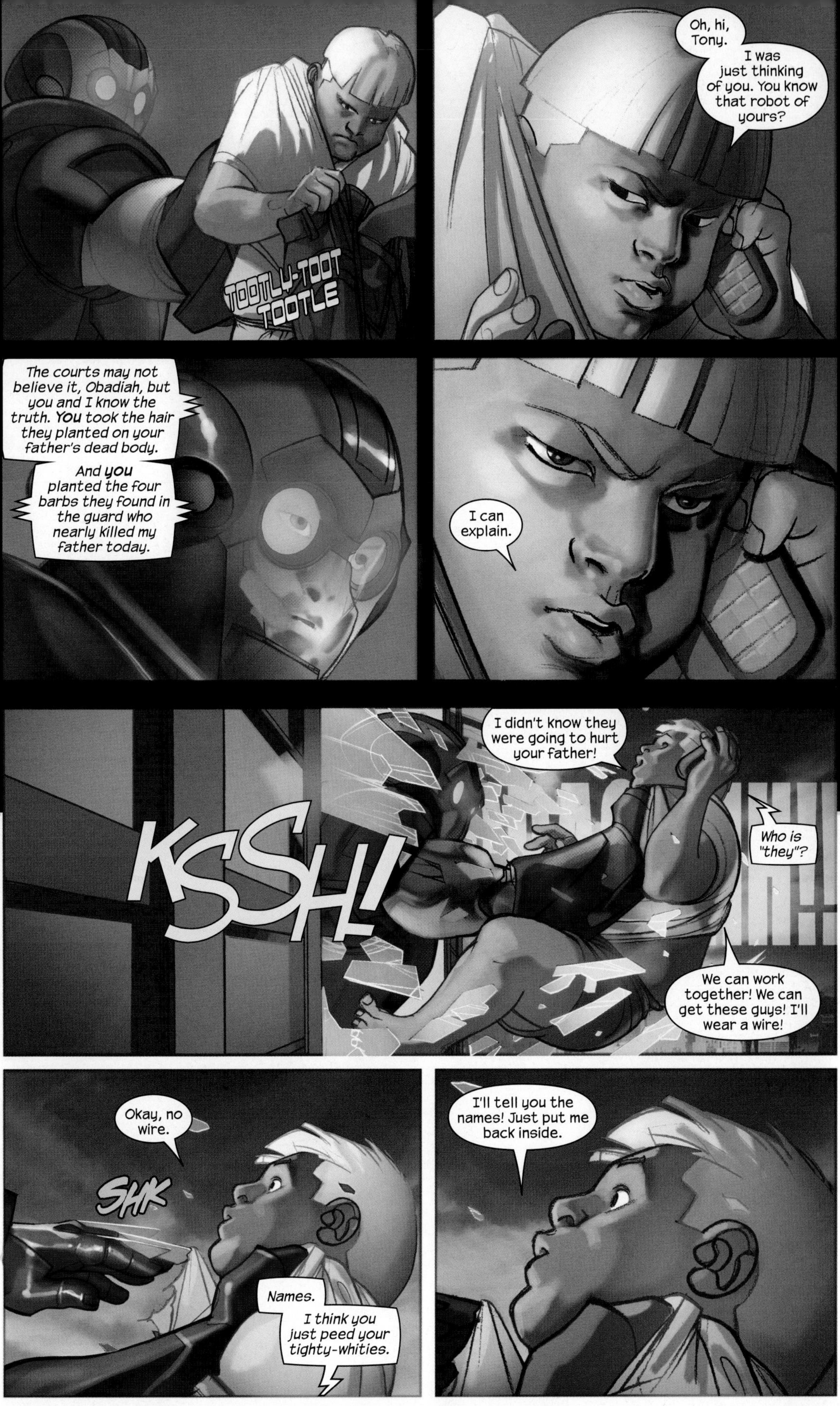
TOOTLY-TOOT TOOTLE
Oh, hi, Tony.
I was just thinking of you. You know that robot of yours?
The courts may not believe it, Obadiah, but you and I know the truth. YOU took the hair they planted on your father's dead body.
And YOU planted the four barbs they found in the guard who nearly killed my father today.
I can explain.
KSSH!
I didn't know they were going to hurt your father!
Who is "they"?
We can work together! We can get these guys! I'll wear a wire!
Okay, no wire.
SHK
Names.
I think you just peed your tighty-whities.
I'll tell you the names! Just put me back inside.

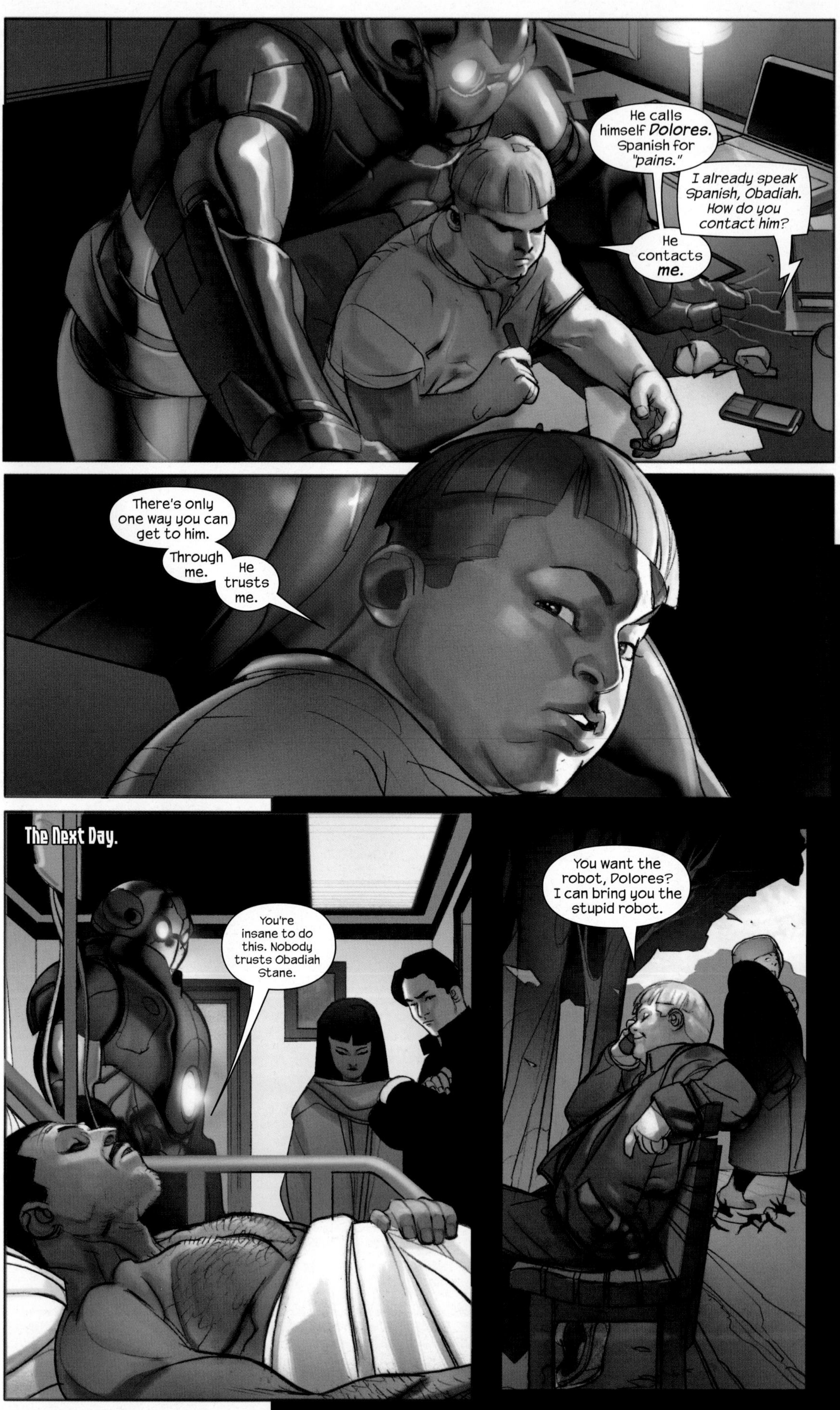
He calls himself Dolores. Spanish for "pains."
I already speak Spanish, Obadiah. How do you contact him?
He contacts me.
There's only one way you can get to him.
Through me.
He trusts me.
The Next Day.
You're insane to do this. Nobody trusts Obadiah Stane.
You want the robot, Dolores? I can bring you the stupid robot.

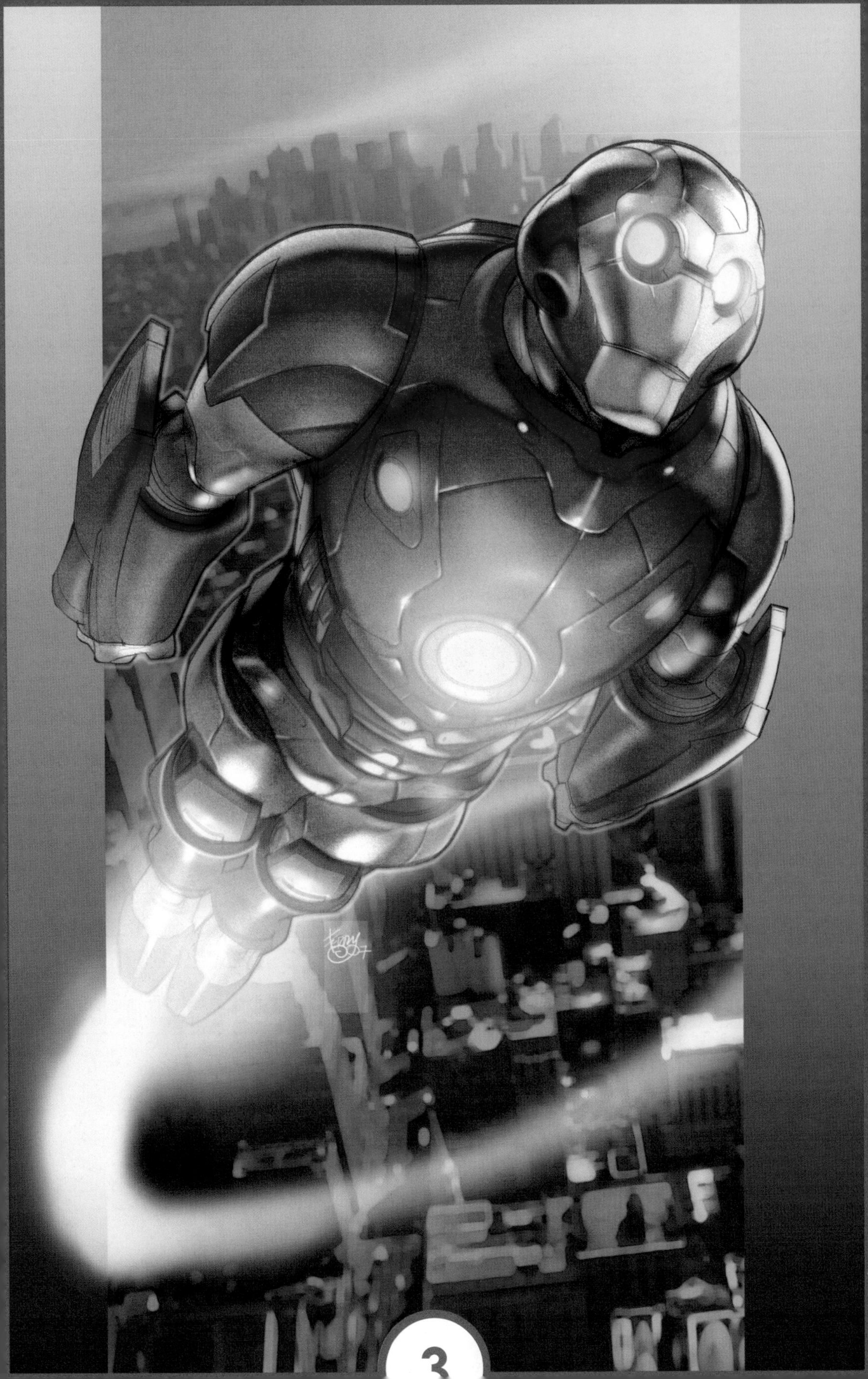

3

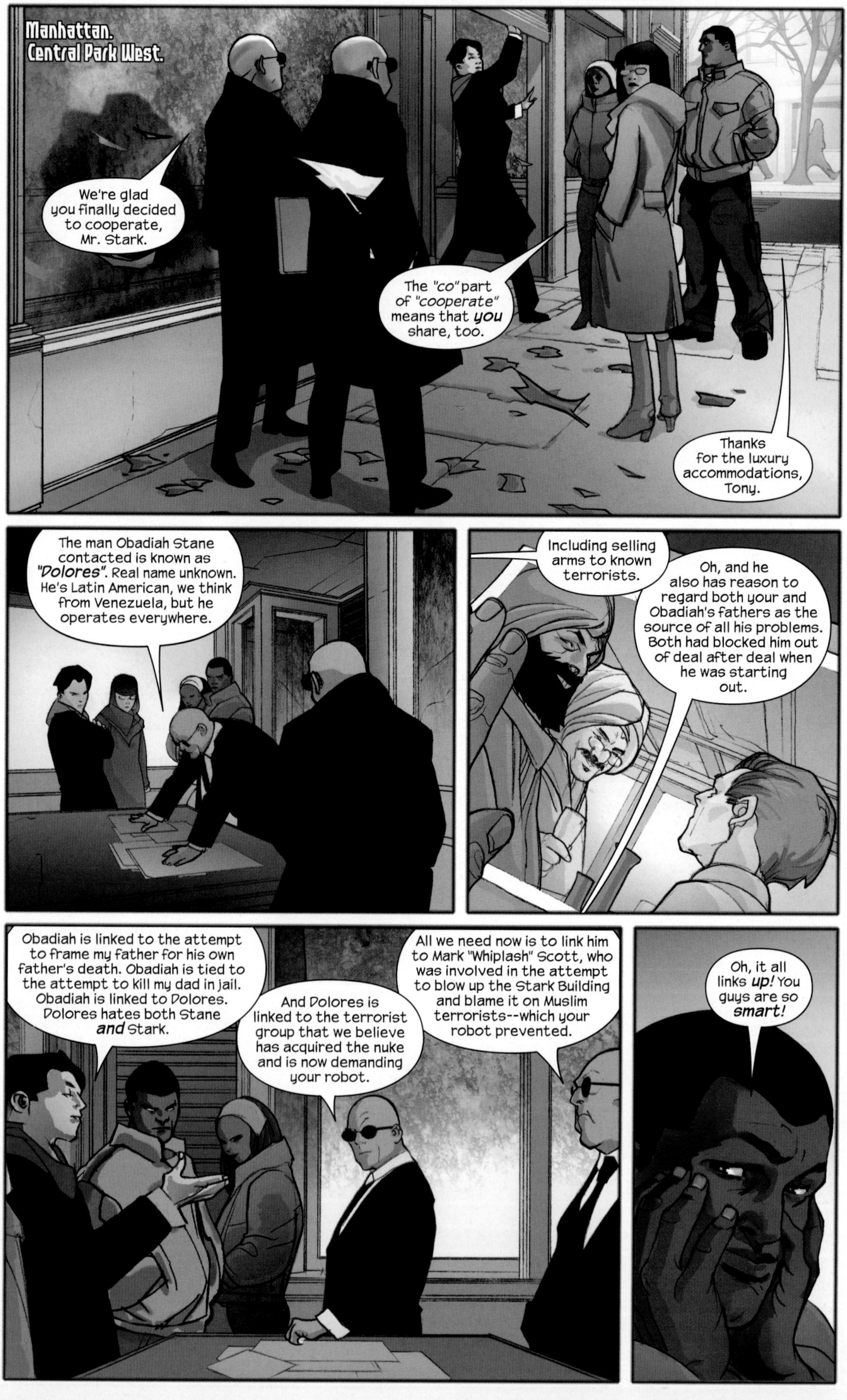
Manhattan.
Central Park West.
We're glad you finally decided to cooperate, Mr. Stark.
The "co" part of "cooperate" means that you share, too.
Thanks for the luxury accommodations, Tony.
The man Obadiah Stane contacted is known as "Dolores". Real name unknown. He's Latin American, we think from Venezuela, but he operates everywhere.
Including selling arms to known terrorists.
Oh, and he also has reason to regard both your and Obadiah's fathers as the source of all his problems. Both had blocked him out of deal after deal when he was starting out.
Obadiah is linked to the attempt to frame my father for his own father's death. Obadiah is tied to the attempt to kill my dad in jail. Obadiah is linked to Dolores. Dolores hates both Stane and Stark.
And Dolores is linked to the terrorist group that we believe has acquired the nuke and is now demanding your robot.
All we need now is to link him to Mark "Whiplash" Scott, who was involved in the attempt to blow up the Stark Building and blame it on Muslim terrorists--which your robot prevented.
Oh, it all links up! You guys are so smart!

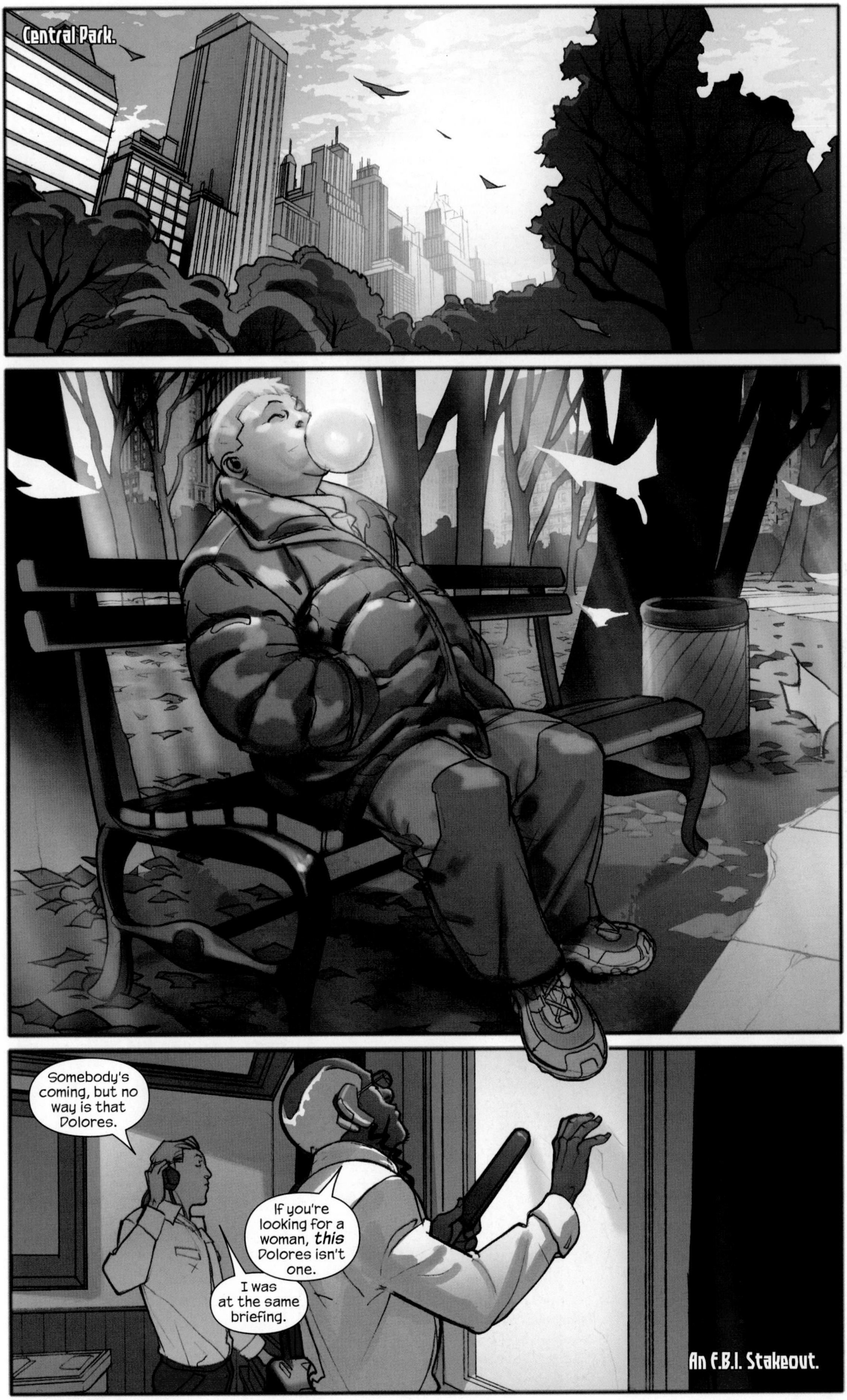
Central Park.
Somebody's coming, but no way is that Dolores.
If you're looking for a woman, *this* Dolores isn't one.
I was at the same briefing.
An F.B.I. Stakeout.

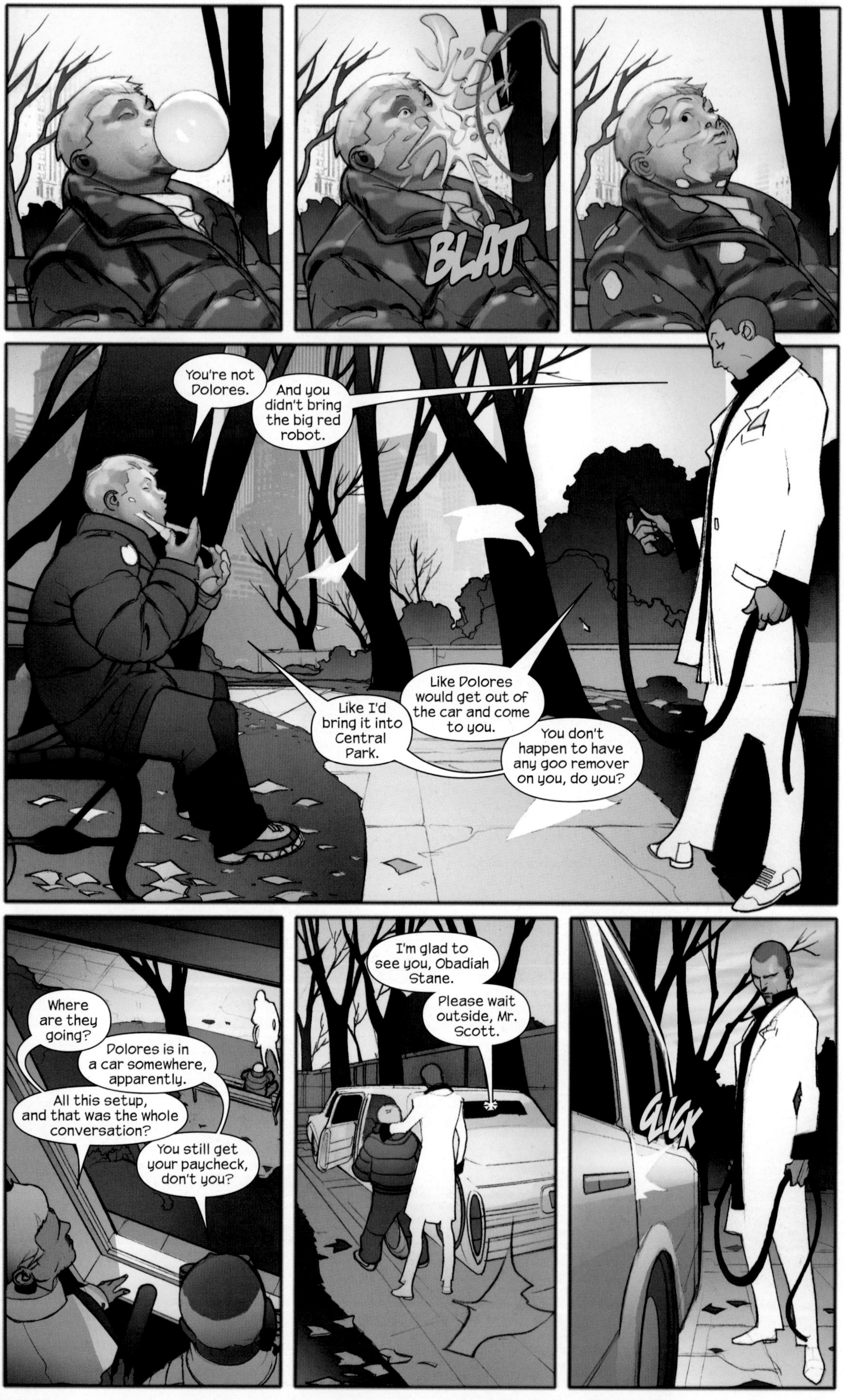
BLAT
You're not Dolores.
And you didn't bring the big red robot.
Like I'd bring it into Central Park.
Like Dolores would get out of the car and come to you.
You don't happen to have any goo remover on you, do you?
Where are they going?
Dolores is in a car somewhere, apparently.
All this setup, and that was the whole conversation?
You still get your paycheck, don't you?
I'm glad to see you, Obadiah Stane.
Please wait outside, Mr. Scott.
CLICK

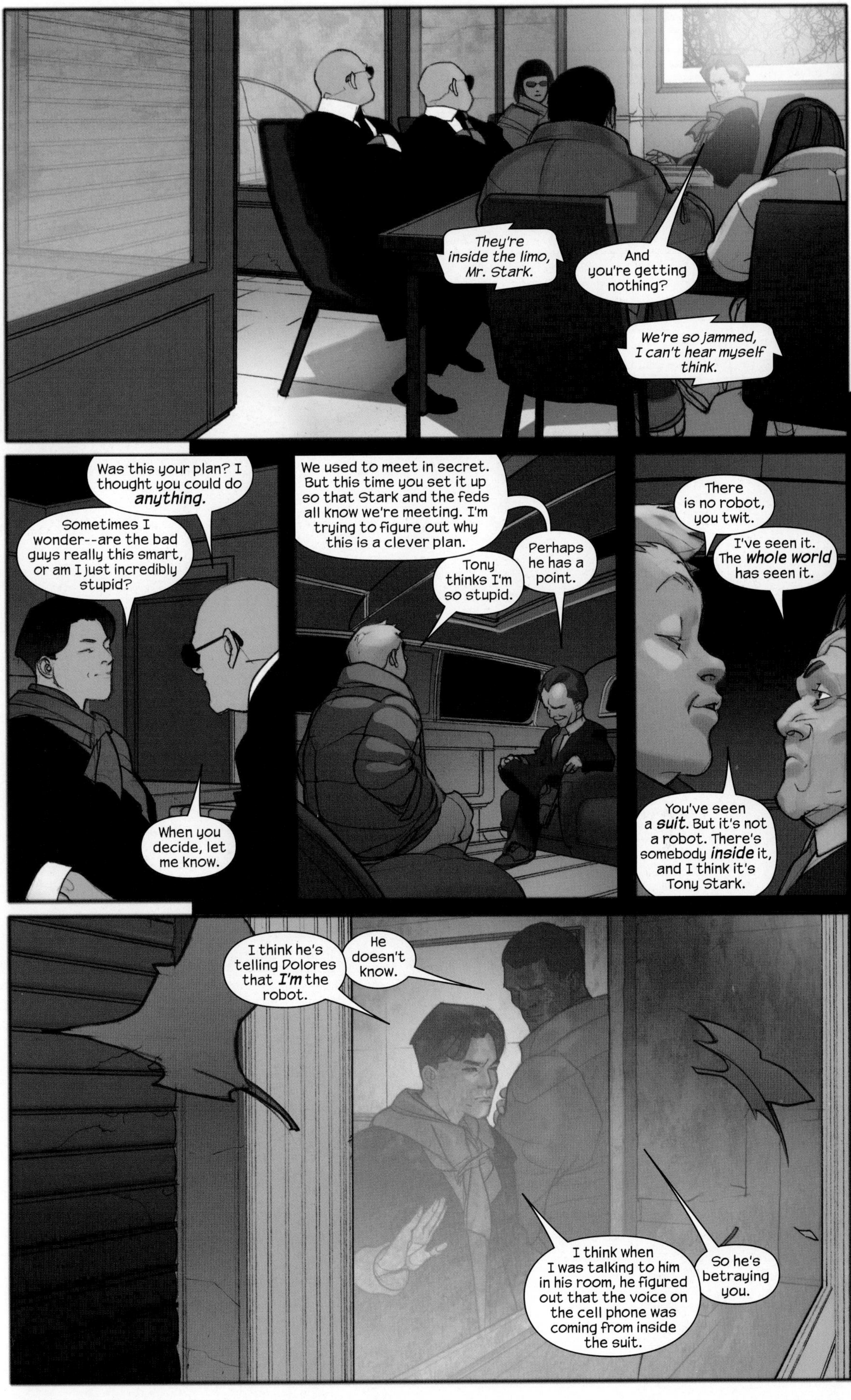
They're inside the limo, Mr. Stark.
And you're getting nothing?
We're so jammed, I can't hear myself think.
Was this your plan? I thought you could do anything.
Sometimes I wonder--are the bad guys really this smart, or am I just incredibly stupid?
When you decide, let me know.
We used to meet in secret. But this time you set it up so that Stark and the feds all know we're meeting. I'm trying to figure out why this is a clever plan.
Perhaps he has a point.
Tony thinks I'm so stupid.
There is no robot, you twit.
I've seen it. The whole world has seen it.
You've seen a suit. But it's not a robot. There's somebody inside it, and I think it's Tony Stark.
I think he's telling Dolores that I'm the robot.
He doesn't know.
I think when I was talking to him in his room, he figured out that the voice on the cell phone was coming from inside the suit.
So he's betraying you.

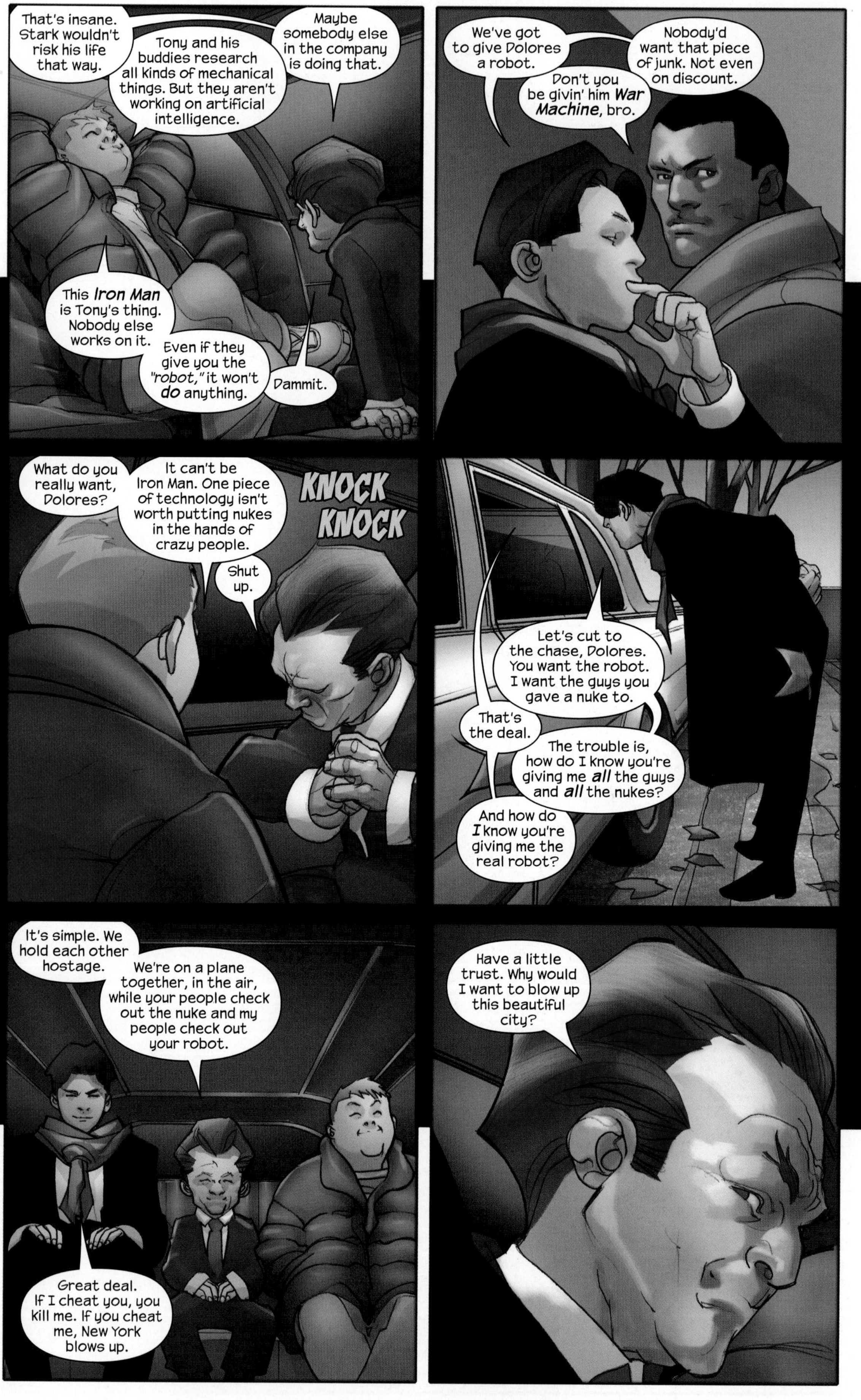

That's insane. Stark wouldn't risk his life that way.
Tony and his buddies research all kinds of mechanical things. But they aren't working on artificial intelligence.
Maybe somebody else in the company is doing that.
This *Iron Man* is Tony's thing. Nobody else works on it.
Even if they give you the *"robot,"* it won't **do** anything.
Dammit.
We've got to give Dolores a robot.
Nobody'd want that piece of junk. Not even on discount.
Don't you be givin' him *War Machine*, bro.
What do you really want, Dolores?
It can't be Iron Man. One piece of technology isn't worth putting nukes in the hands of crazy people.
KNOCK KNOCK
Shut up.
Let's cut to the chase, Dolores. You want the robot. I want the guys you gave a nuke to.
That's the deal.
The trouble is, how do I know you're giving me *all* the guys and *all* the nukes?
And how do *I* know you're giving me the real robot?
It's simple. We hold each other hostage.
We're on a plane together, in the air, while your people check out the nuke and my people check out your robot.
Great deal. If I cheat you, you kill me. If you cheat me, New York blows up.
Have a little trust. Why would I want to blow up this beautiful city?

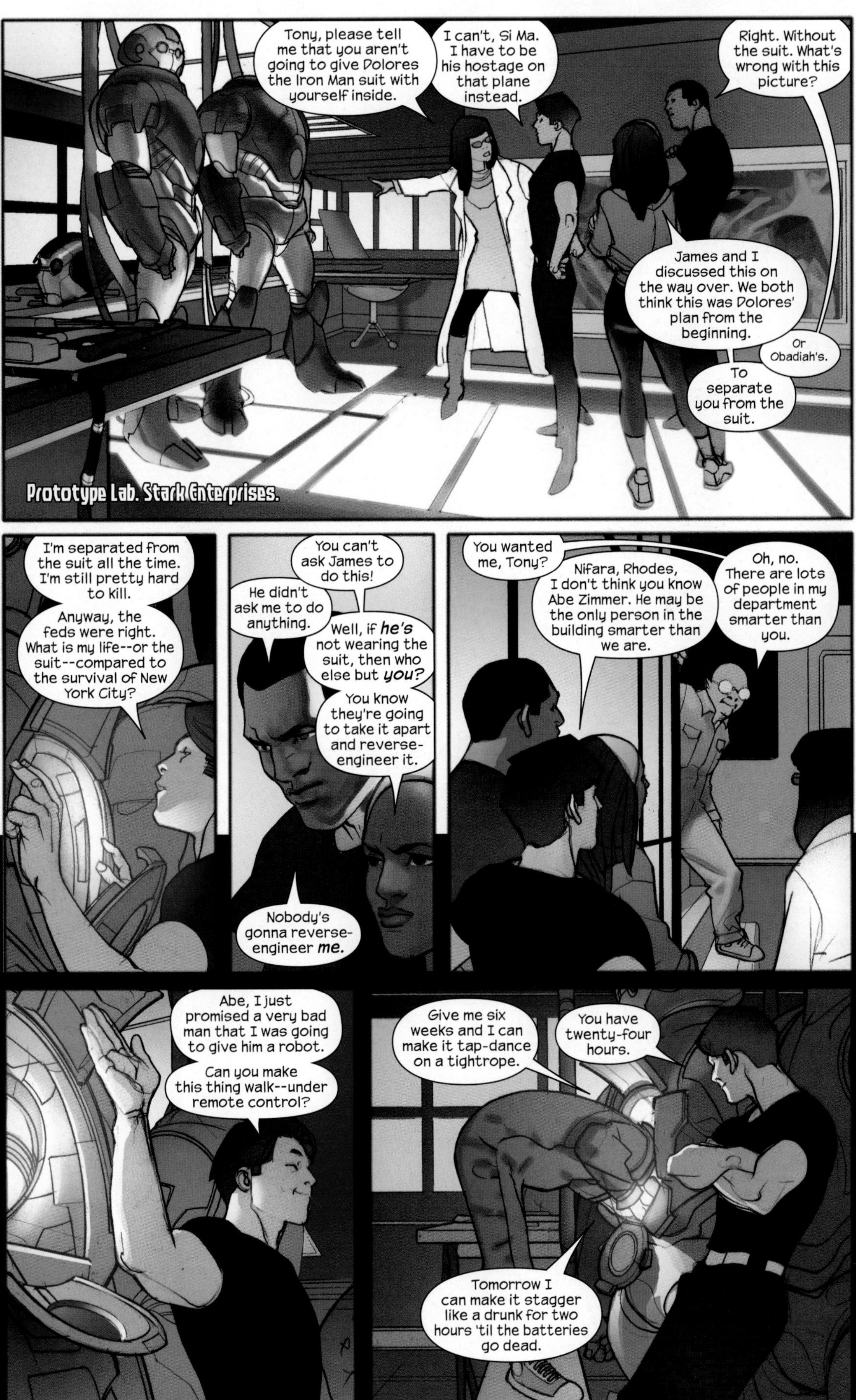
Tony, please tell me that you aren't going to give Dolores the Iron Man suit with yourself inside.
I can't, Si Ma. I have to be his hostage on that plane instead.
Right. Without the suit. What's wrong with this picture?
James and I discussed this on the way over. We both think this was Dolores' plan from the beginning.
Or Obadiah's.
To separate you from the suit.
Prototype Lab. Stark Enterprises.
I'm separated from the suit all the time. I'm still pretty hard to kill.
Anyway, the feds were right. What is my life--or the suit--compared to the survival of New York City?
You can't ask James to do this!
He didn't ask me to do anything.
Well, if he's not wearing the suit, then who else but you?
You know they're going to take it apart and reverse-engineer it.
Nobody's gonna reverse-engineer me.
You wanted me, Tony?
Nifara, Rhodes, I don't think you know Abe Zimmer. He may be the only person in the building smarter than we are.
Oh, no. There are lots of people in my department smarter than you.
Abe, I just promised a very bad man that I was going to give him a robot.
Can you make this thing walk--under remote control?
Give me six weeks and I can make it tap-dance on a tightrope.
You have twenty-four hours.
Tomorrow I can make it stagger like a drunk for two hours 'til the batteries go dead.

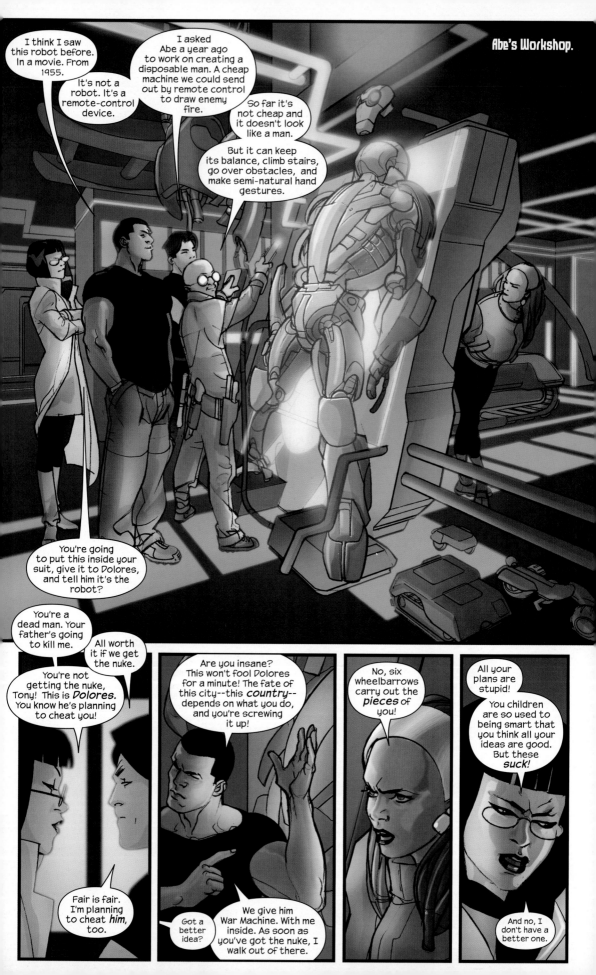

I think I saw this robot before. In a movie. From 1955.

It's not a robot. It's a remote-control device.

I asked Abe a year ago to work on creating a disposable man. A cheap machine we could send out by remote control to draw enemy fire.

So far it's not cheap and it doesn't look like a man.

But it can keep its balance, climb stairs, go over obstacles, and make semi-natural hand gestures.

You're going to put this inside your suit, give it to Dolores, and tell him it's the robot?

You're a dead man. Your father's going to kill me.

All worth it if we get the nuke.

You're not getting the nuke, Tony! This is Dolores. You know he's planning to cheat you!

Fair is fair. I'm planning to cheat him, too.

Are you insane? This won't fool Dolores for a minute! The fate of this city--this country-- depends on what you do, and you're screwing it up!

Got a better idea?

We give him War Machine. With me inside. As soon as you've got the nuke, I walk out of there.

No, six wheelbarrows carry out the pieces of you!

All your plans are stupid! You children are so used to being smart that you think all your ideas are good. But these suck!

And no, I don't have a better one.

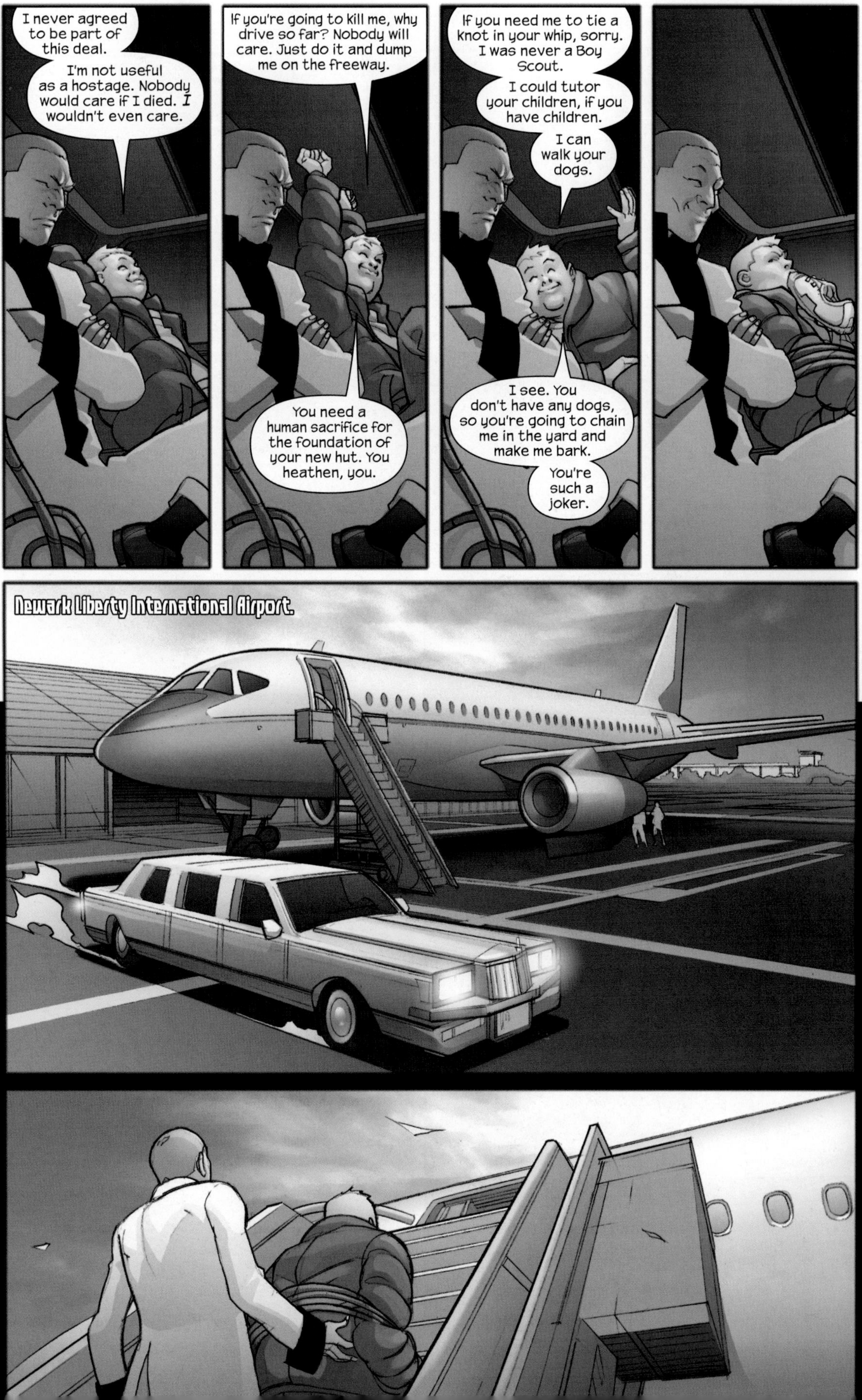
I never agreed to be part of this deal.
I'm not useful as a hostage. Nobody would care if I died. *I* wouldn't even care.
If you're going to kill me, why drive so far? Nobody will care. Just do it and dump me on the freeway.
You need a human sacrifice for the foundation of your new hut. You heathen, you.
If you need me to tie a knot in your whip, sorry. I was never a Boy Scout.
I could tutor your children, if you have children.
I can walk your dogs.
I see. You don't have any dogs, so you're going to chain me in the yard and make me bark.
You're such a joker.
Newark Liberty International Airport.

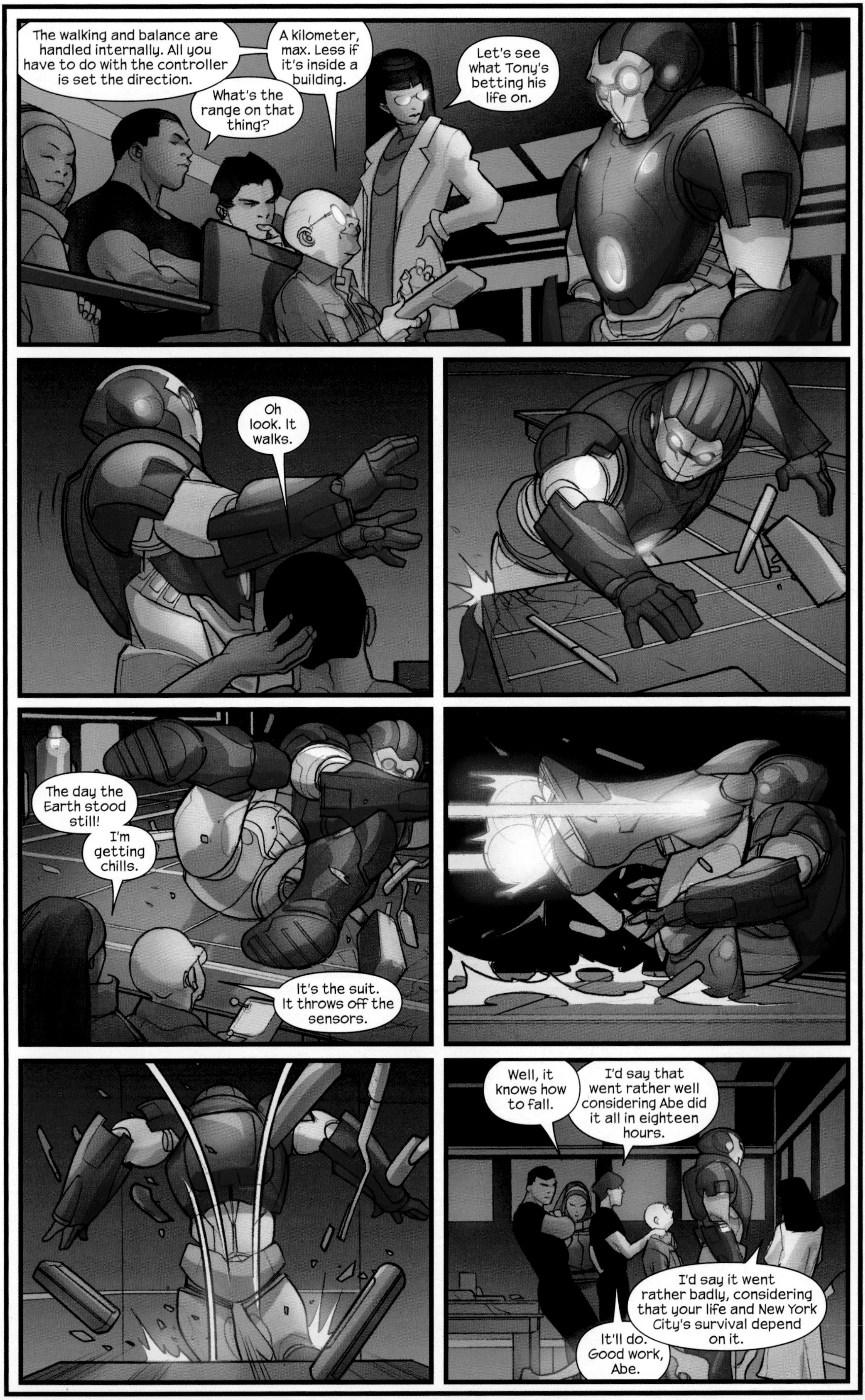

The walking and balance are handled internally. All you have to do with the controller is set the direction.
What's the range on that thing?
A kilometer, max. Less if it's inside a building.
Let's see what Tony's betting his life on.
Oh look. It walks.
The day the Earth stood still!
I'm getting chills.
It's the suit. It throws off the sensors.
Well, it knows how to fall.
I'd say that went rather well considering Abe did it all in eighteen hours.
I'd say it went rather badly, considering that your life and New York City's survival depend on it.
It'll do. Good work, Abe.

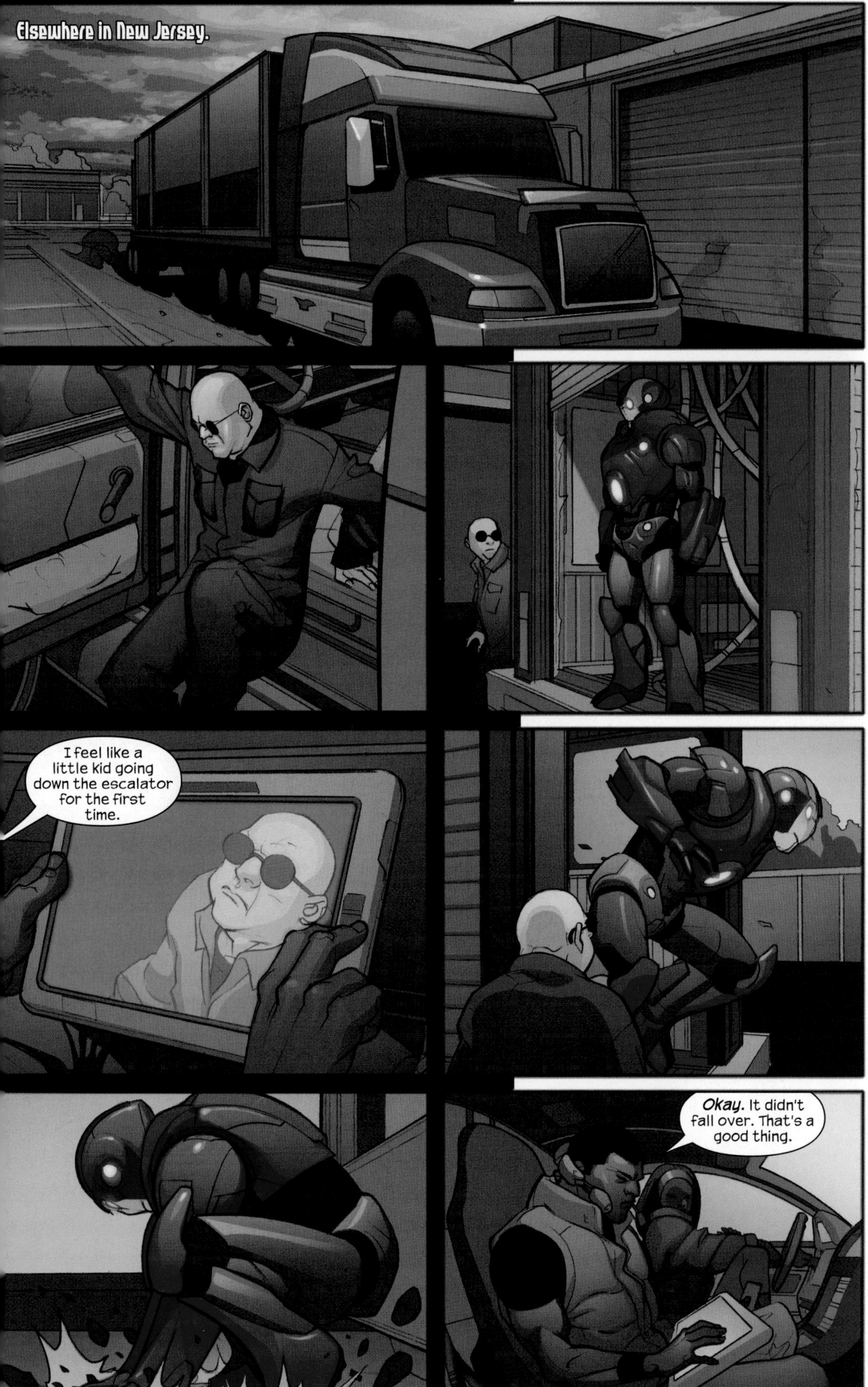
Elsewhere in New Jersey.
I feel like a little kid going down the escalator for the first time.
Okay. It didn't fall over. That's a good thing.

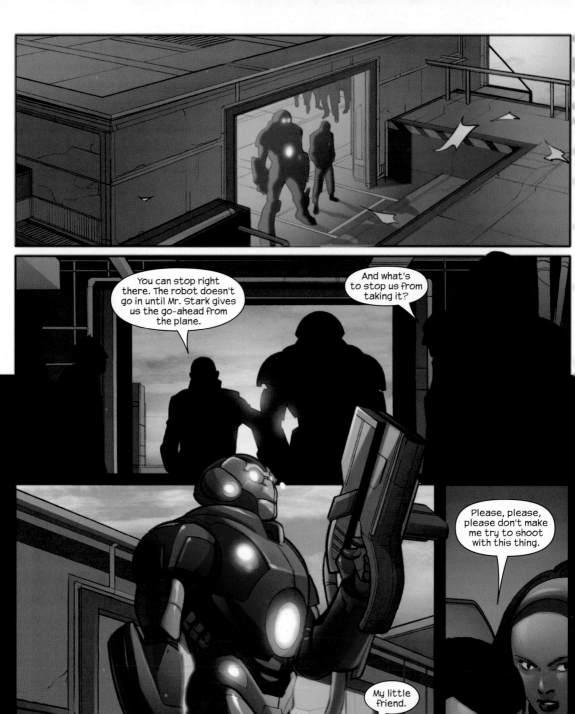

You can stop right there. The robot doesn't go in until Mr. Stark gives us the go-ahead from the plane.

And what's to stop us from taking it?

Please, please, please don't make me try to shoot with this thing.

My little friend.

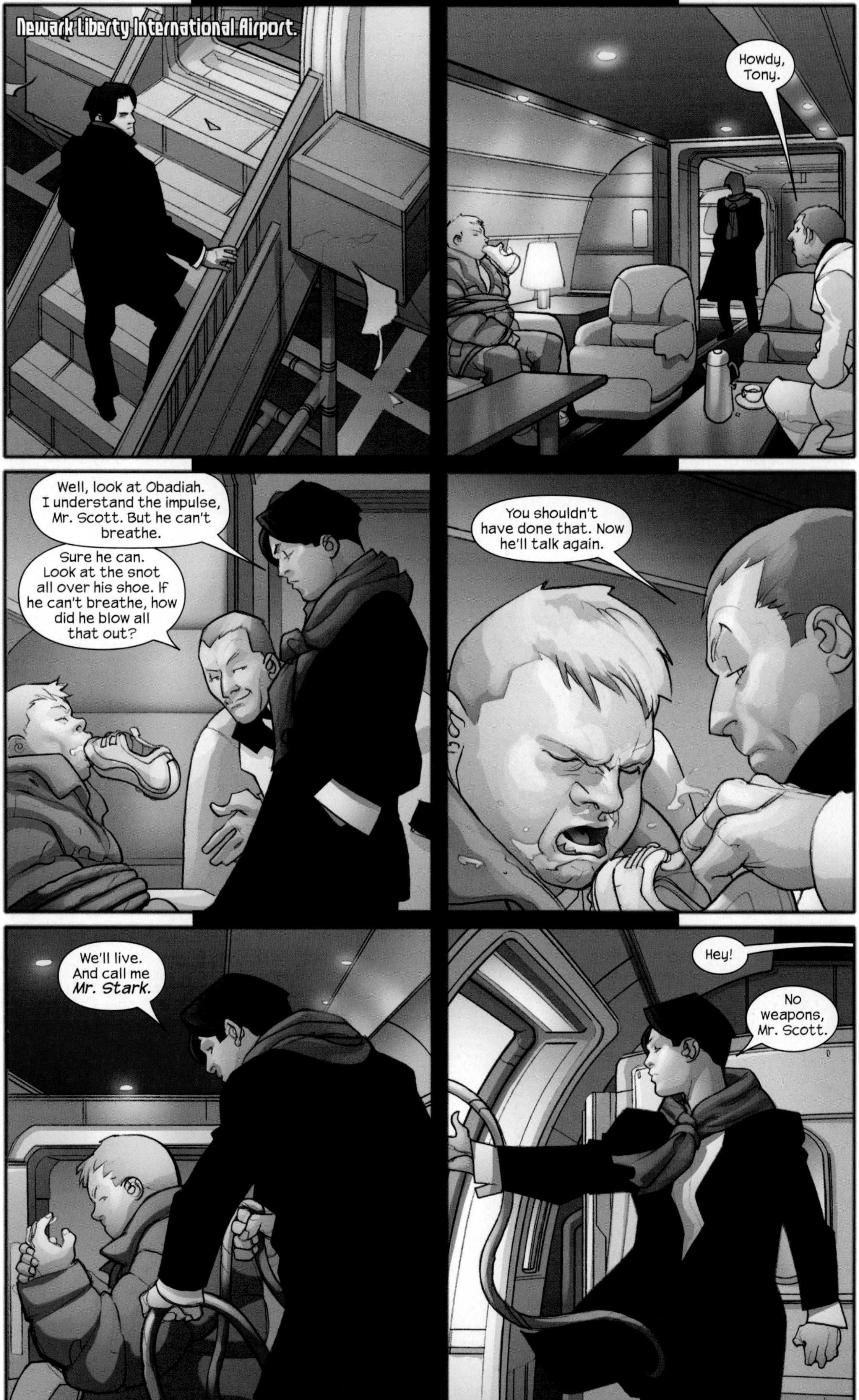
Newark Liberty International Airport.
Howdy, Tony.
Well, look at Obadiah. I understand the impulse, Mr. Scott. But he can't breathe.
Sure he can. Look at the snot all over his shoe. If he can't breathe, how did he blow all that out?
You shouldn't have done that. Now he'll talk again.
We'll live. And call me *Mr. Stark.*
Hey!
No weapons, Mr. Scott.

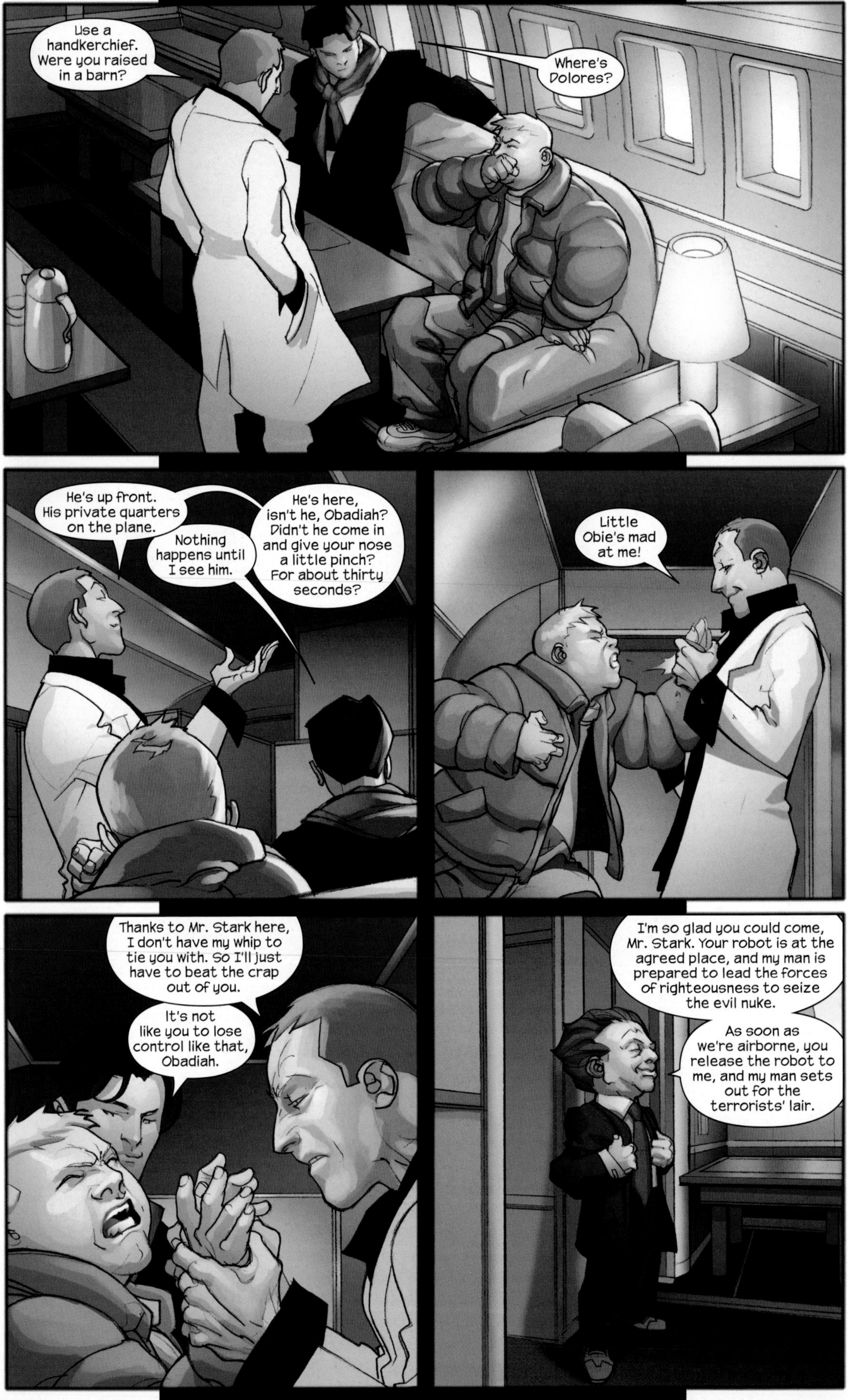
Use a handkerchief. Were you raised in a barn?
Where's Dolores?
He's up front. His private quarters on the plane.
Nothing happens until I see him.
He's here, isn't he, Obadiah? Didn't he come in and give your nose a little pinch? For about thirty seconds?
Little Obie's mad at me!
Thanks to Mr. Stark here, I don't have my whip to tie you with. So I'll just have to beat the crap out of you.
It's not like you to lose control like that, Obadiah.
I'm so glad you could come, Mr. Stark. Your robot is at the agreed place, and my man is prepared to lead the forces of righteousness to seize the evil nuke.
As soon as we're airborne, you release the robot to me, and my man sets out for the terrorists' lair.

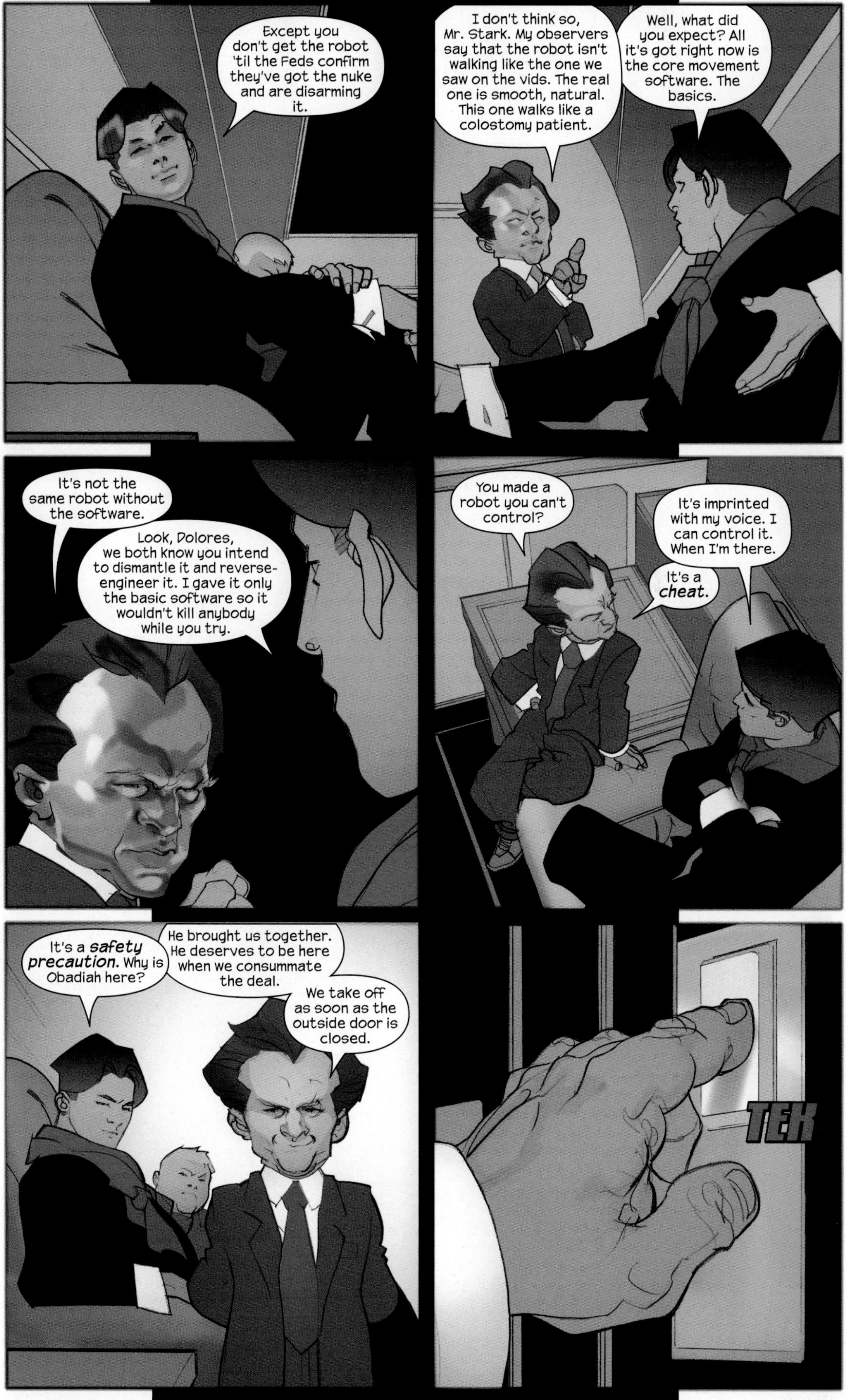
Except you don't get the robot 'til the Feds confirm they've got the nuke and are disarming it.
I don't think so, Mr. Stark. My observers say that the robot isn't walking like the one we saw on the vids. The real one is smooth, natural. This one walks like a colostomy patient.
Well, what did you expect? All it's got right now is the core movement software. The basics.
It's not the same robot without the software.
Look, Dolores, we both know you intend to dismantle it and reverse-engineer it. I gave it only the basic software so it wouldn't kill anybody while you try.
You made a robot you can't control?
It's imprinted with my voice. I can control it. When I'm there.
It's a *cheat*.
It's a *safety precaution*. Why is Obadiah here?
He brought us together. He deserves to be here when we consummate the deal.
We take off as soon as the outside door is closed.
TEK

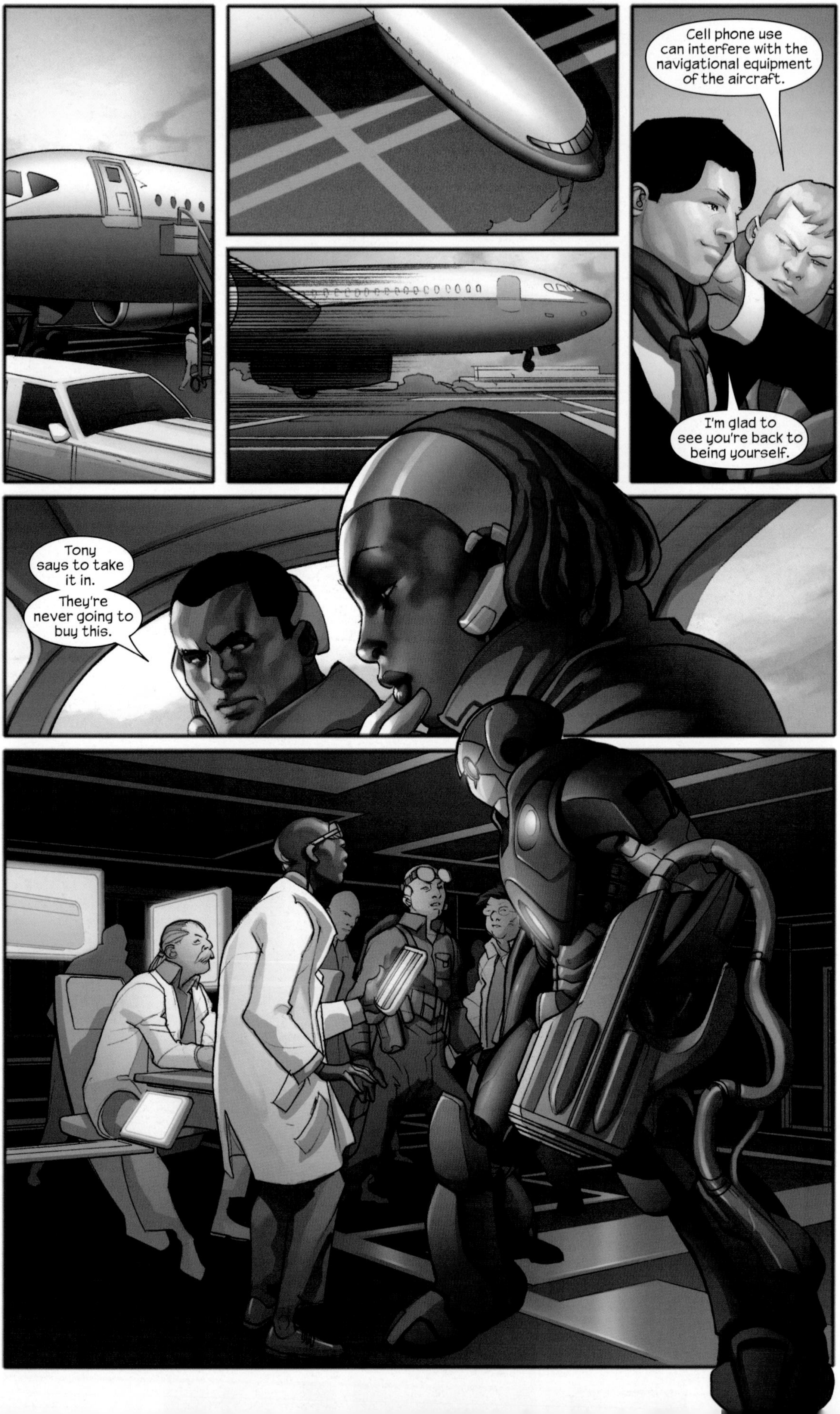
Cell phone use can interfere with the navigational equipment of the aircraft.
I'm glad to see you're back to being yourself.
Tony says to take it in.
They're never going to buy this.

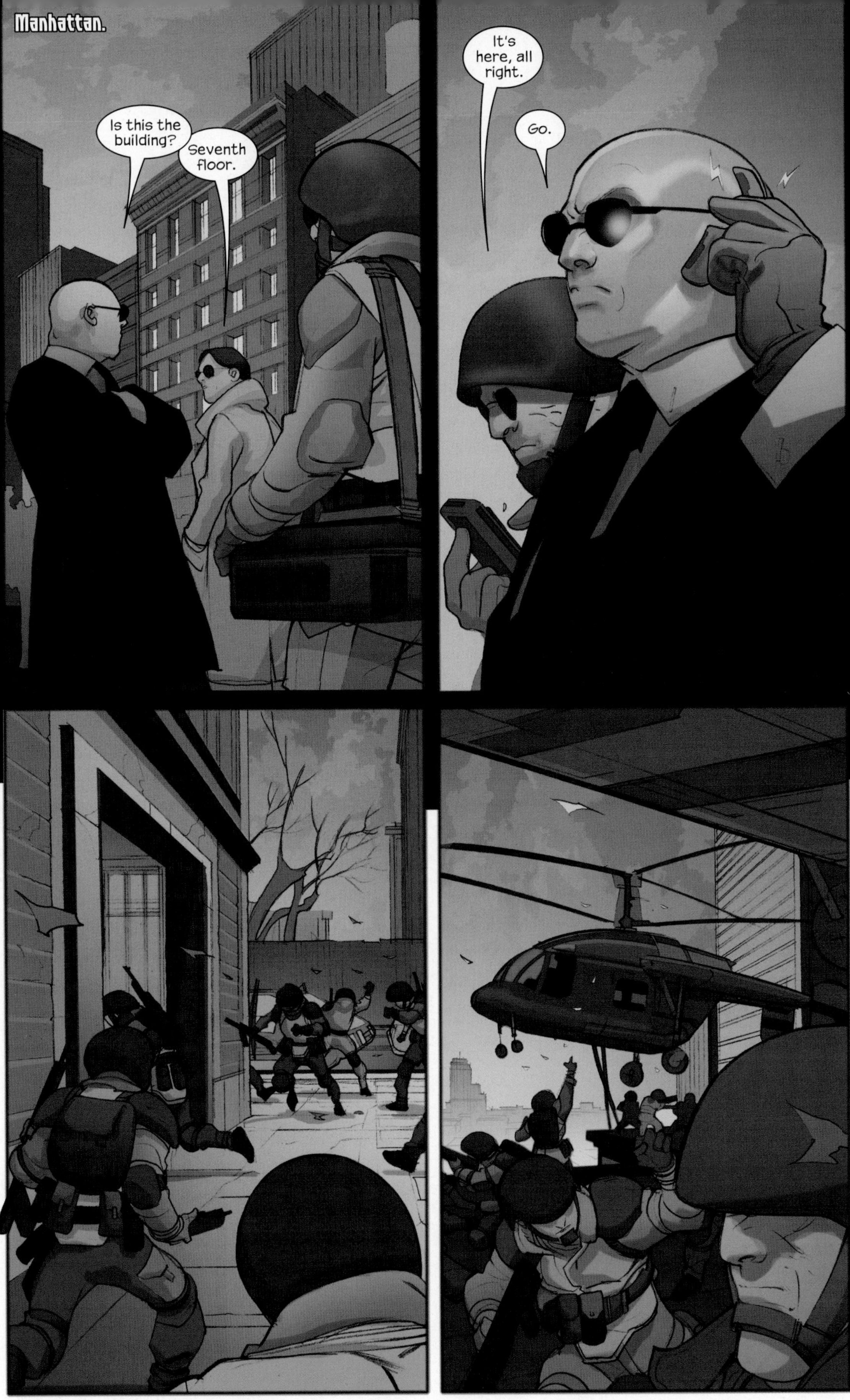
Manhattan.
Is this the building?
Seventh floor.
It's here, all right.
Go.

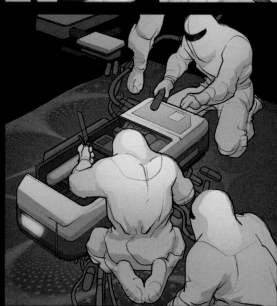

It's here. It's real. But we've got it defused.

Good. Excellent.

Except the bomb is all we got. Not a soul here. They knew we were coming and they're gone.

If they were ever there. We only have Dolores' word that there **were** any terrorists.

Be careful, Tony.

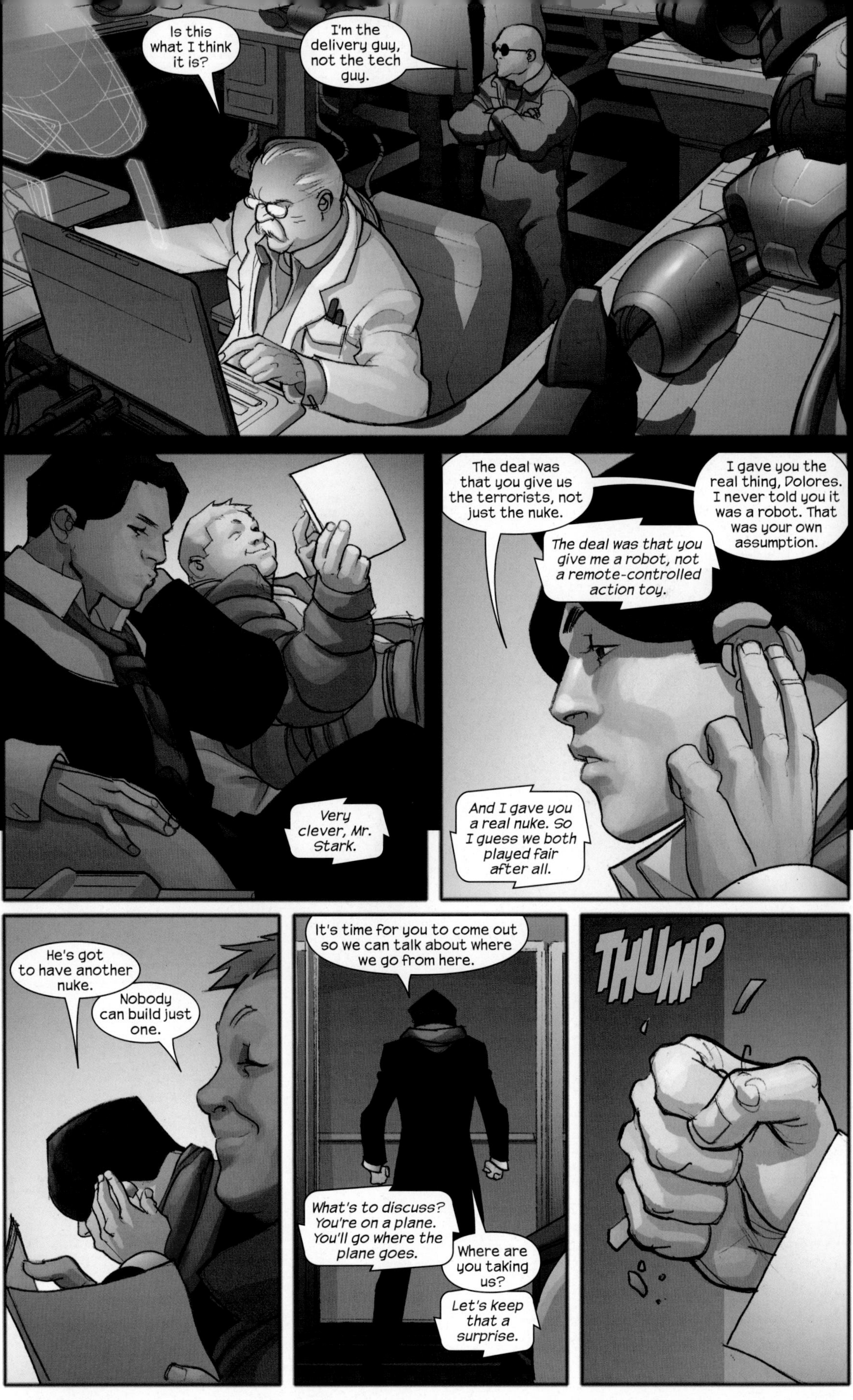
Is this what I think it is?
I'm the delivery guy, not the tech guy.
The deal was that you give us the terrorists, not just the nuke.
I gave you the real thing, Dolores. I never told you it was a robot. That was your own assumption.
The deal was that you give me a robot, not a remote-controlled action toy.
Very clever, Mr. Stark.
And I gave you a real nuke. So I guess we both played fair after all.
He's got to have another nuke.
Nobody can build just one.
It's time for you to come out so we can talk about where we go from here.
What's to discuss? You're on a plane. You'll go where the plane goes.
Where are you taking us?
Let's keep that a surprise.
THUMP

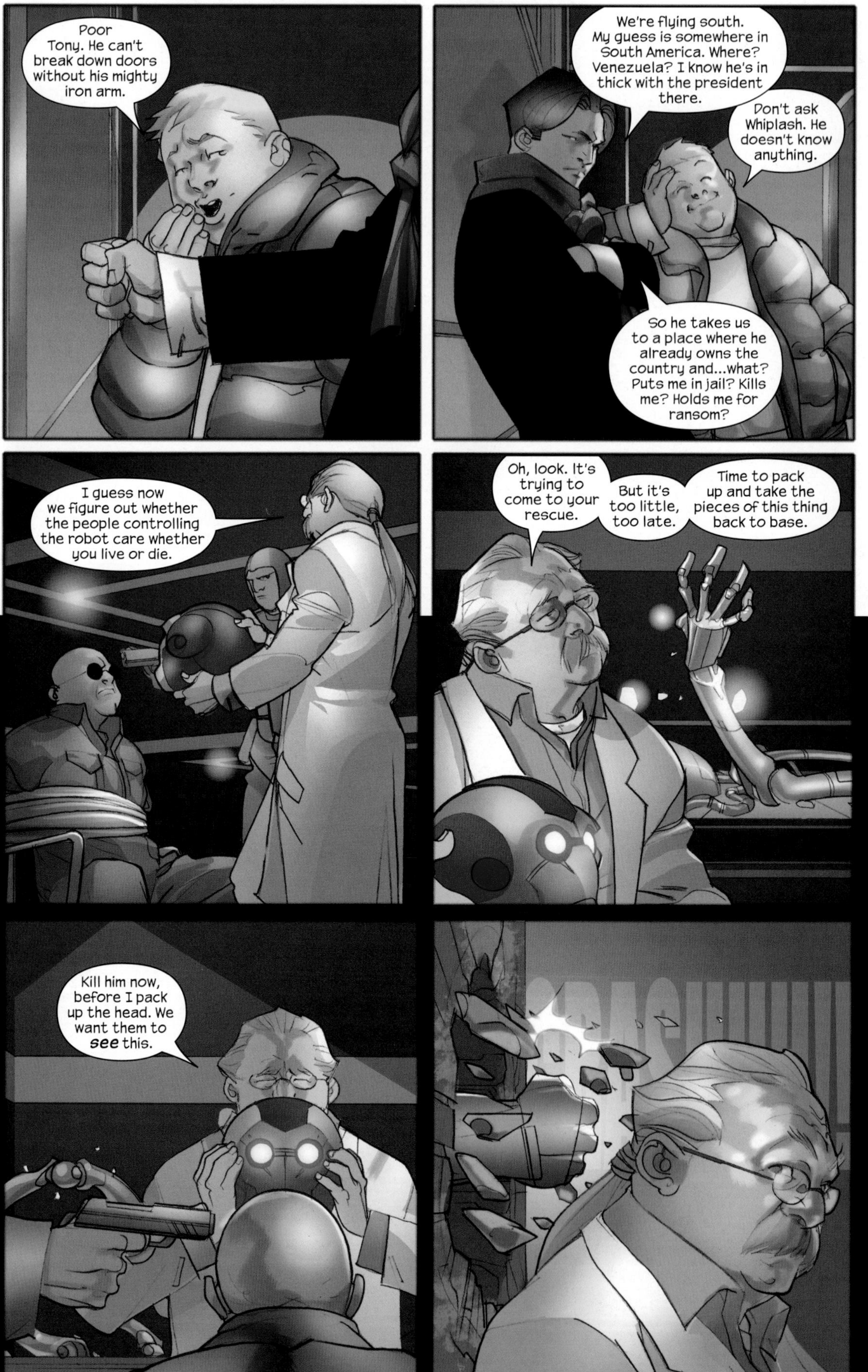
Poor Tony. He can't break down doors without his mighty iron arm.
We're flying south. My guess is somewhere in South America. Where? Venezuela? I know he's in thick with the president there.
Don't ask Whiplash. He doesn't know anything.
So he takes us to a place where he already owns the country and...what? Puts me in jail? Kills me? Holds me for ransom?
I guess now we figure out whether the people controlling the robot care whether you live or die.
Oh, look. It's trying to come to your rescue.
But it's too little, too late.
Time to pack up and take the pieces of this thing back to base.
Kill him now, before I pack up the head. We want them to *see* this.

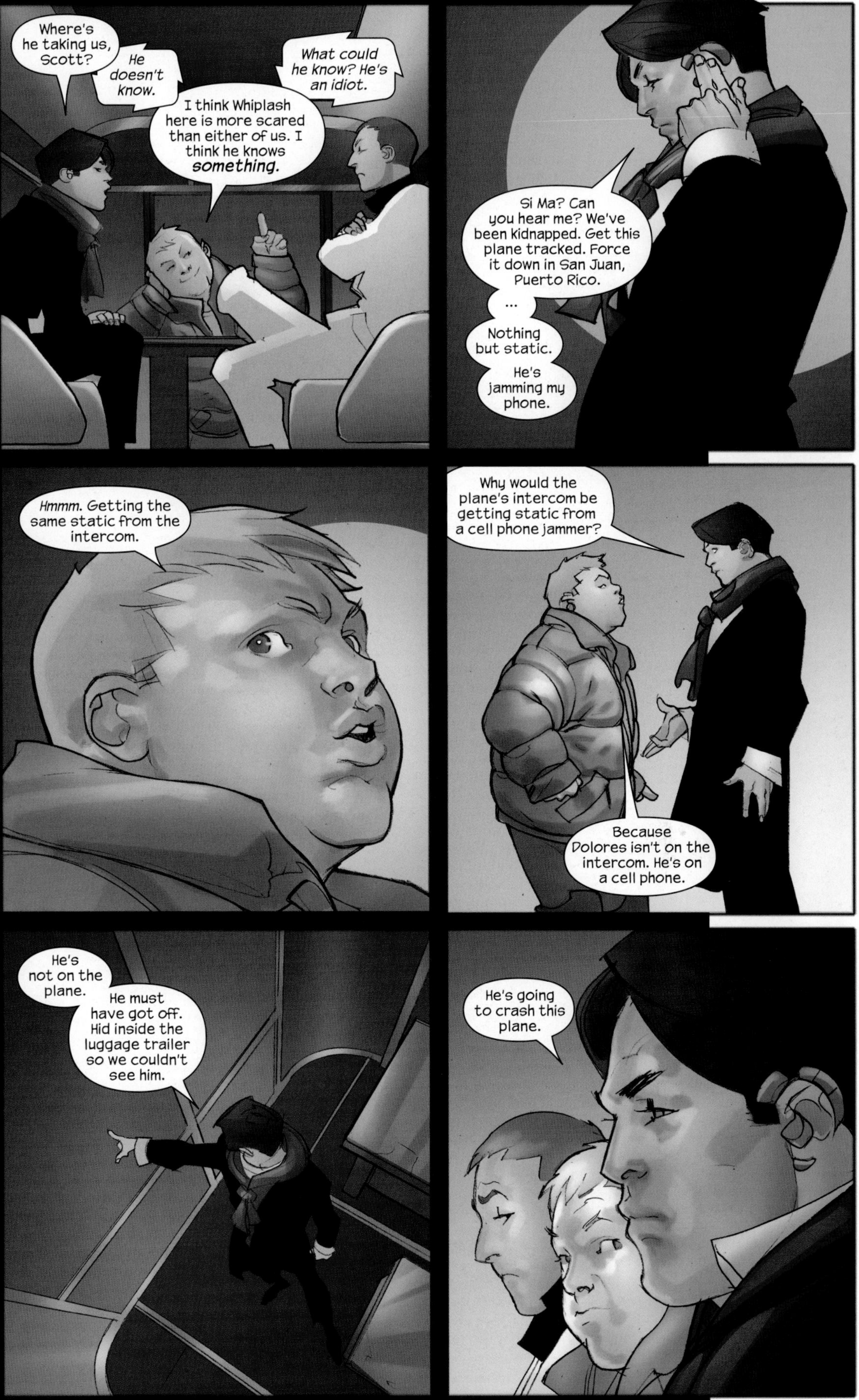
Where's he taking us, Scott?
He doesn't know.
What could he know? He's an idiot.
I think Whiplash here is more scared than either of us. I think he knows *something.*
Si Ma? Can you hear me? We've been kidnapped. Get this plane tracked. Force it down in San Juan, Puerto Rico.
...
Nothing but static.
He's jamming my phone.
Hmmm. Getting the same static from the intercom.
Why would the plane's intercom be getting static from a cell phone jammer?
Because Dolores isn't on the intercom. He's on a cell phone.
He's not on the plane.
He must have got off. Hid inside the luggage trailer so we couldn't see him.
He's going to crash this plane.

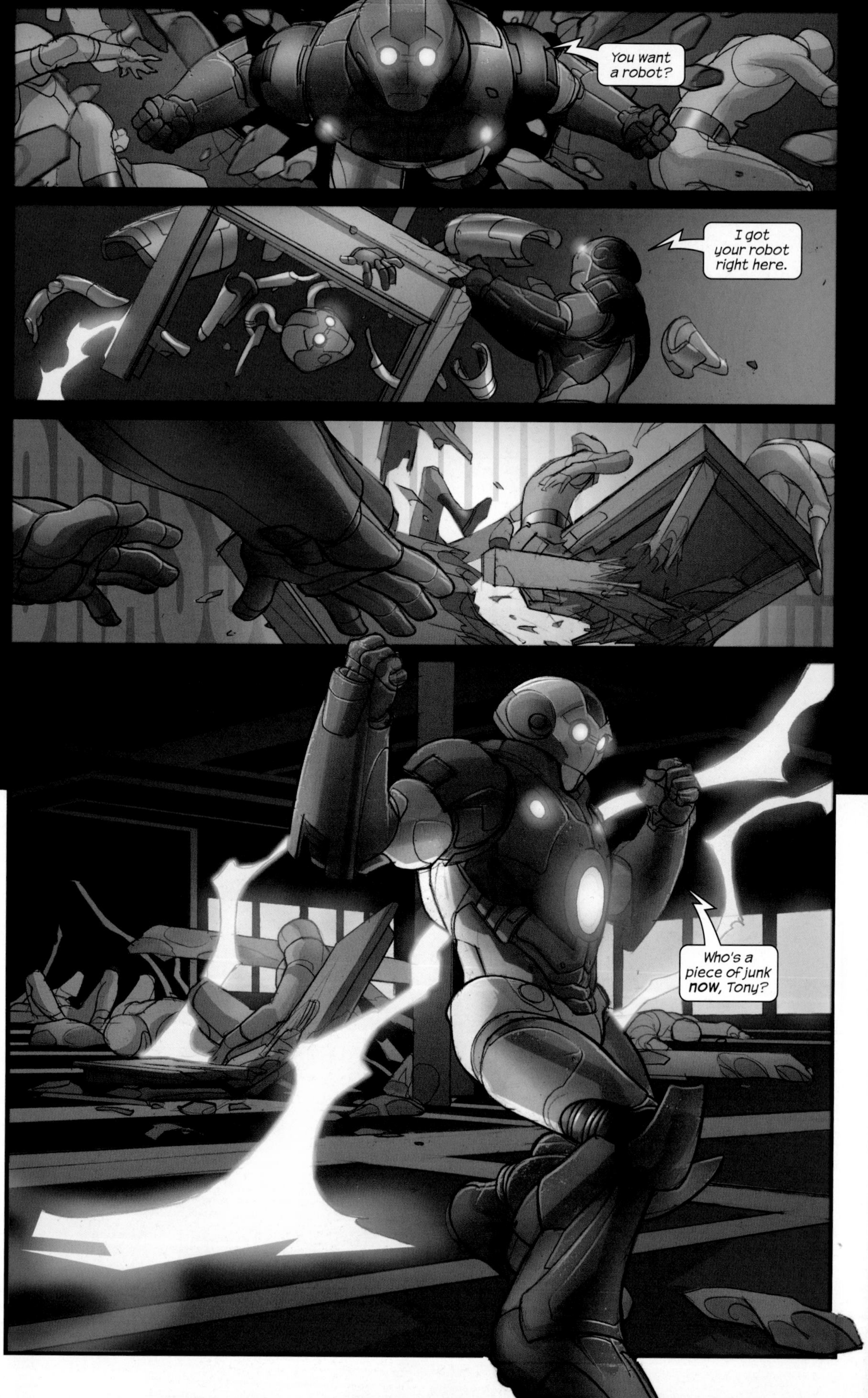
You want a robot?
I got your robot right here.
Who's a piece of junk NOW, Tony?

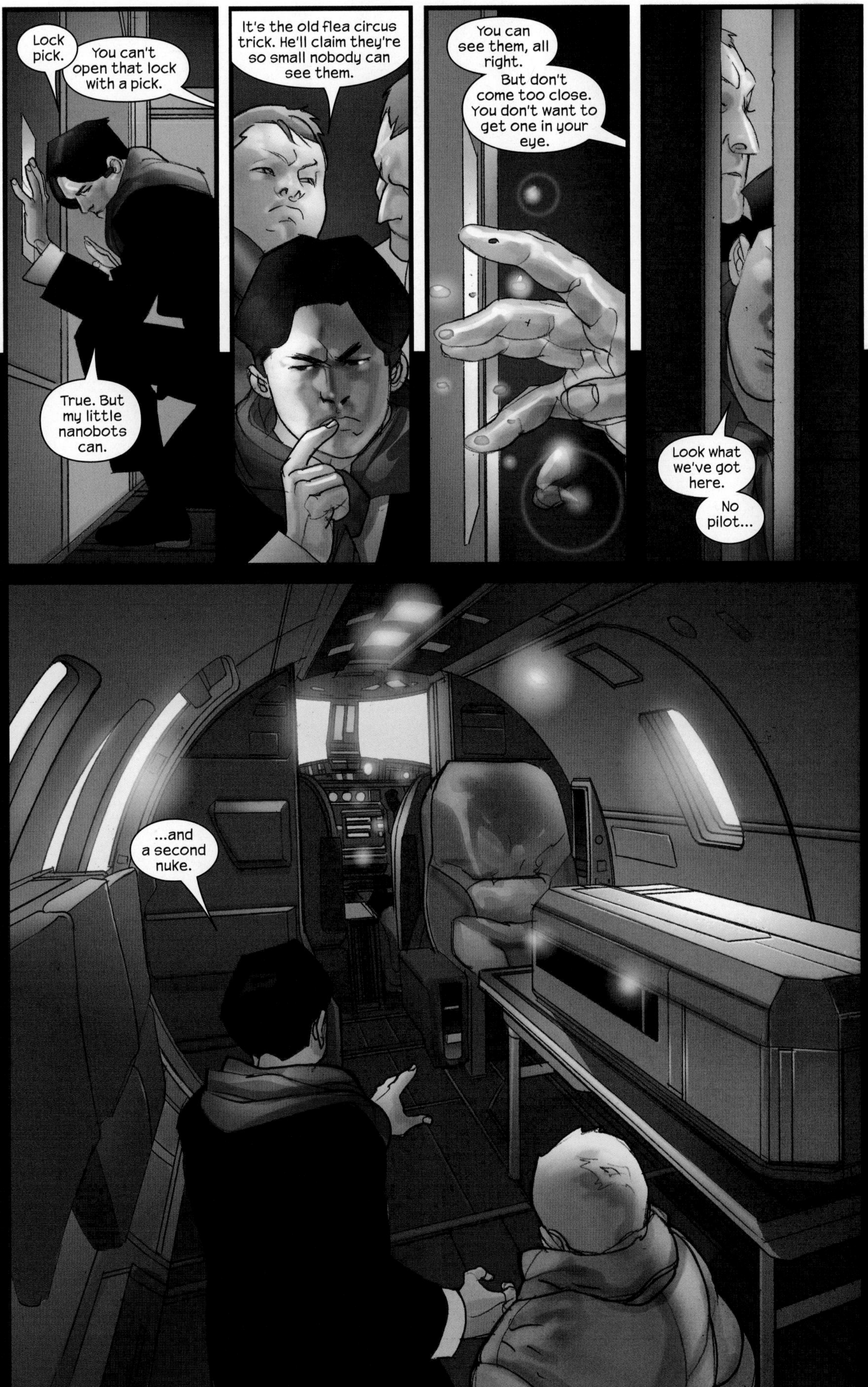
Lock pick.
You can't open that lock with a pick.
True. But my little nanobots can.
It's the old flea circus trick. He'll claim they're so small nobody can see them.
You can see them, all right.
But don't come too close. You don't want to get one in your eye.
Look what we've got here.
No pilot...
...and a second nuke.

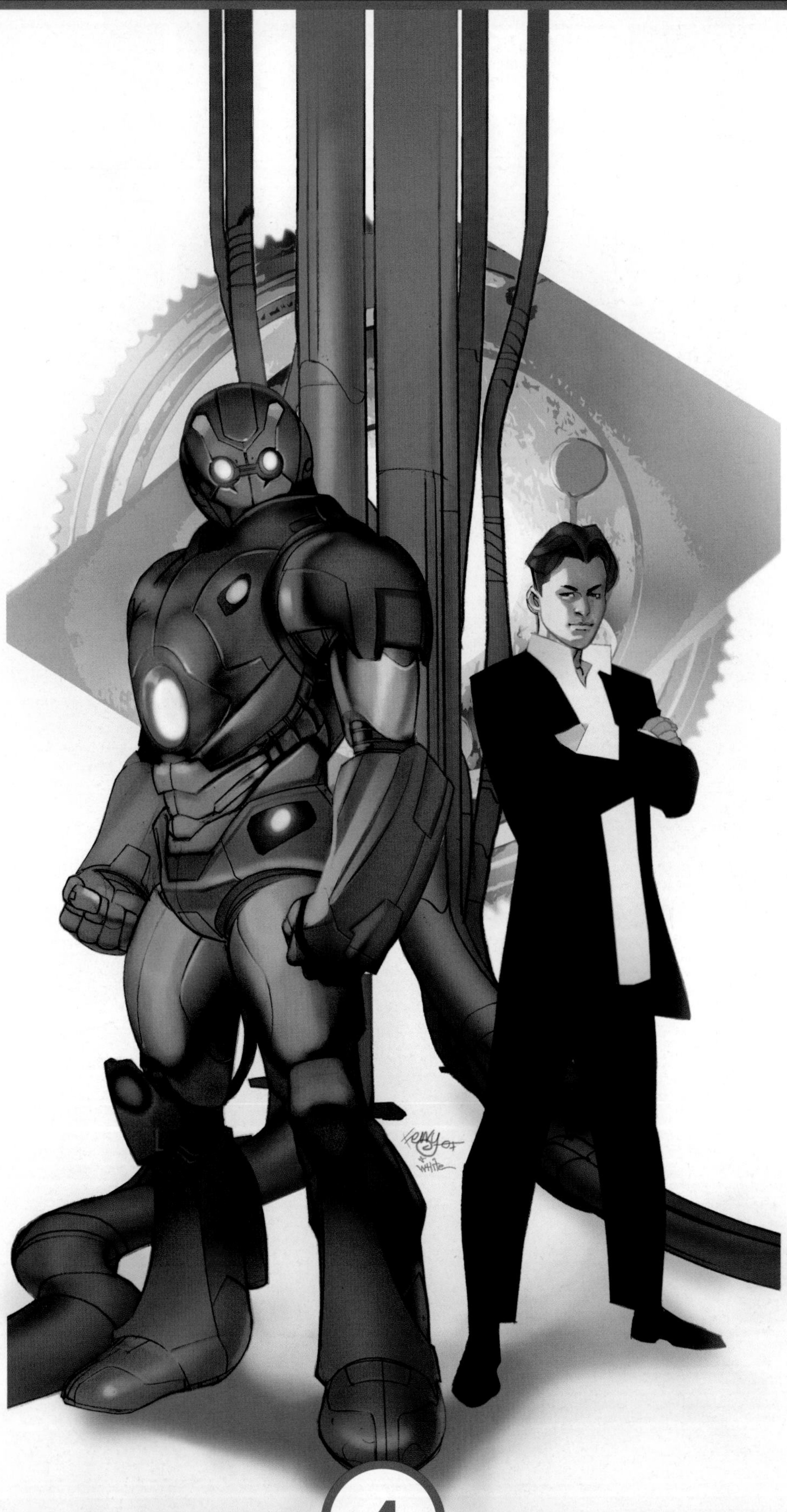

4

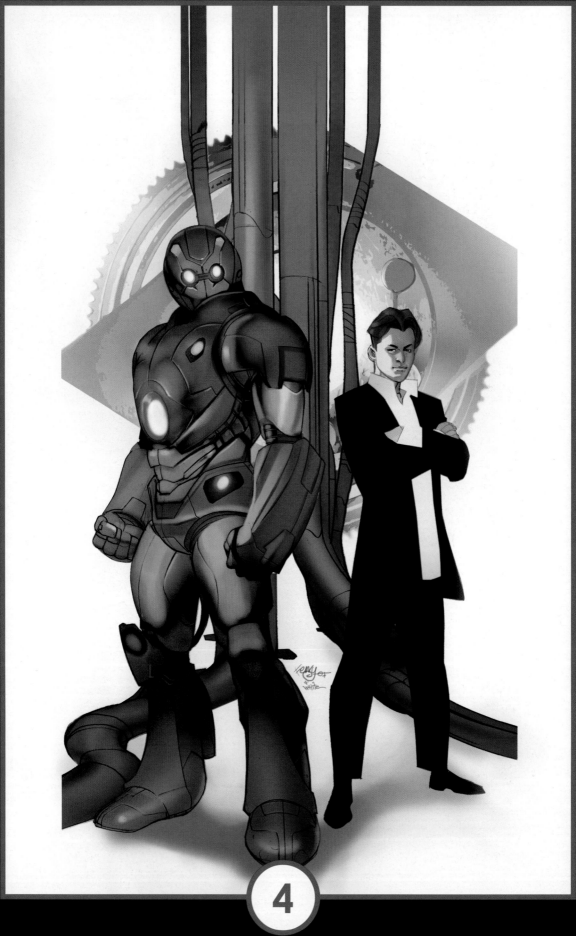

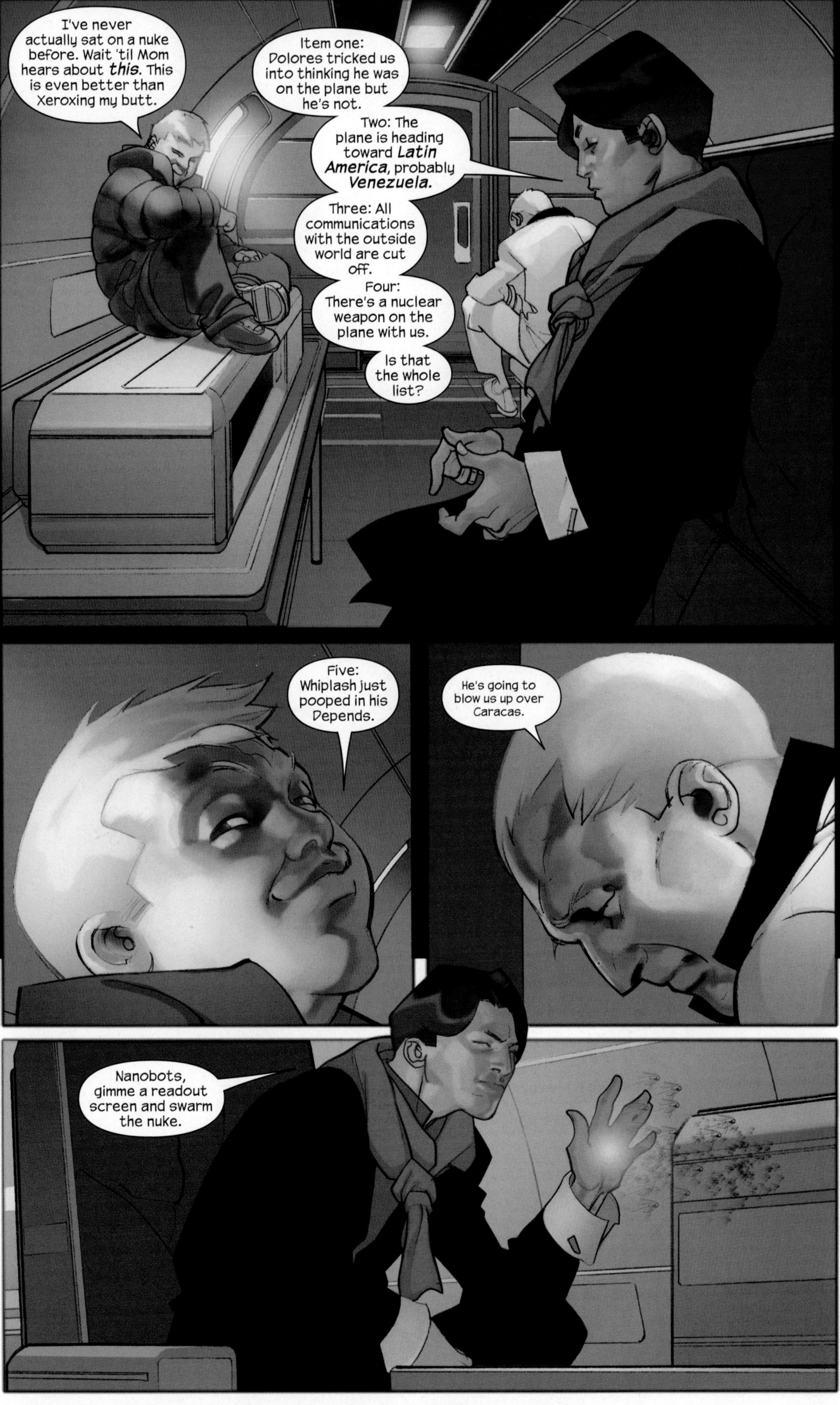
I've never actually sat on a nuke before. Wait 'til Mom hears about *this*. This is even better than Xeroxing my butt.
Item one: Dolores tricked us into thinking he was on the plane but he's not.
Two: The plane is heading toward *Latin America*, probably *Venezuela.*
Three: All communications with the outside world are cut off.
Four: There's a nuclear weapon on the plane with us.
Is that the whole list?
Five: Whiplash just pooped in his Depends.
He's going to blow us up over Caracas.
Nanobots, gimme a readout screen and swarm the nuke.

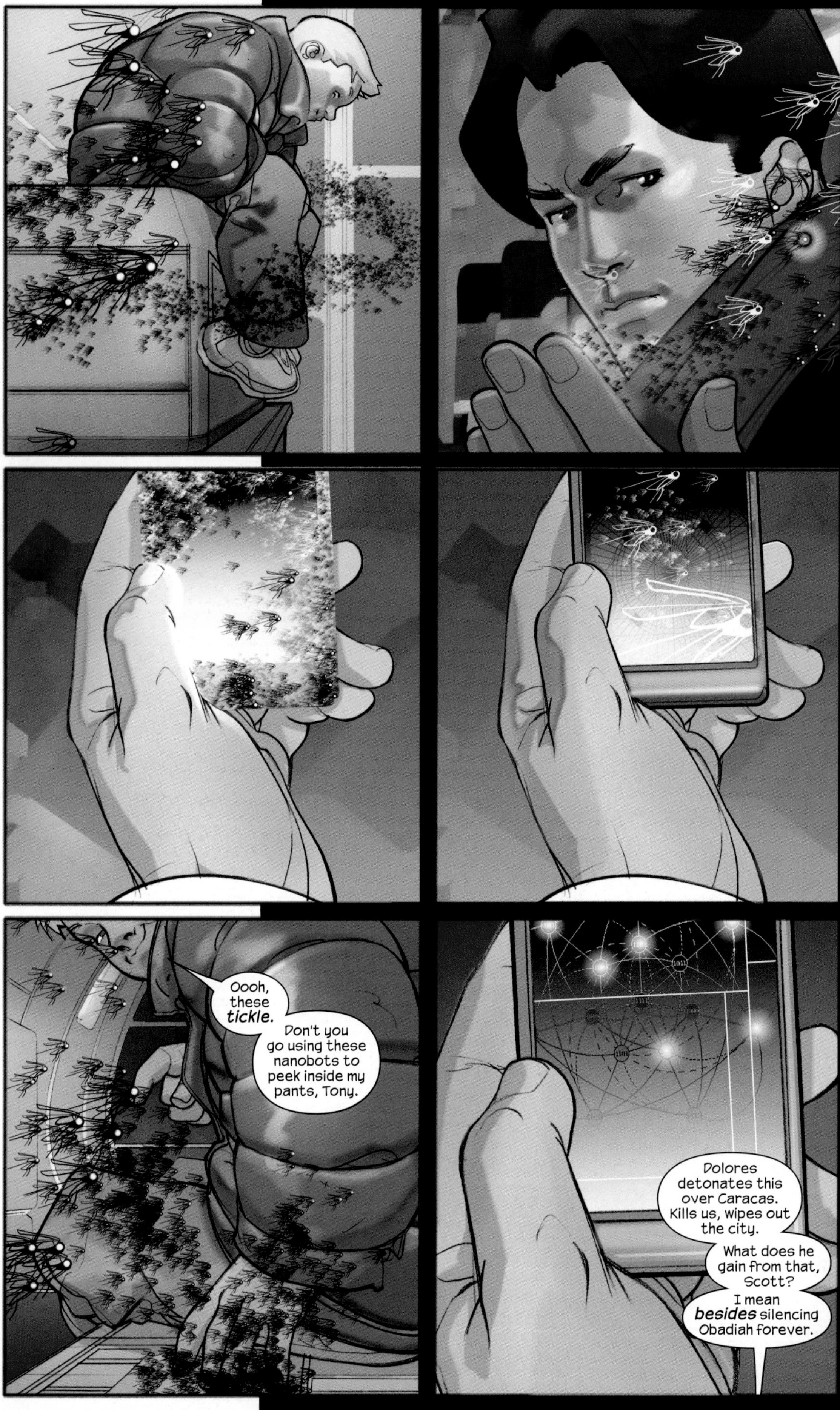
Oooh, these *tickle.*
Don't you go using these nanobots to peek inside my pants, Tony.
Dolores detonates this over Caracas. Kills us, wipes out the city.
What does he gain from that, Scott?
I mean ***besides*** silencing Obadiah forever.

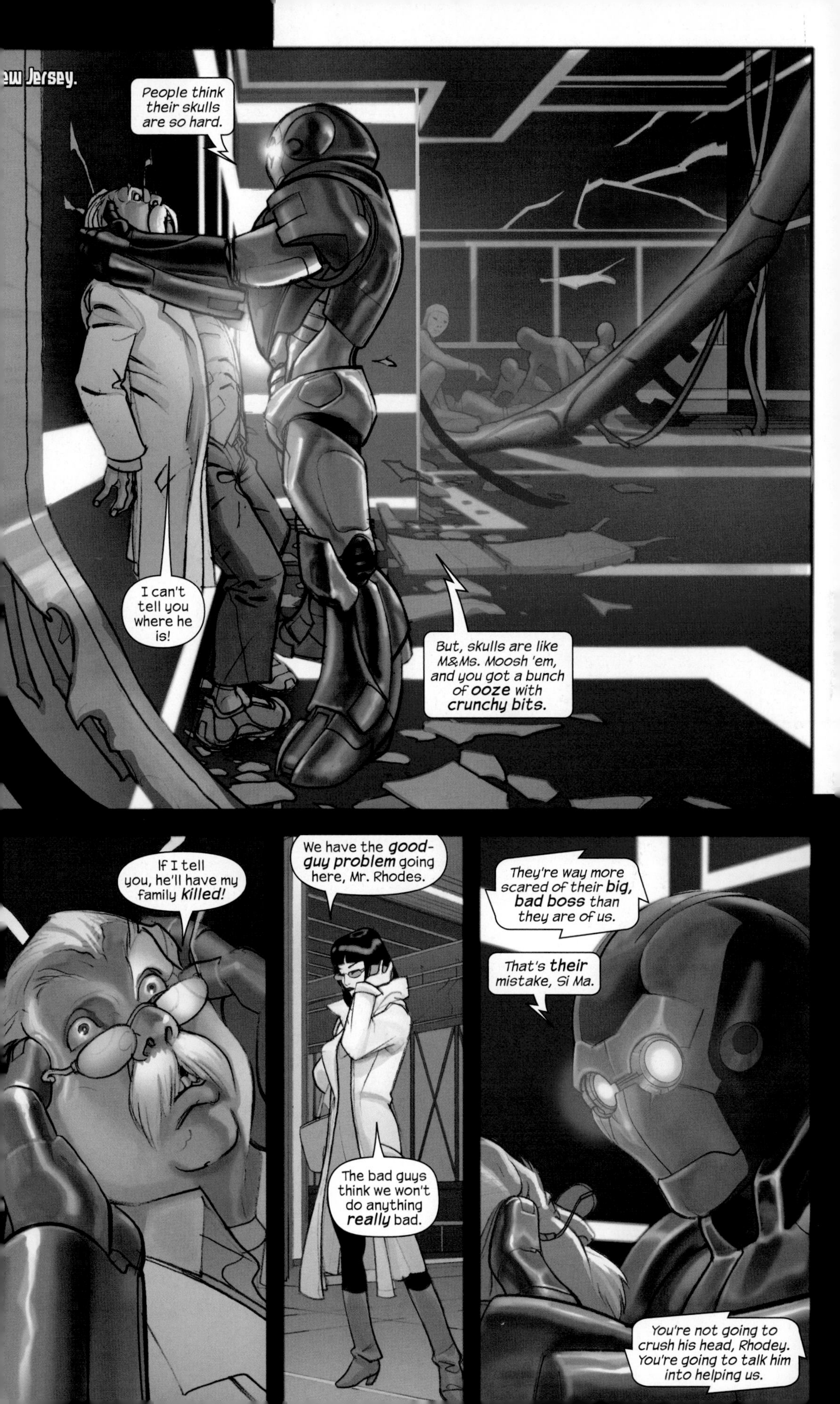

ew Jersey.
People think their skulls are so hard.
I can't tell you where he is!
But, skulls are like M&Ms. Moosh 'em, and you got a bunch of ooze with crunchy bits.
If I tell you, he'll have my family killed!
We have the good-guy problem going here, Mr. Rhodes.
The bad guys think we won't do anything really bad.
They're way more scared of their big, bad boss than they are of us.
That's their mistake, Si Ma.
You're not going to crush his head, Rhodey. You're going to talk him into helping us.

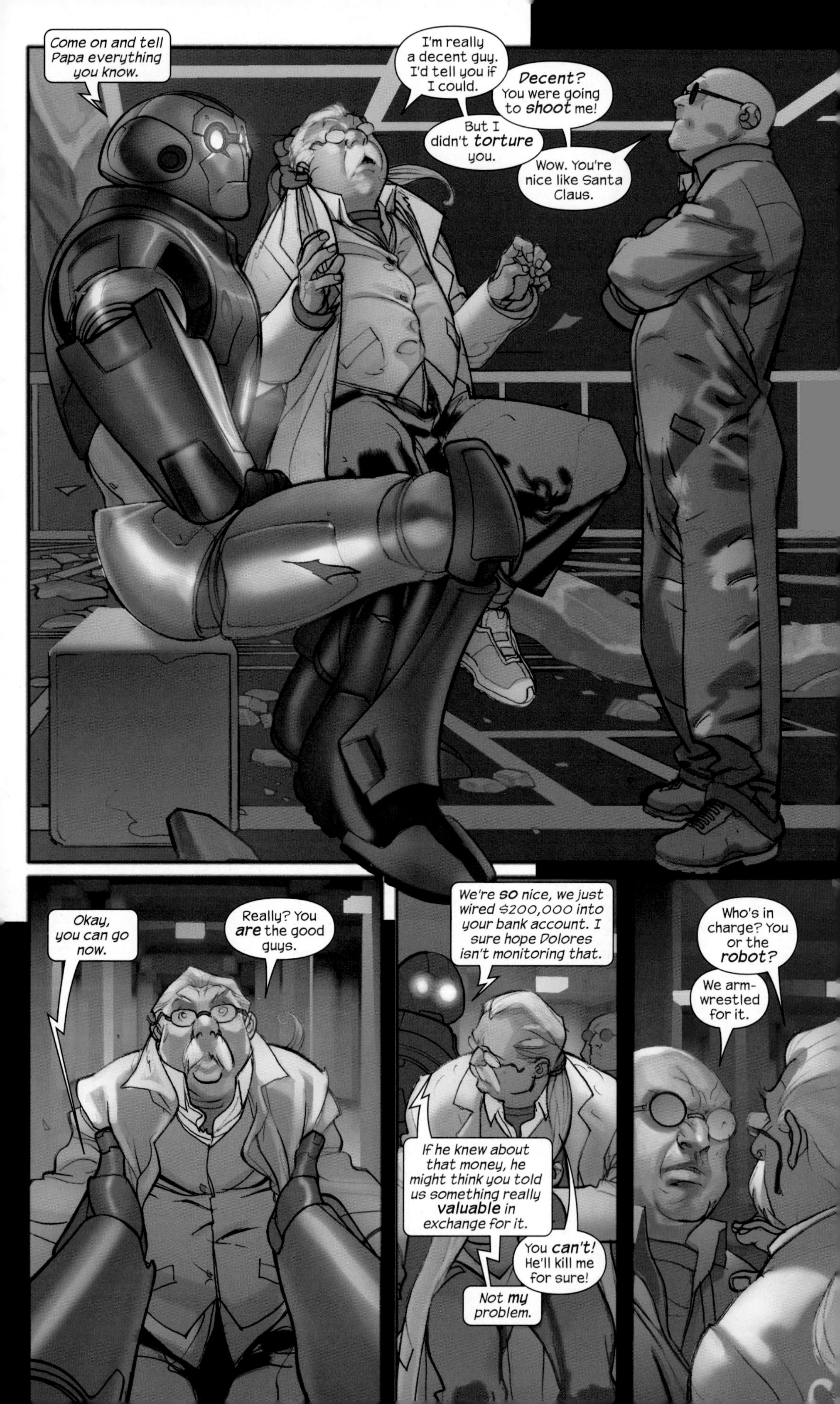

Come on and tell Papa everything you know.
I'm really a decent guy. I'd tell you if I could.
But I didn't **torture** you.
Decent? You were going to ***shoot*** me!
Wow. You're nice like Santa Claus.
Okay, you can go now.
Really? You ***are*** the good guys.
We're ***so*** nice, we just wired $200,000 into your bank account. I sure hope Dolores isn't monitoring that.
If he knew about that money, he might think you told us something really **valuable** in exchange for it.
You ***can't!*** He'll kill me for sure!
Not ***my*** problem.
Who's in charge? You or the ***robot?***
We arm-wrestled for it.

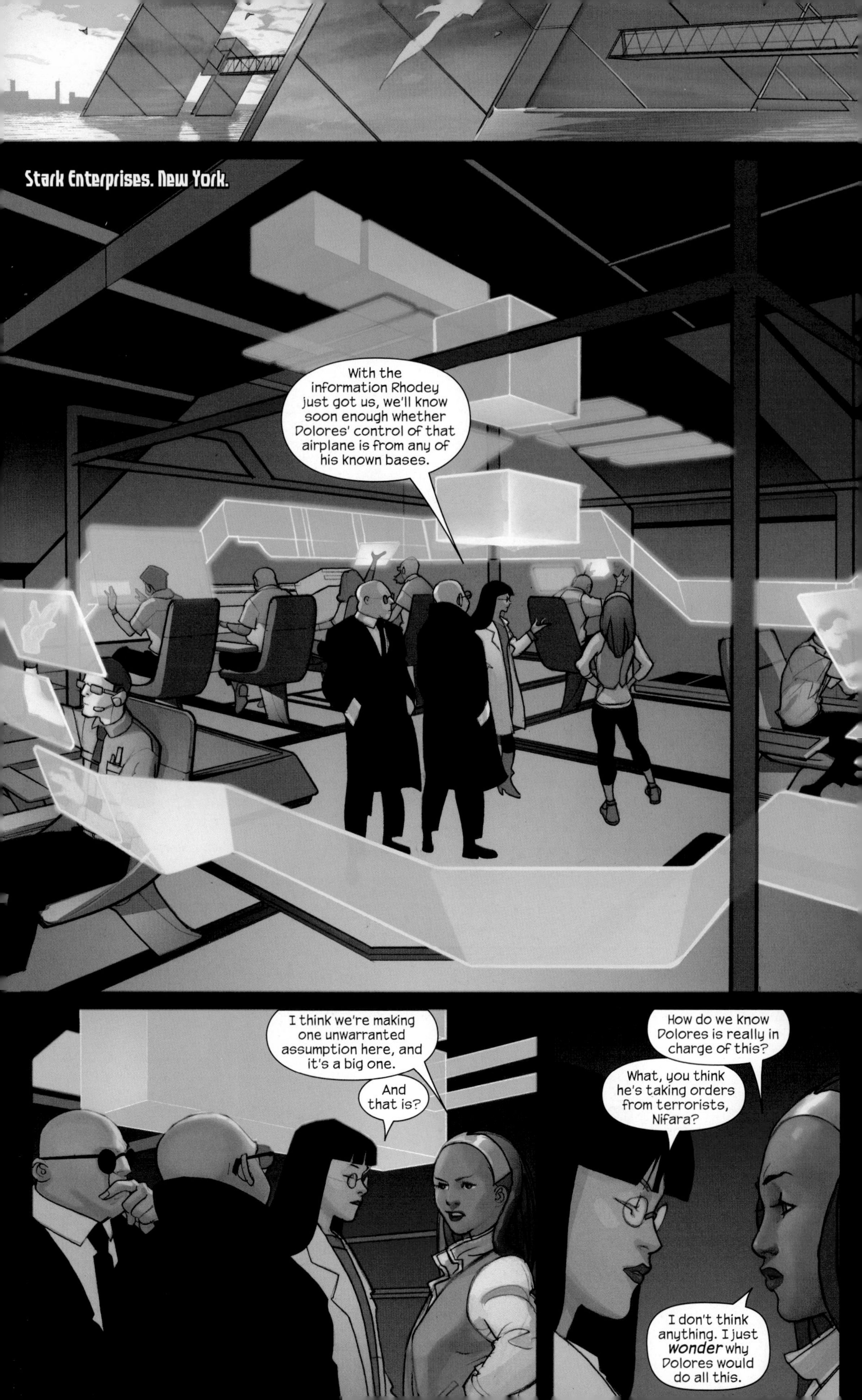
Stark Enterprises. New York.
With the information Rhodey just got us, we'll know soon enough whether Dolores' control of that airplane is from any of his known bases.
I think we're making one unwarranted assumption here, and it's a big one.
And that is?
How do we know Dolores is really in charge of this?
What, you think he's taking orders from terrorists, Nifara?
I don't think anything. I just *wonder* why Dolores would do all this.

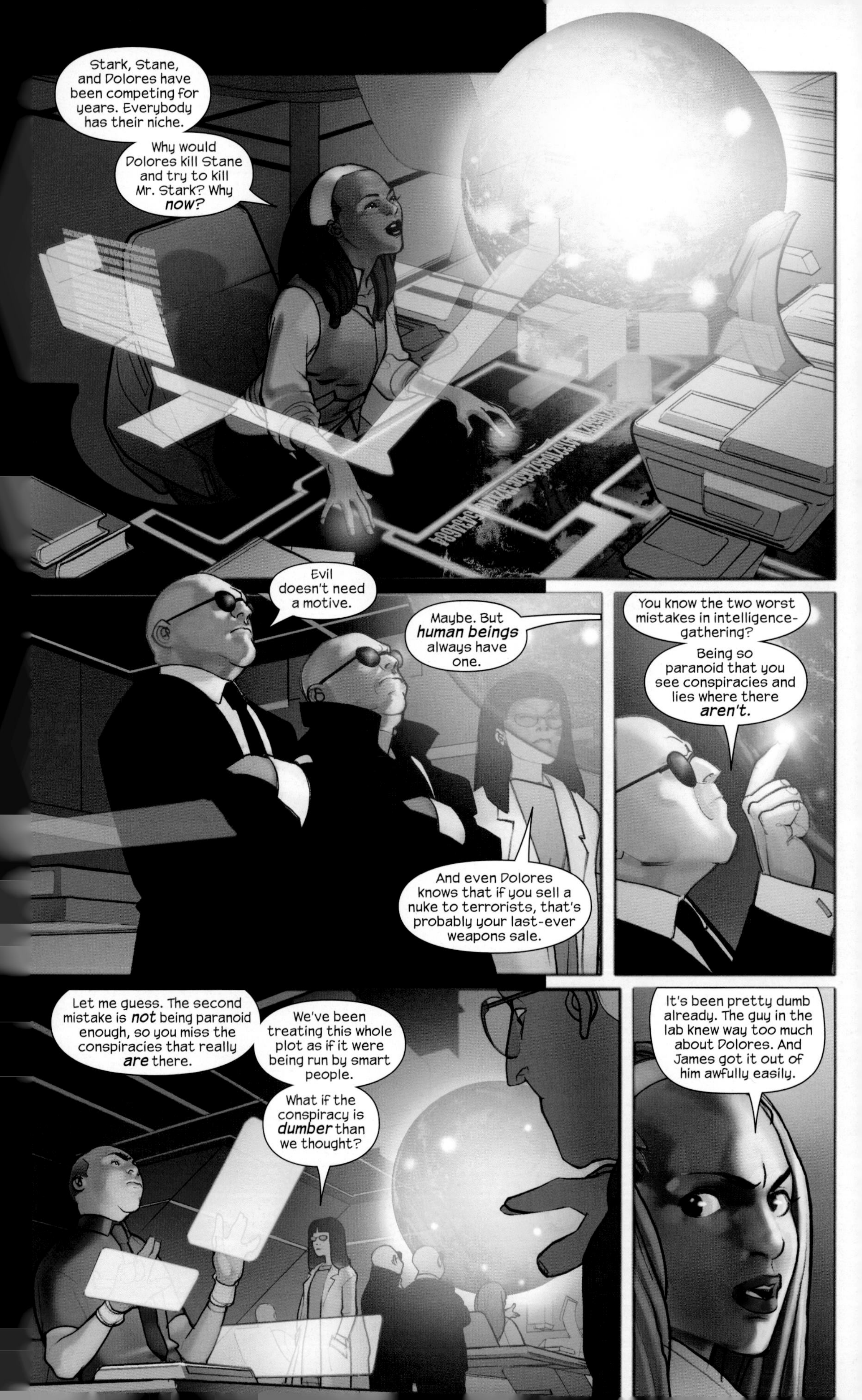
Stark, Stane, and Dolores have been competing for years. Everybody has their niche.
Why would Dolores kill Stane and try to kill Mr. Stark? Why now?
Evil doesn't need a motive.
Maybe. But human beings always have one.
And even Dolores knows that if you sell a nuke to terrorists, that's probably your last-ever weapons sale.
You know the two worst mistakes in intelligence-gathering?
Being so paranoid that you see conspiracies and lies where there aren't.
Let me guess. The second mistake is not being paranoid enough, so you miss the conspiracies that really are there.
We've been treating this whole plot as if it were being run by smart people.
What if the conspiracy is dumber than we thought?
It's been pretty dumb already. The guy in the lab knew way too much about Dolores. And James got it out of him awfully easily.

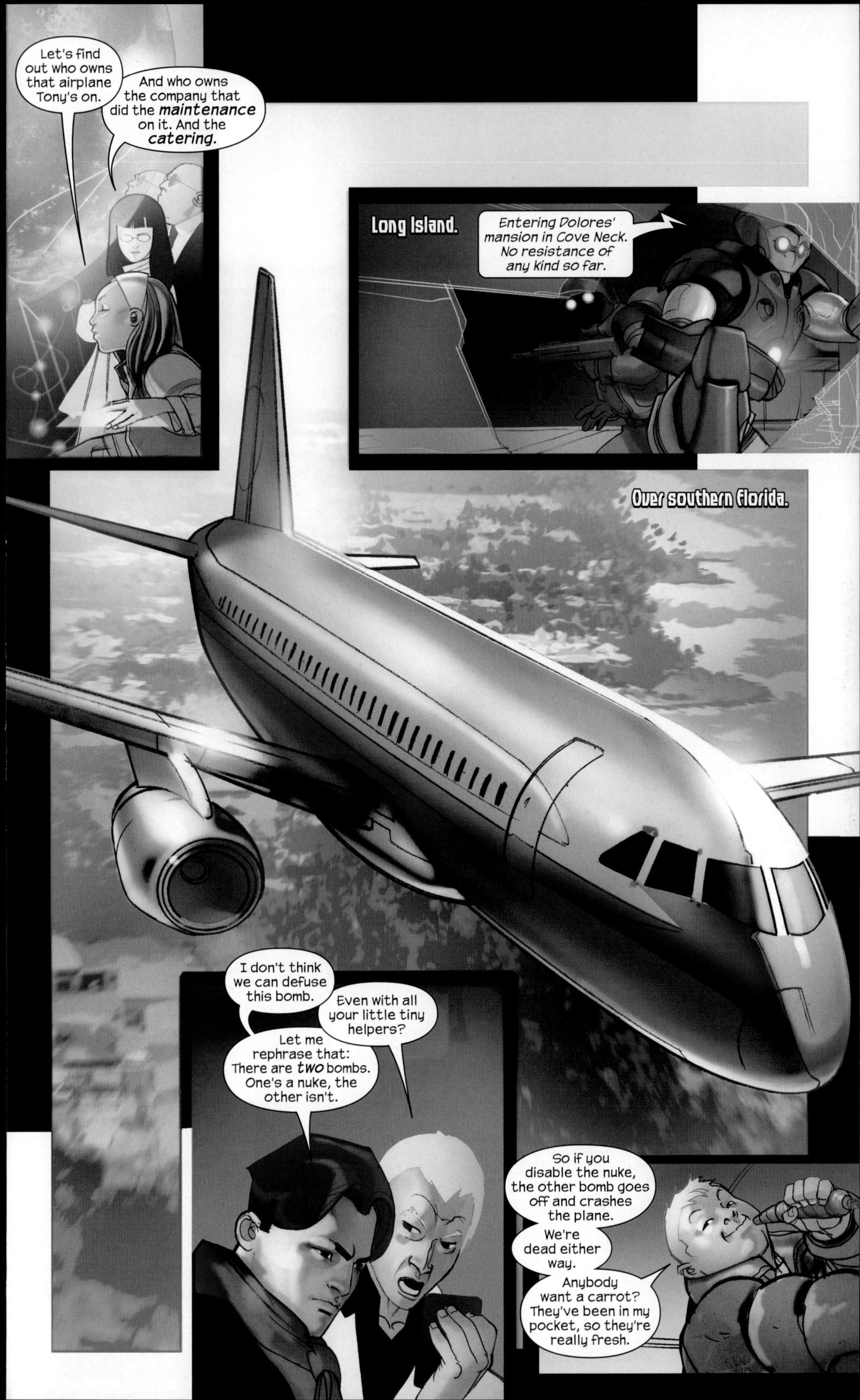
Let's find out who owns that airplane Tony's on.
And who owns the company that did the *maintenance* on it. And the *catering.*
Long Island.
Entering Dolores' mansion in Cove Neck. No resistance of any kind so far.
Over southern Florida.
I don't think we can defuse this bomb.
Even with all your little tiny helpers?
Let me rephrase that: There are *two* bombs. One's a nuke, the other isn't.
So if you disable the nuke, the other bomb goes off and crashes the plane.
We're dead either way.
Anybody want a carrot? They've been in my pocket, so they're really fresh.

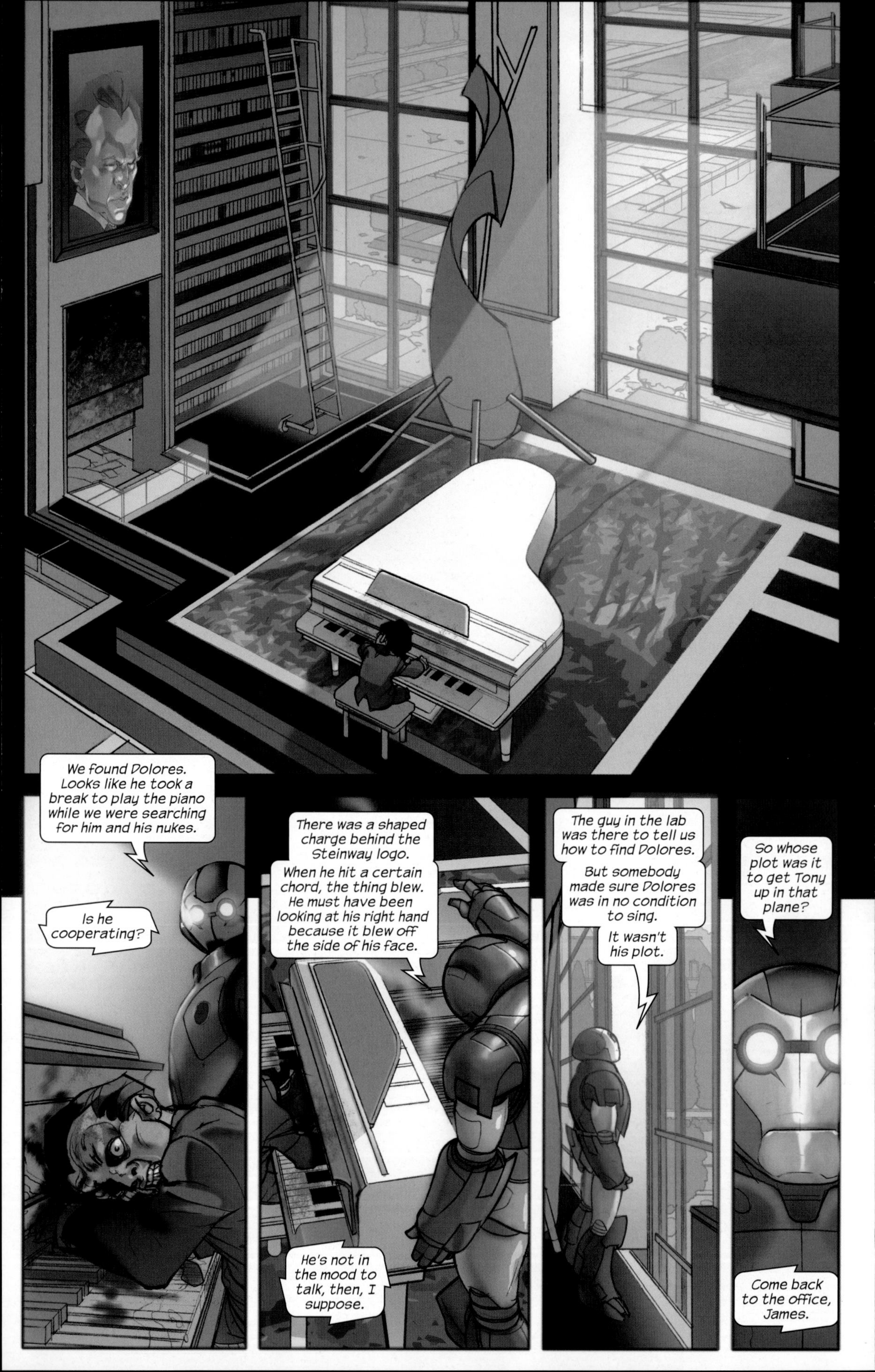
We found Dolores. Looks like he took a break to play the piano while we were searching for him and his nukes.
Is he cooperating?
There was a shaped charge behind the Steinway logo.
When he hit a certain chord, the thing blew. He must have been looking at his right hand because it blew off the side of his face.
He's not in the mood to talk, then, I suppose.
The guy in the lab was there to tell us how to find Dolores.
But somebody made sure Dolores was in no condition to sing.
It wasn't his plot.
So whose plot was it to get Tony up in that plane?
Come back to the office, James.

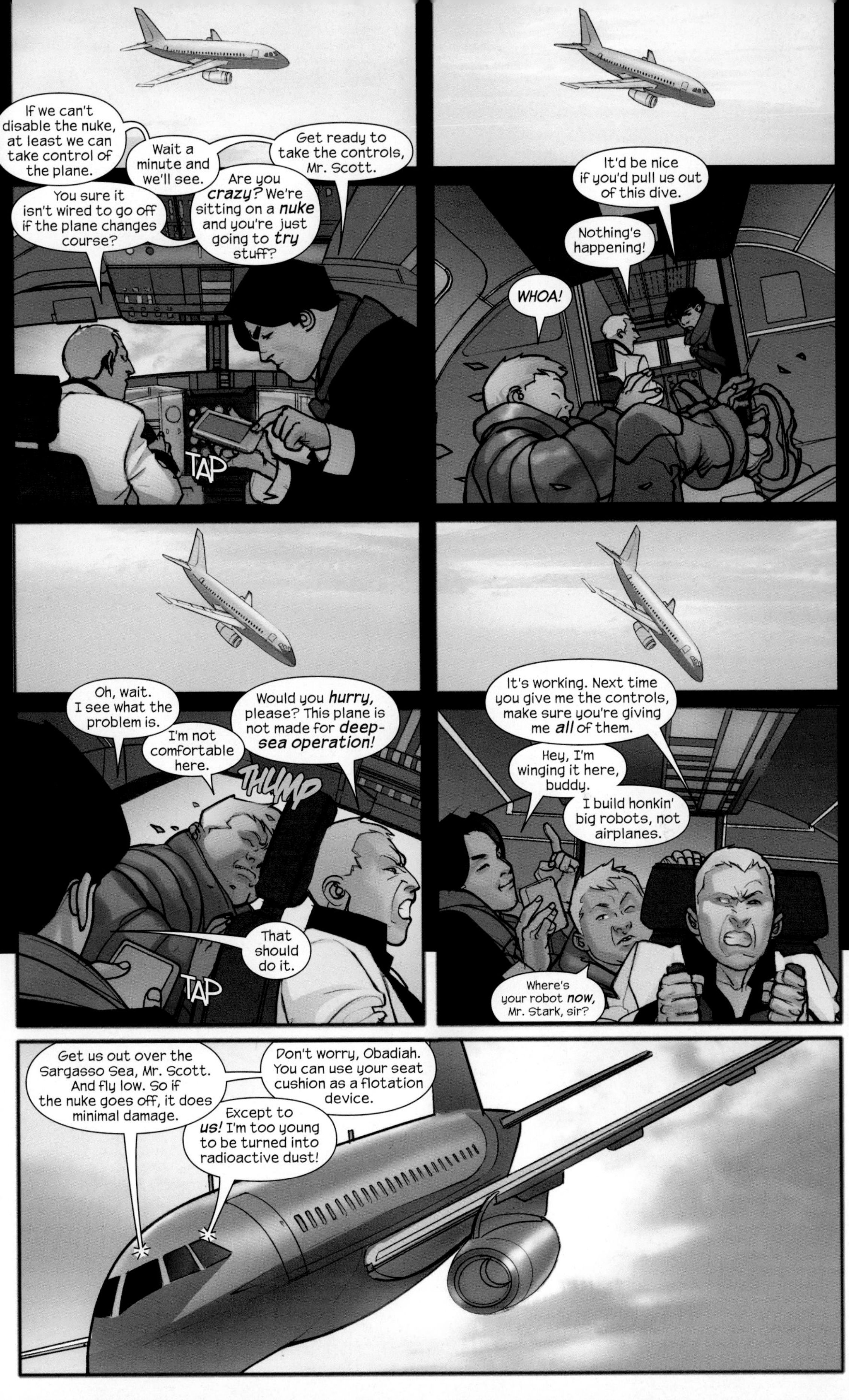
If we can't disable the nuke, at least we can take control of the plane.
Wait a minute and we'll see.
Get ready to take the controls, Mr. Scott.
You sure it isn't wired to go off if the plane changes course?
Are you *crazy?* We're sitting on a *nuke* and you're just going to *try* stuff?
TAP
It'd be nice if you'd pull us out of this dive.
Nothing's happening!
WHOA!
Oh, wait. I see what the problem is.
I'm not comfortable here.
Would you *hurry,* please? This plane is not made for *deep-sea operation!*
THUMP
That should do it.
TAP
It's working. Next time you give me the controls, make sure you're giving me *all* of them.
Hey, I'm winging it here, buddy.
I build honkin' big robots, not airplanes.
Where's your robot *now,* Mr. Stark, sir?
Get us out over the Sargasso Sea, Mr. Scott. And fly low. So if the nuke goes off, it does minimal damage.
Don't worry, Obadiah. You can use your seat cushion as a flotation device.
Except to *us!* I'm too young to be turned into radioactive dust!

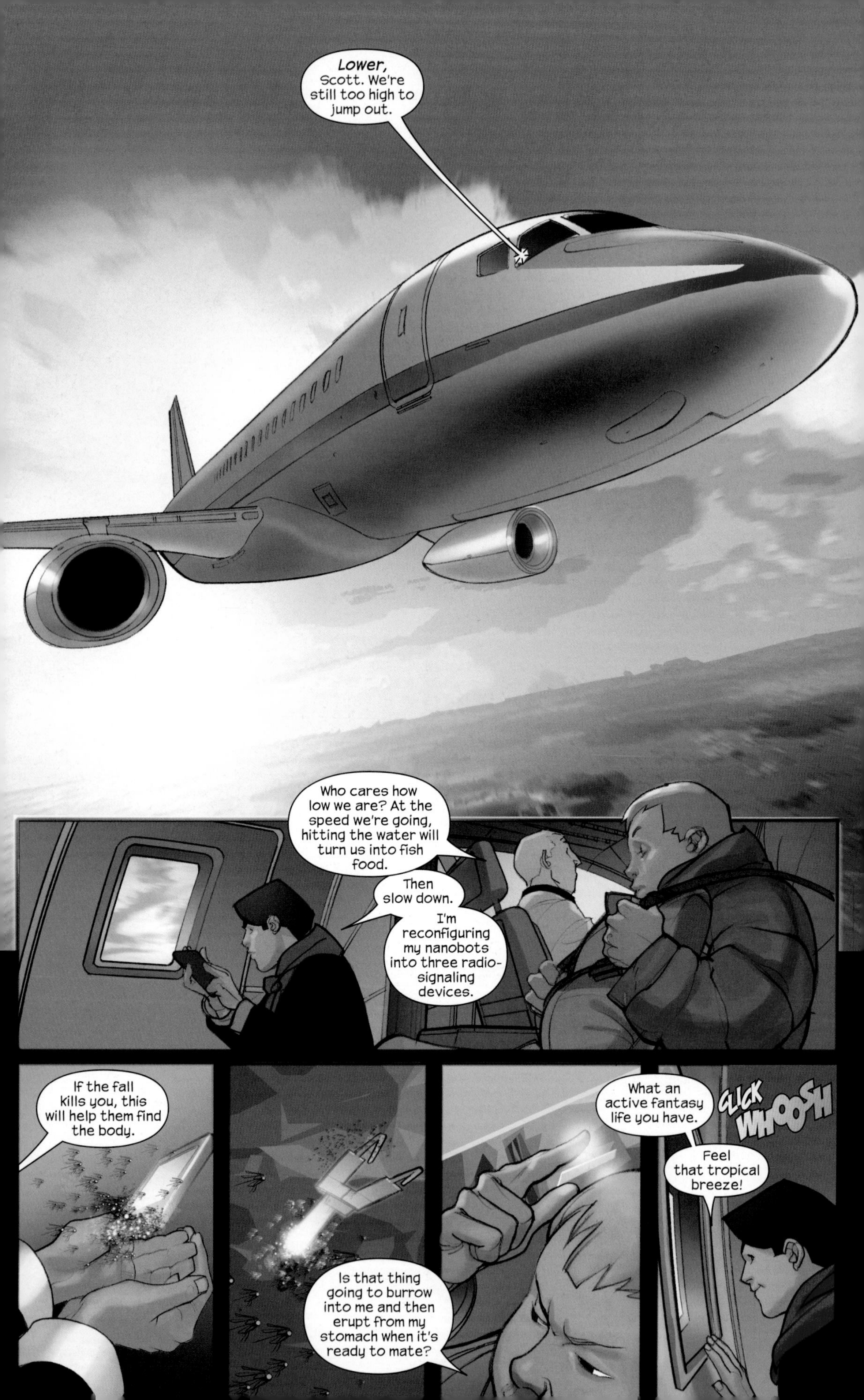
Lower, Scott. We're still too high to jump out.
Who cares how low we are? At the speed we're going, hitting the water will turn us into fish food.
Then slow down.
I'm reconfiguring my nanobots into three radio-signaling devices.
If the fall kills you, this will help them find the body.
Is that thing going to burrow into me and then erupt from my stomach when it's ready to mate?
What an active fantasy life you have.
CLICK
WHOOSH
Feel that tropical breeze!

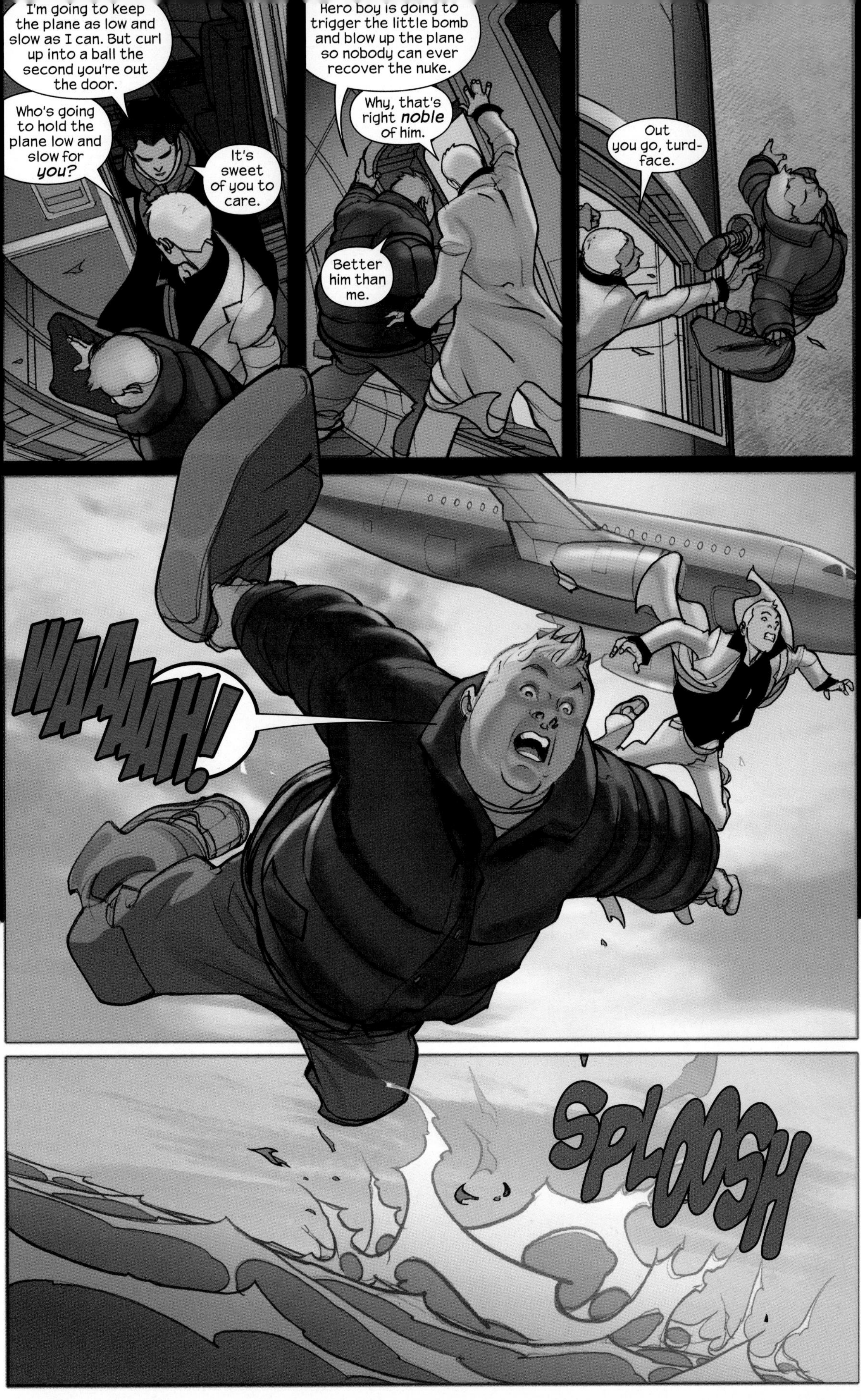

I'm going to keep the plane as low and slow as I can. But curl up into a ball the second you're out the door.
Who's going to hold the plane low and slow for *you*?
It's sweet of you to care.
Hero boy is going to trigger the little bomb and blow up the plane so nobody can ever recover the nuke.
Why, that's right *noble* of him.
Better him than me.
Out you go, turd-face.
WAAAAAH!
SPLOOSH

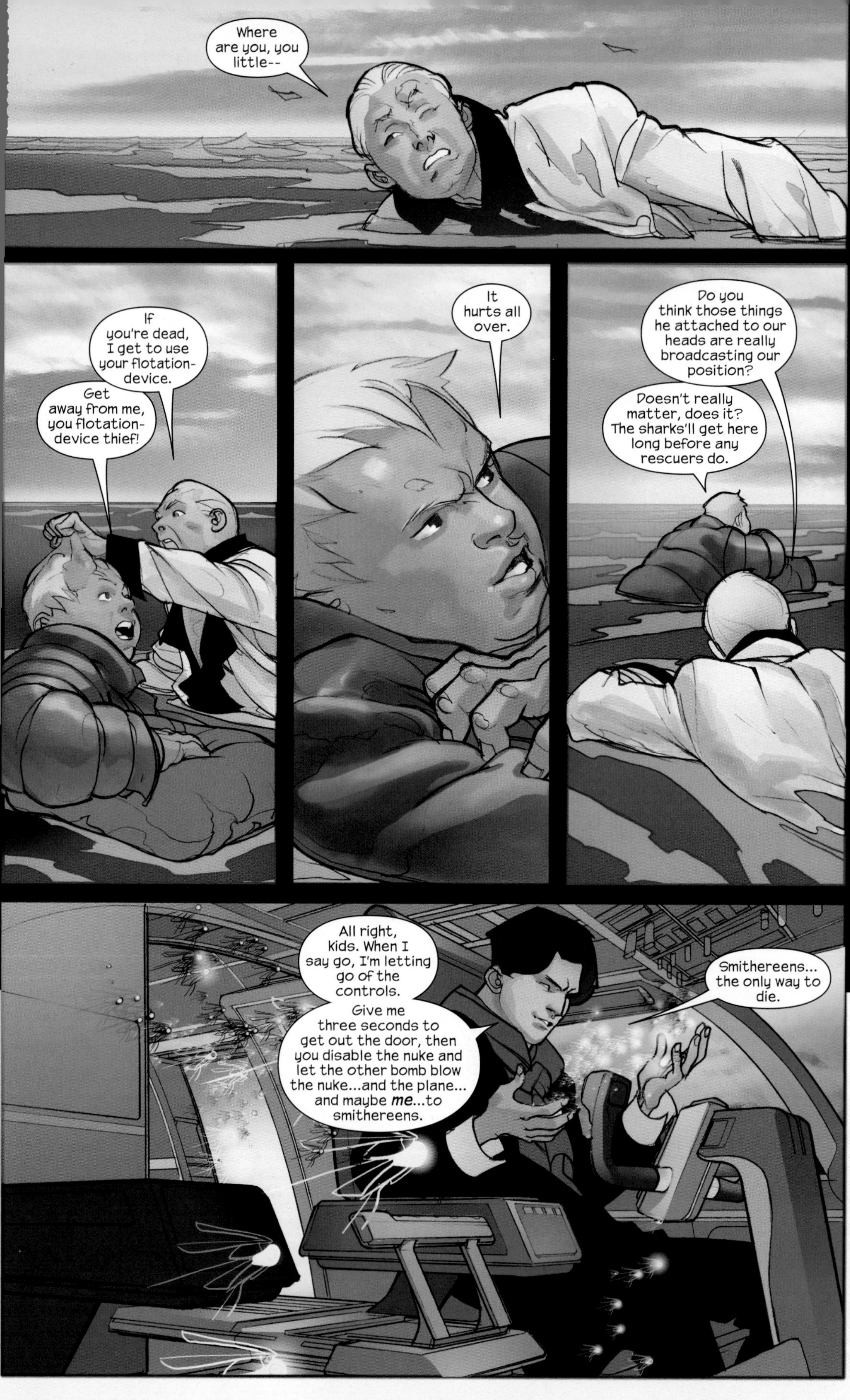
Where are you, you little--
If you're dead, I get to use your flotation-device.
Get away from me, you flotation-device thief!
It hurts all over.
Do you think those things he attached to our heads are really broadcasting our position?
Doesn't really matter, does it? The sharks'll get here long before any rescuers do.
All right, kids. When I say go, I'm letting go of the controls.
Give me three seconds to get out the door, then you disable the nuke and let the other bomb blow the nuke...and the plane... and maybe *me*...to smithereens.
Smithereens... the only way to die.

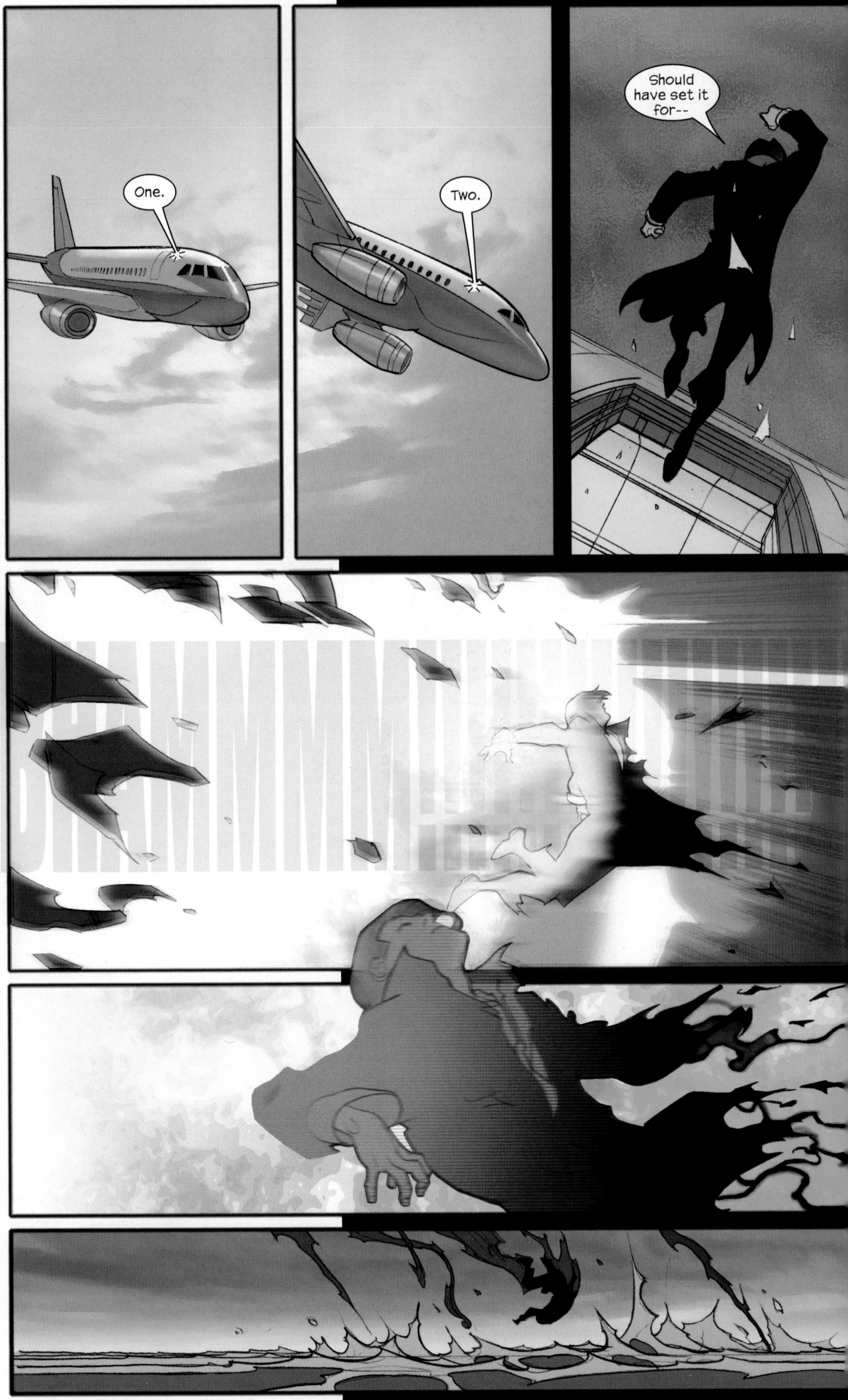
One.
Two.
Should have set it for--
BHAMMMMM

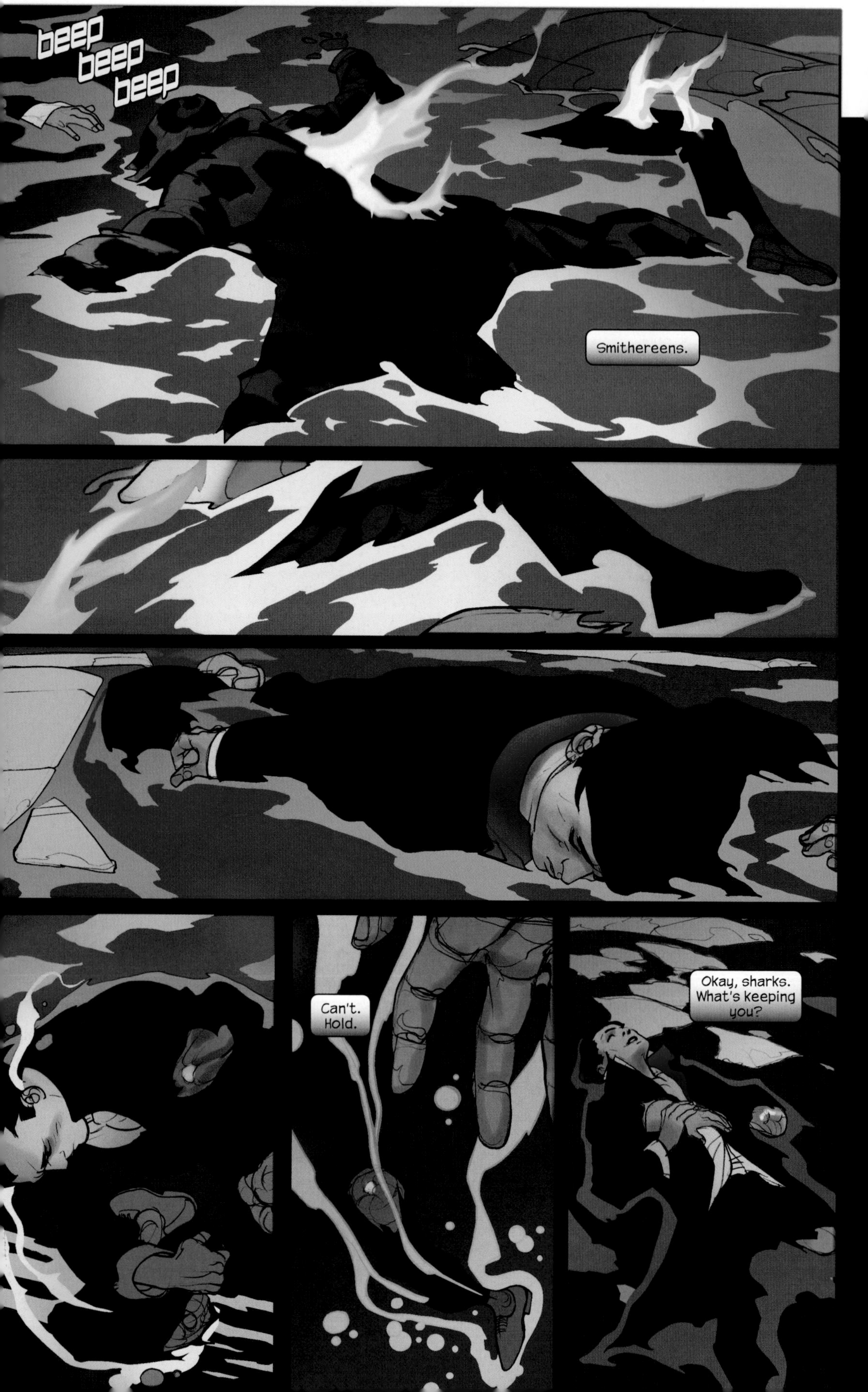
beep
beep
beep
Smithereens.
Can't. Hold.
Okay, sharks. What's keeping you?

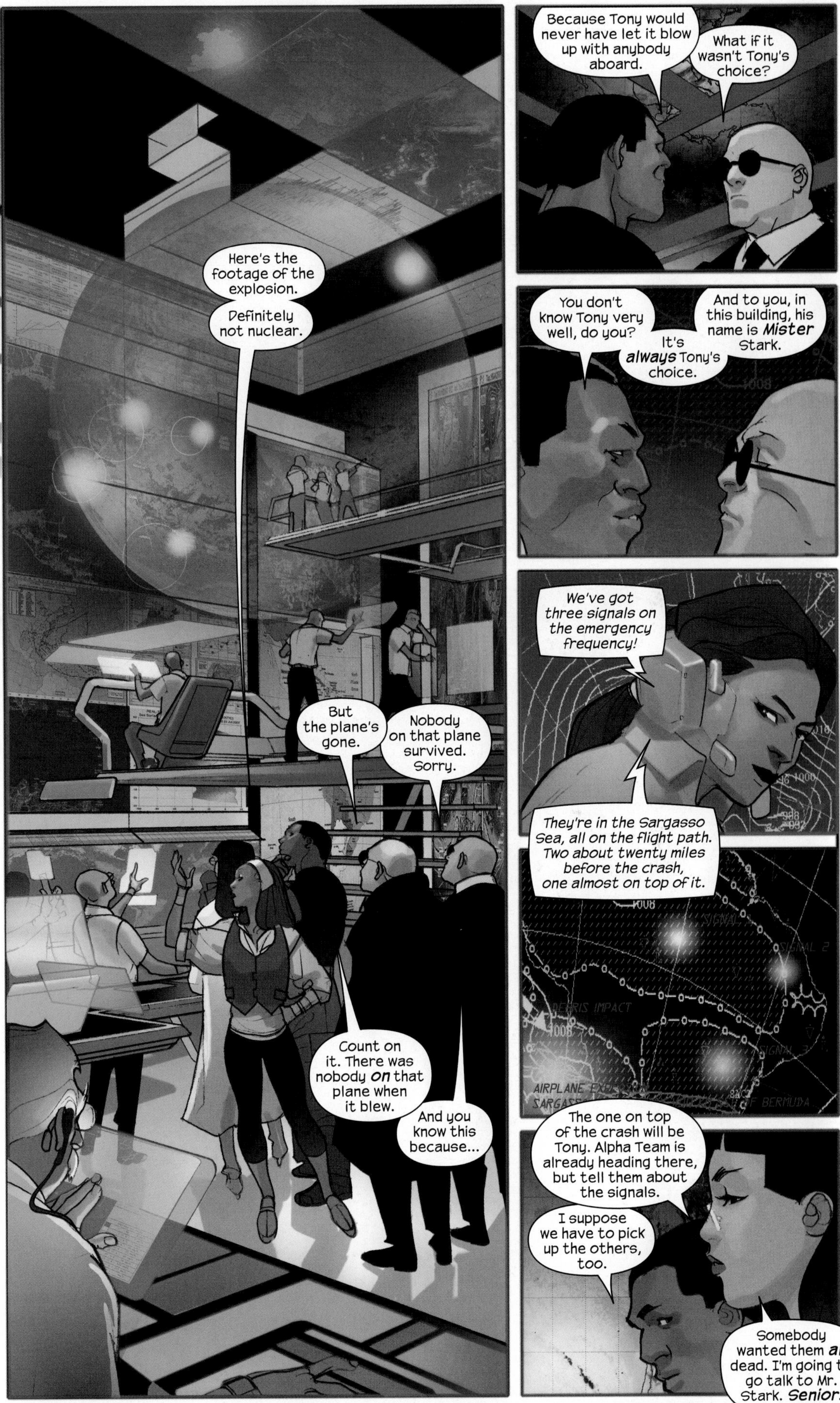
Here's the footage of the explosion.
Definitely not nuclear.
But the plane's gone.
Nobody on that plane survived. Sorry.
Count on it. There was nobody *on* that plane when it blew.
And you know this because...
Because Tony would never have let it blow up with anybody aboard.
What if it wasn't Tony's choice?
You don't know Tony very well, do you?
It's *always* Tony's choice.
And to you, in this building, his name is *Mister* Stark.
We've got three signals on the emergency frequency!
They're in the Sargasso Sea, all on the flight path. Two about twenty miles before the crash, one almost on top of it.
The one on top of the crash will be Tony. Alpha Team is already heading there, but tell them about the signals.
I suppose we have to pick up the others, too.
Somebody wanted them *all* dead. I'm going to go talk to Mr. Stark. *Senior.*

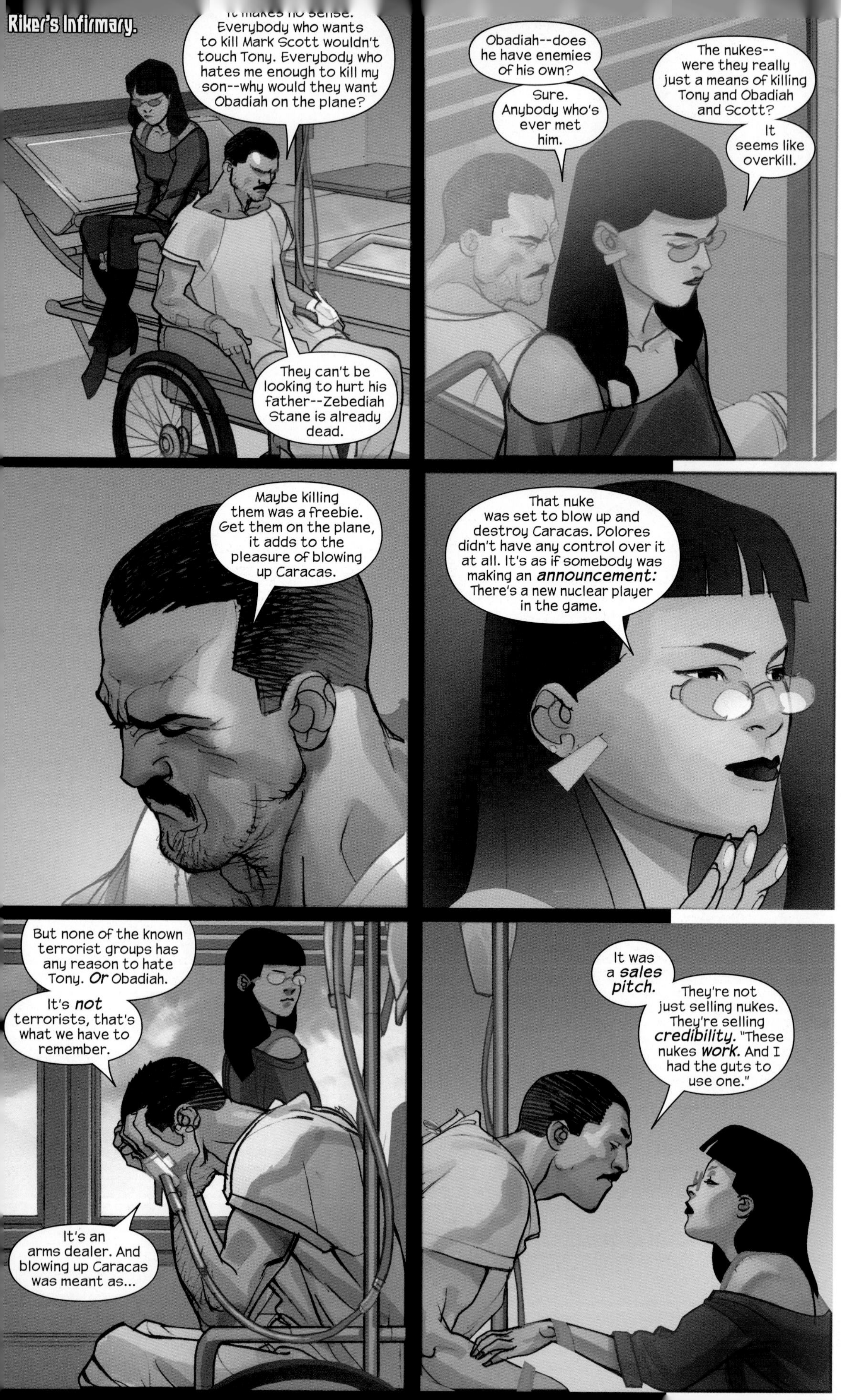
Riker's Infirmary.
Everybody who wants to kill Mark Scott wouldn't touch Tony. Everybody who hates me enough to kill my son--why would they want Obadiah on the plane?
They can't be looking to hurt his father--Zebediah Stane is already dead.
Obadiah--does he have enemies of his own?
Sure. Anybody who's ever met him.
The nukes--were they really just a means of killing Tony and Obadiah and Scott?
It seems like overkill.
Maybe killing them was a freebie. Get them on the plane, it adds to the pleasure of blowing up Caracas.
That nuke was set to blow up and destroy Caracas. Dolores didn't have any control over it at all. It's as if somebody was making an *announcement:* There's a new nuclear player in the game.
But none of the known terrorist groups has any reason to hate Tony. *Or* Obadiah.
It's *not* terrorists, that's what we have to remember.
It's an arms dealer. And blowing up Caracas was meant as...
It was a *sales pitch.*
They're not just selling nukes. They're selling *credibility.* "These nukes *work.* And I had the guts to use one."

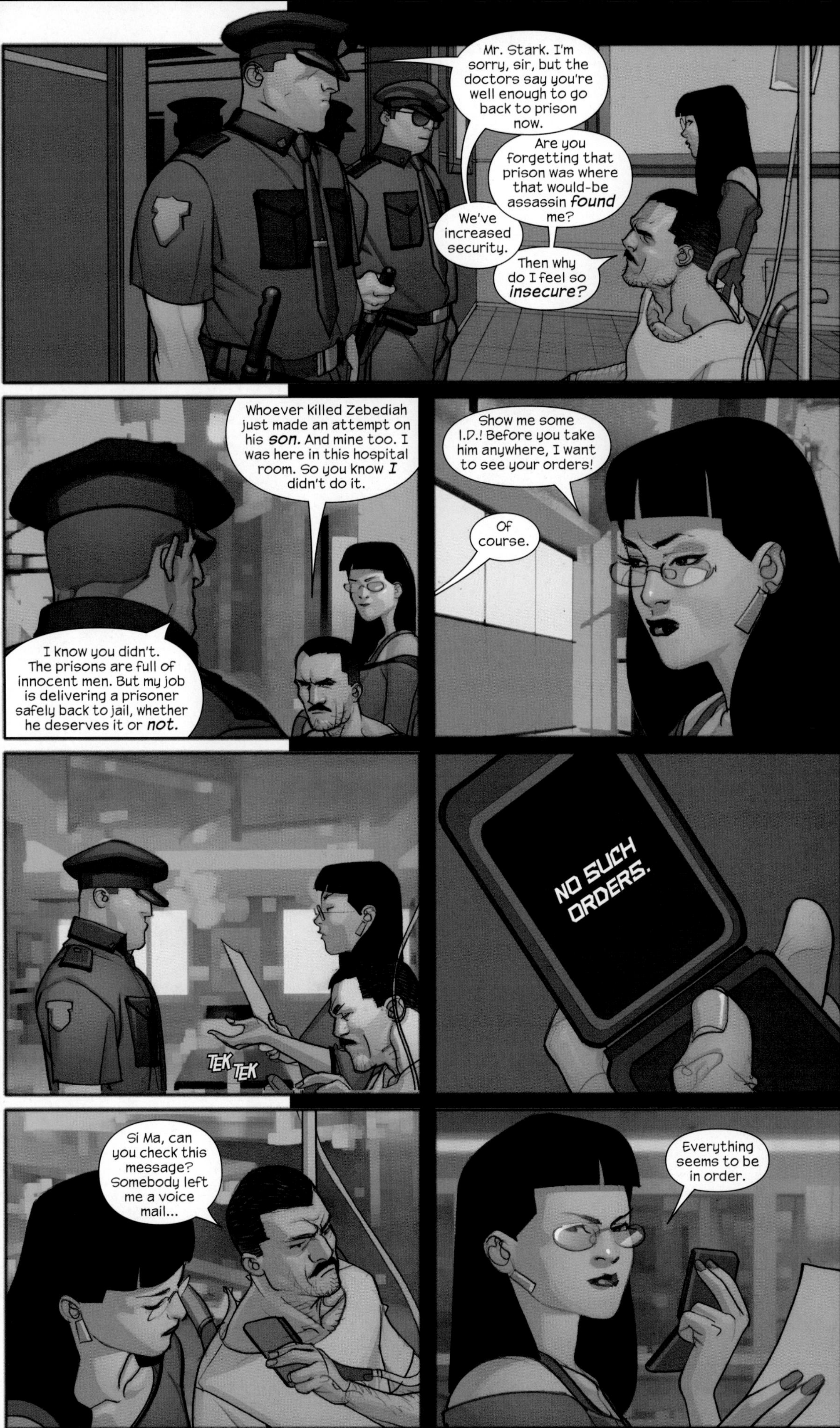
Mr. Stark. I'm sorry, sir, but the doctors say you're well enough to go back to prison now.
Are you forgetting that prison was where that would-be assassin *found* me?
We've increased security.
Then why do I feel so *insecure?*
Whoever killed Zebediah just made an attempt on his *son.* And mine too. I was here in this hospital room. So you know *I* didn't do it.
I know you didn't. The prisons are full of innocent men. But my job is delivering a prisoner safely back to jail, whether he deserves it or *not.*
Show me some I.D.! Before you take him anywhere, I want to see your orders!
Of course.
TEK TEK
NO SUCH ORDERS.
Si Ma, can you check this message? Somebody left me a voice mail...
Everything seems to be in order.

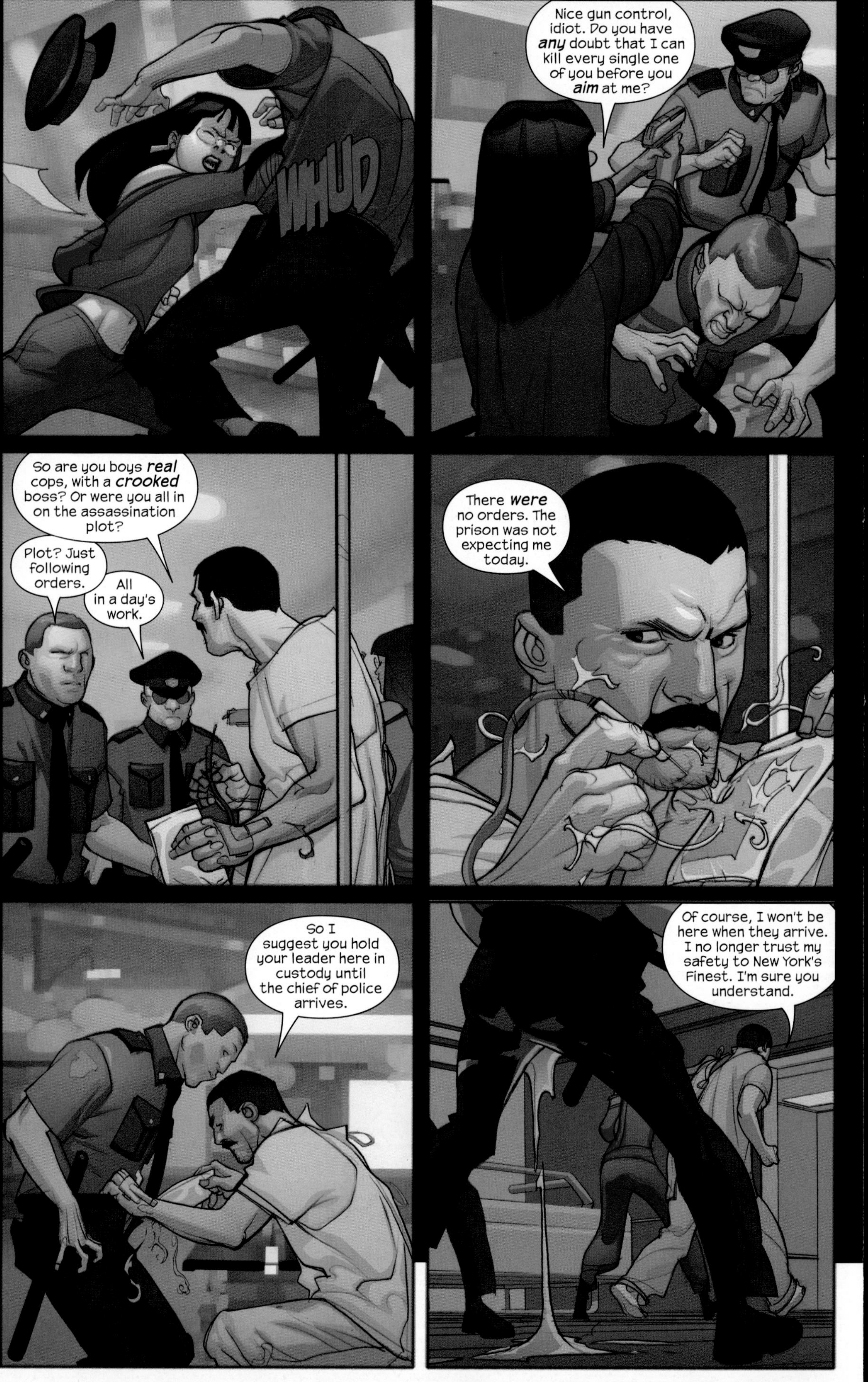
WHUD
Nice gun control, idiot. Do you have *any* doubt that I can kill every single one of you before you *aim* at me?
So are you boys *real* cops, with a *crooked* boss? Or were you all in on the assassination plot?
Plot? Just following orders.
All in a day's work.
There *were* no orders. The prison was not expecting me today.
So I suggest you hold your leader here in custody until the chief of police arrives.
Of course, I won't be here when they arrive. I no longer trust my safety to New York's Finest. I'm sure you understand.

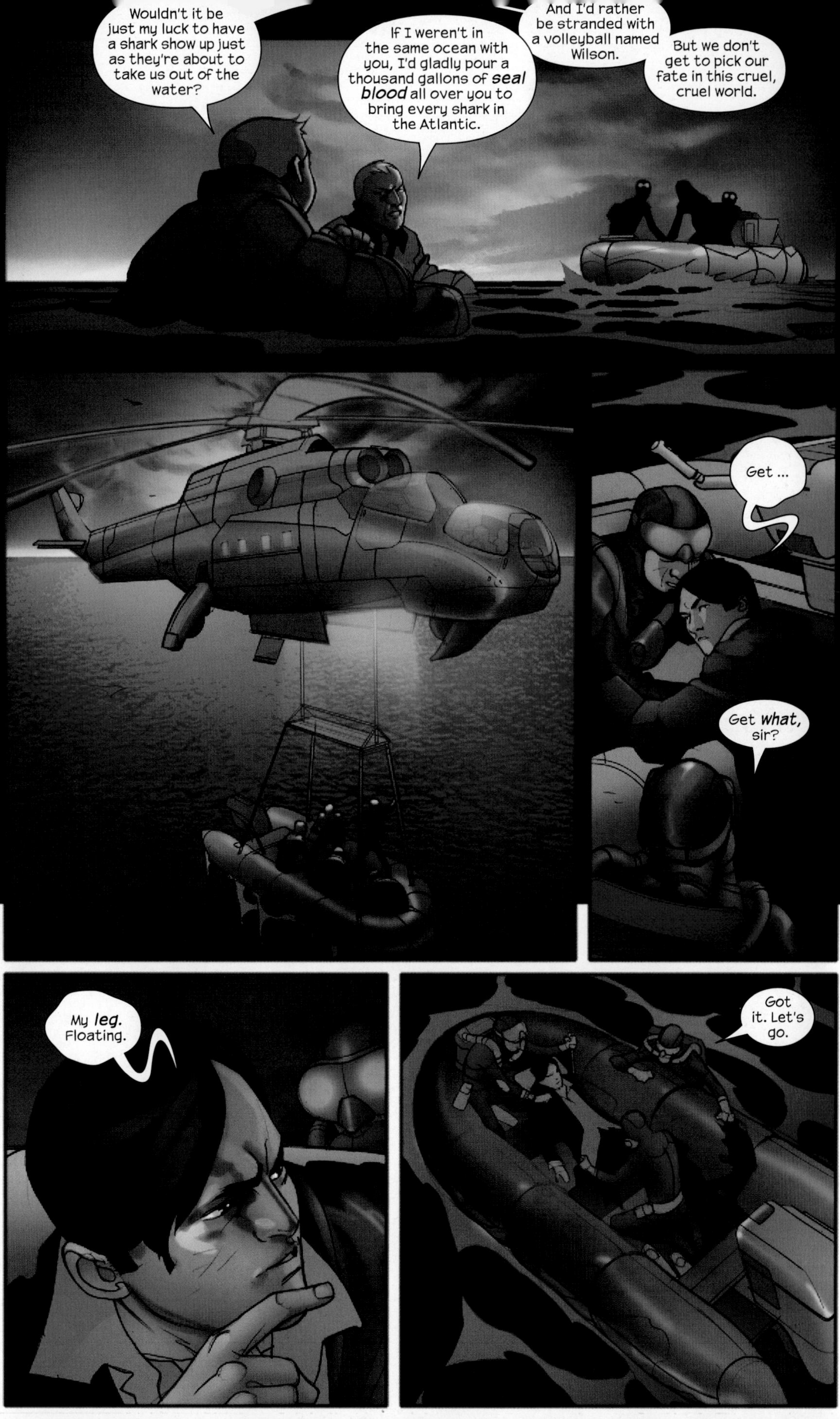
Wouldn't it be just my luck to have a shark show up just as they're about to take us out of the water?
If I weren't in the same ocean with you, I'd gladly pour a thousand gallons of *seal blood* all over you to bring every shark in the Atlantic.
And I'd rather be stranded with a volleyball named Wilson.
But we don't get to pick our fate in this cruel, cruel world.
Get ...
Get *what,* sir?
My *leg.* Floating.
Got it. Let's go.

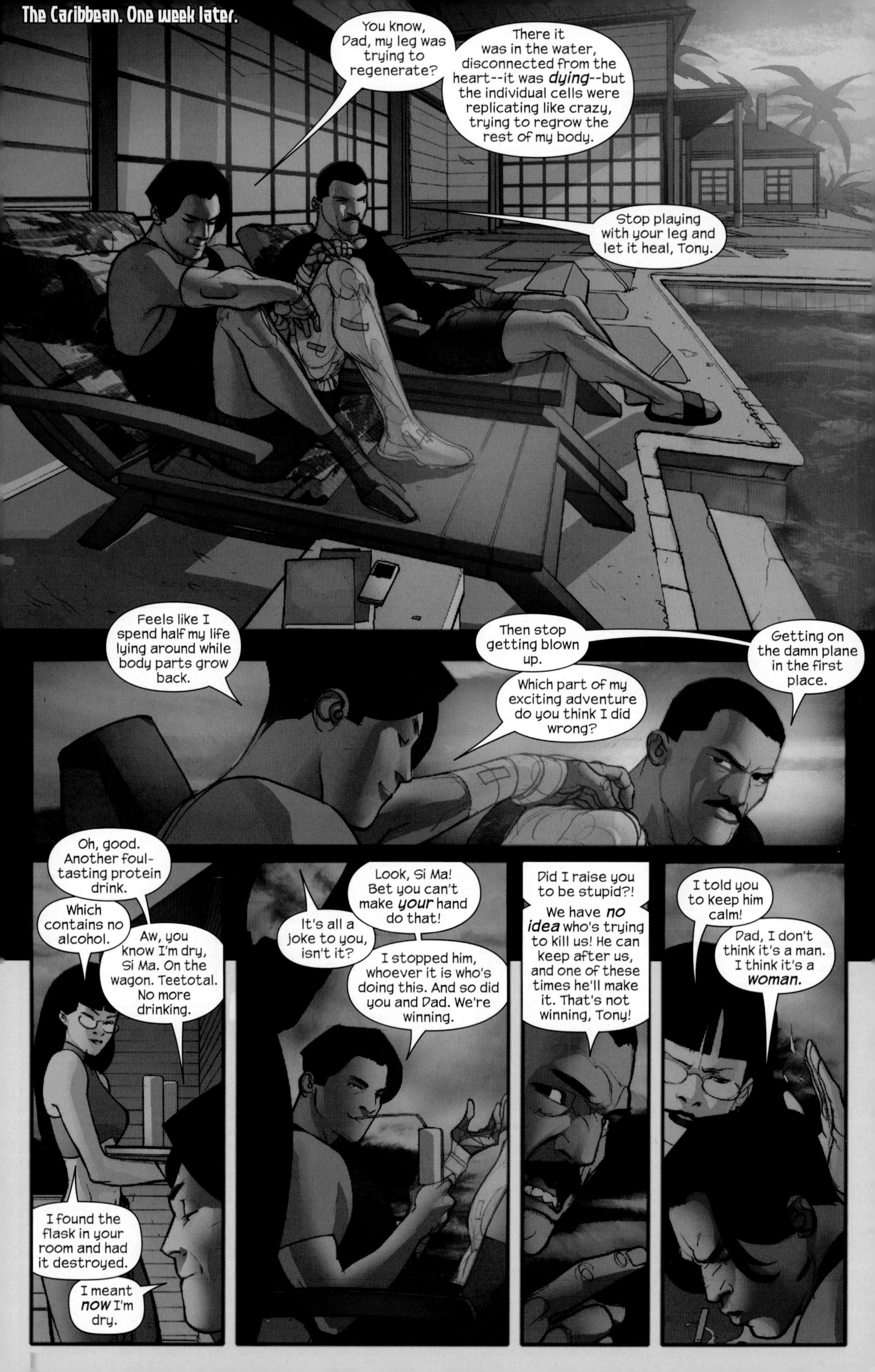
The Caribbean. One week later.
You know, Dad, my leg was trying to regenerate?
There it was in the water, disconnected from the heart--it was *dying*--but the individual cells were replicating like crazy, trying to regrow the rest of my body.
Stop playing with your leg and let it heal, Tony.
Feels like I spend half my life lying around while body parts grow back.
Then stop getting blown up.
Which part of my exciting adventure do you think I did wrong?
Getting on the damn plane in the first place.
Oh, good. Another foul-tasting protein drink.
Which contains no alcohol.
Aw, you know I'm dry, Si Ma. On the wagon. Teetotal. No more drinking.
I found the flask in your room and had it destroyed.
I meant *now* I'm dry.
It's all a joke to you, isn't it?
Look, Si Ma! Bet you can't make *your* hand do that!
I stopped him, whoever it is who's doing this. And so did you and Dad. We're winning.
Did I raise you to be stupid?!
We have *no idea* who's trying to kill us! He can keep after us, and one of these times he'll make it. That's not winning, Tony!
I told you to keep him calm!
Dad, I don't think it's a man. I think it's a ***woman.***

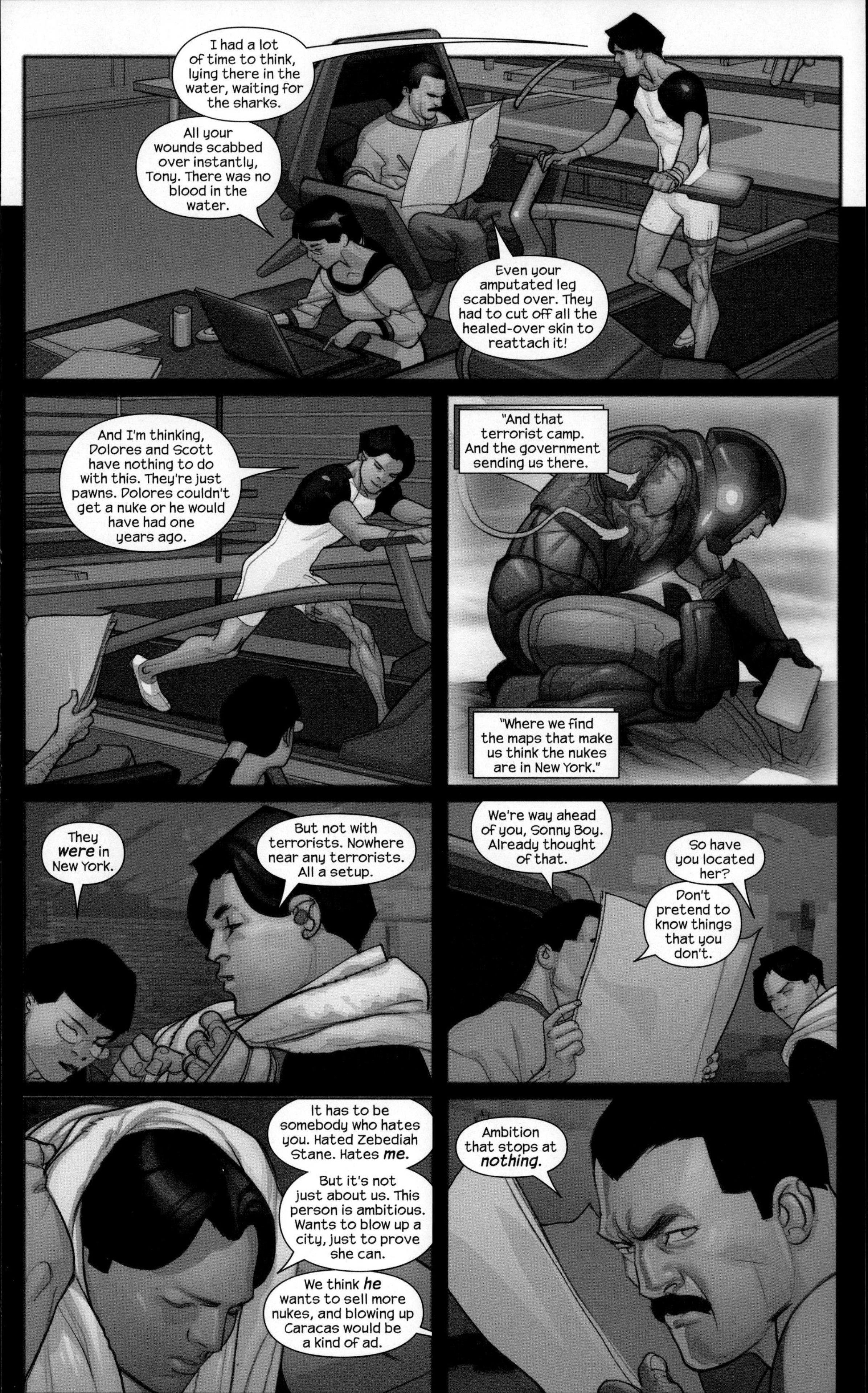

I had a lot of time to think, lying there in the water, waiting for the sharks.
All your wounds scabbed over instantly, Tony. There was no blood in the water.
Even your amputated leg scabbed over. They had to cut off all the healed-over skin to reattach it!
And I'm thinking, Dolores and Scott have nothing to do with this. They're just pawns. Dolores couldn't get a nuke or he would have had one years ago.
"And that terrorist camp. And the government sending us there.
"Where we find the maps that make us think the nukes are in New York."
They *were* in New York.
But not with terrorists. Nowhere near any terrorists. All a setup.
We're way ahead of you, Sonny Boy. Already thought of that.
So have you located her?
Don't pretend to know things that you don't.
It has to be somebody who hates you. Hated Zebediah Stane. Hates *me*.
But it's not just about us. This person is ambitious. Wants to blow up a city, just to prove she can.
We think *he* wants to sell more nukes, and blowing up Caracas would be a kind of ad.
Ambition that stops at *nothing*.

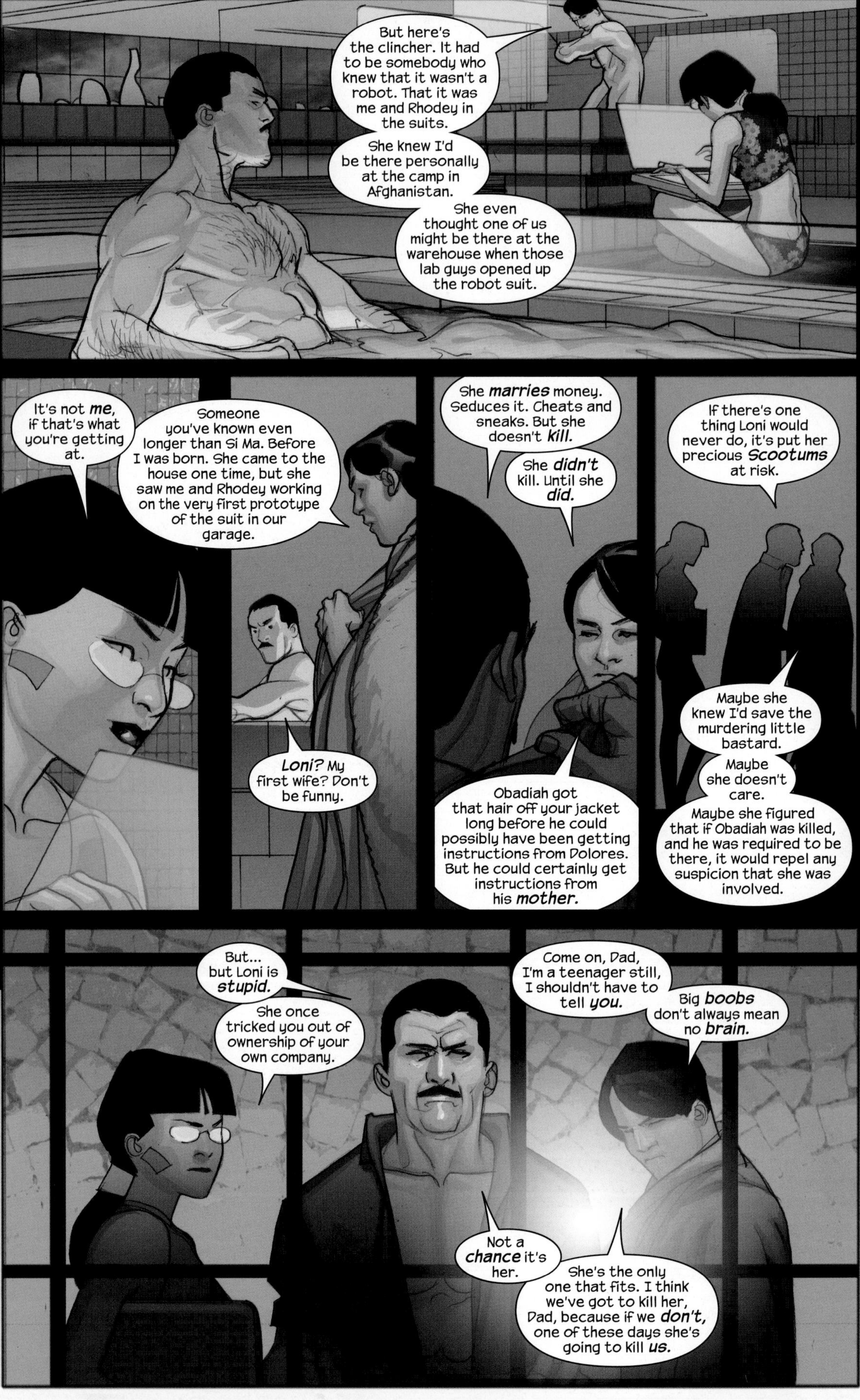

But here's the clincher. It had to be somebody who knew that it wasn't a robot. That it was me and Rhodey in the suits.
She knew I'd be there personally at the camp in Afghanistan.
She even thought one of us might be there at the warehouse when those lab guys opened up the robot suit.
It's not me, if that's what you're getting at.
Someone you've known even longer than Si Ma. Before I was born. She came to the house one time, but she saw me and Rhodey working on the very first prototype of the suit in our garage.
Loni? My first wife? Don't be funny.
She marries money. Seduces it. Cheats and sneaks. But she doesn't kill.
She didn't kill. Until she did.
Obadiah got that hair off your jacket long before he could possibly have been getting instructions from Dolores. But he could certainly get instructions from his mother.
If there's one thing Loni would never do, it's put her precious Scootums at risk.
Maybe she knew I'd save the murdering little bastard.
Maybe she doesn't care.
Maybe she figured that if Obadiah was killed, and he was required to be there, it would repel any suspicion that she was involved.
But... but Loni is stupid.
She once tricked you out of ownership of your own company.
Come on, Dad, I'm a teenager still, I shouldn't have to tell you.
Big boobs don't always mean no brain.
Not a chance it's her.
She's the only one that fits. I think we've got to kill her, Dad, because if we don't, one of these days she's going to kill us.

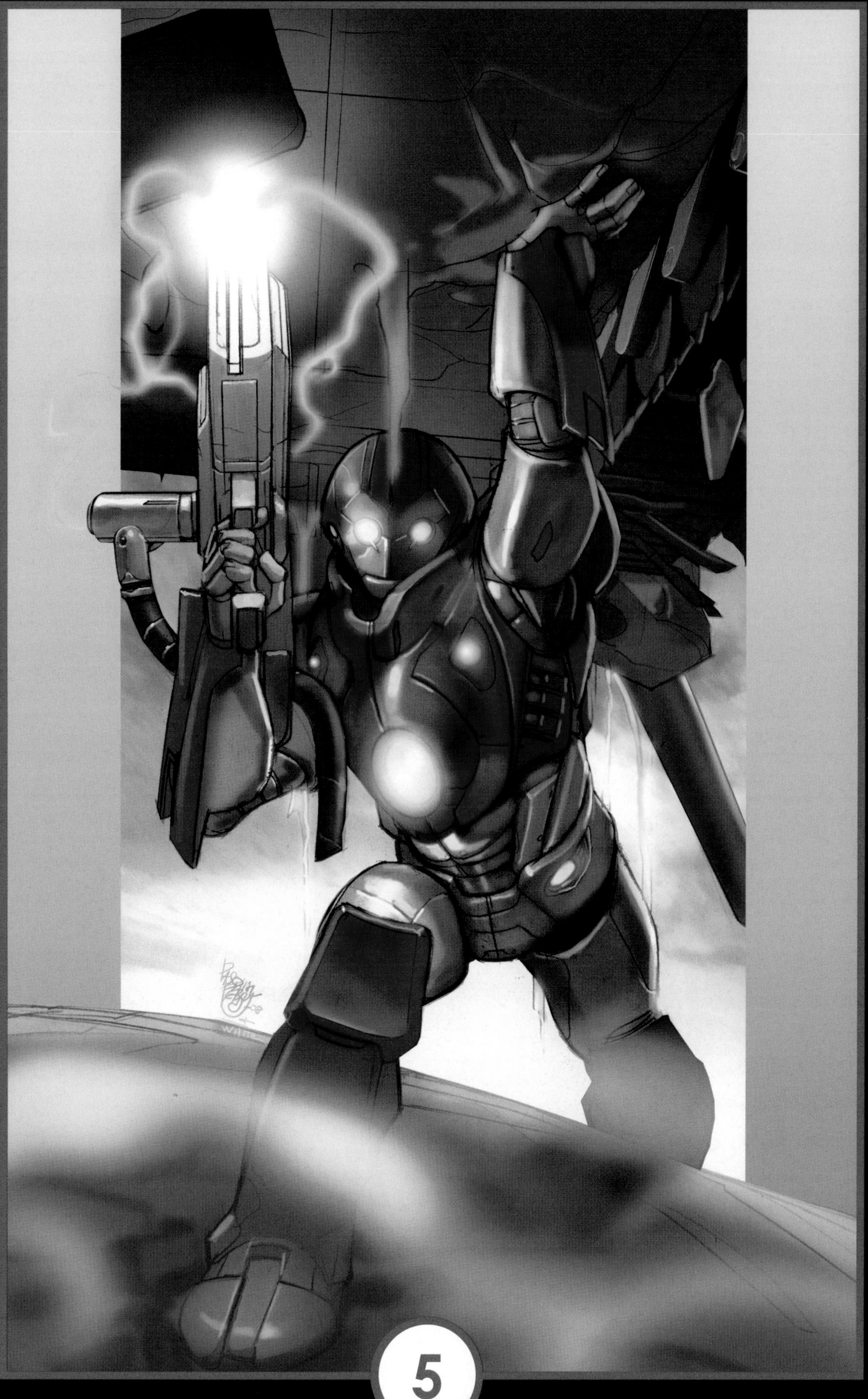

5

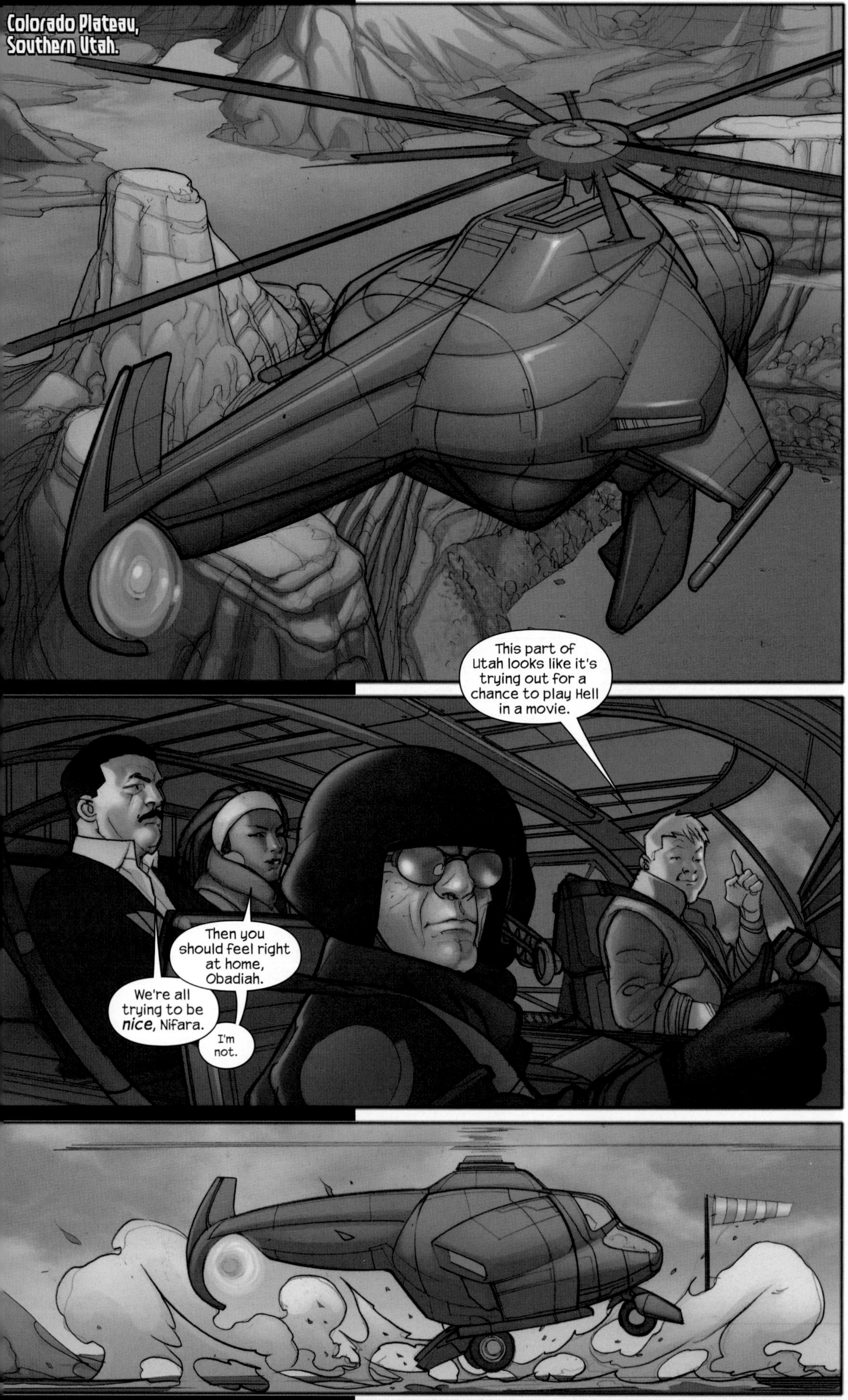
Colorado Plateau,
Southern Utah.
This part of Utah looks like it's trying out for a chance to play Hell in a movie.
Then you should feel right at home, Obadiah.
We're all trying to be *nice*, Nifara.
I'm not.

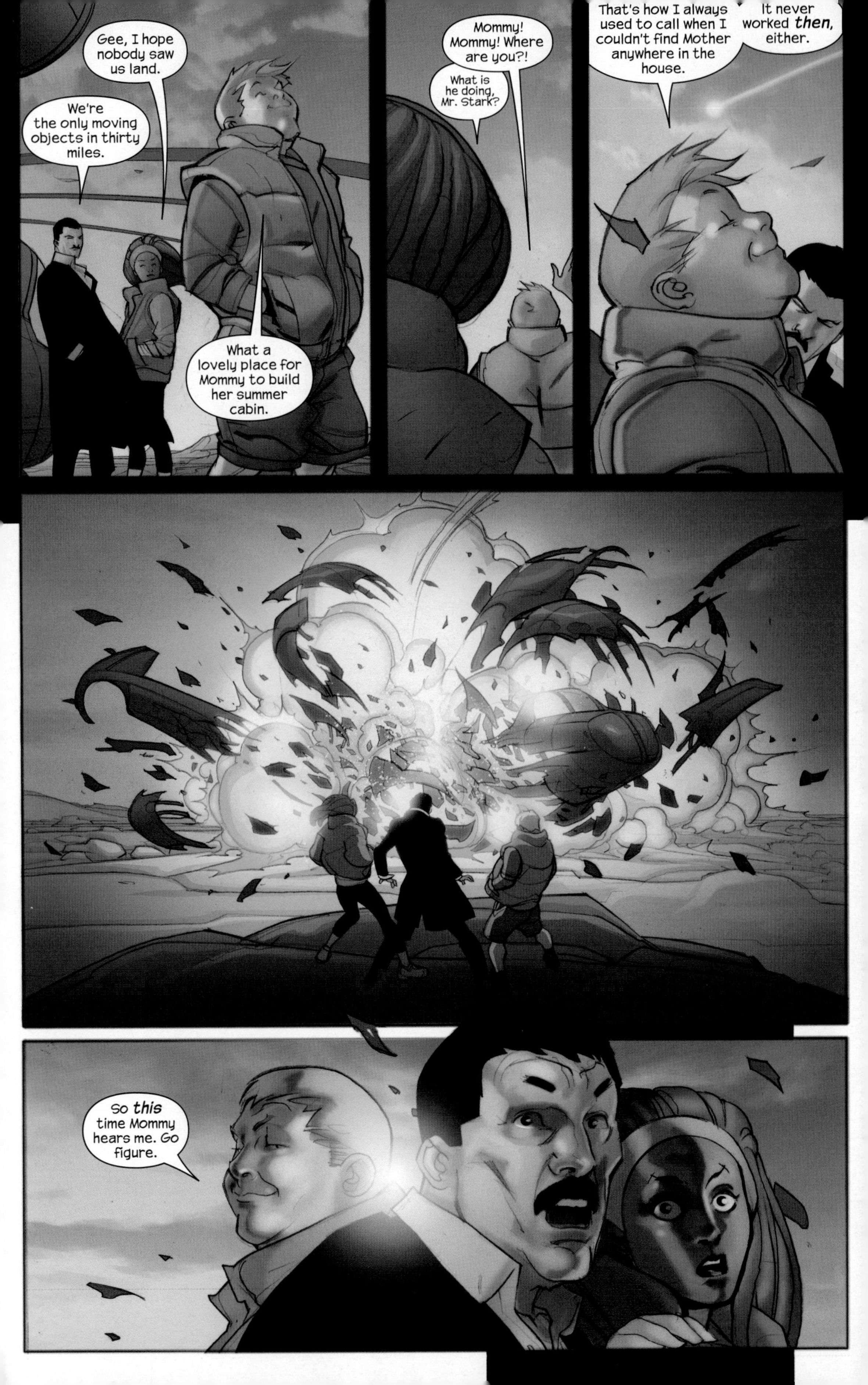
Gee, I hope nobody saw us land.
We're the only moving objects in thirty miles.
What a lovely place for Mommy to build her summer cabin.
Mommy! Mommy! Where are you?!
What is he doing, Mr. Stark?
That's how I always used to call when I couldn't find Mother anywhere in the house.
It never worked *then*, either.
So *this* time Mommy hears me. Go figure.

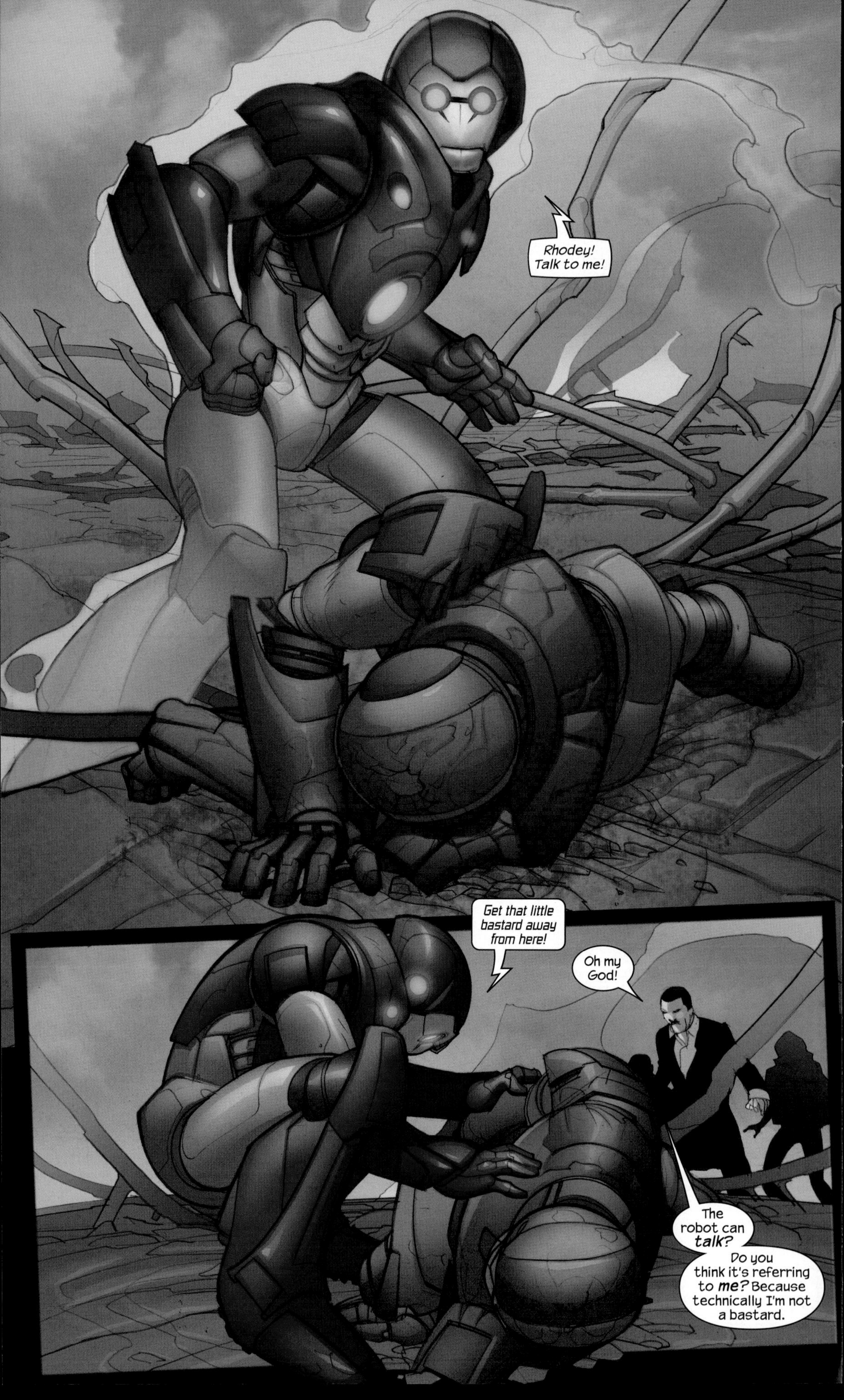
Rhodey! Talk to me!
Get that little bastard away from here!
Oh my God!
The robot can talk?
Do you think it's referring to me? Because technically I'm not a bastard.

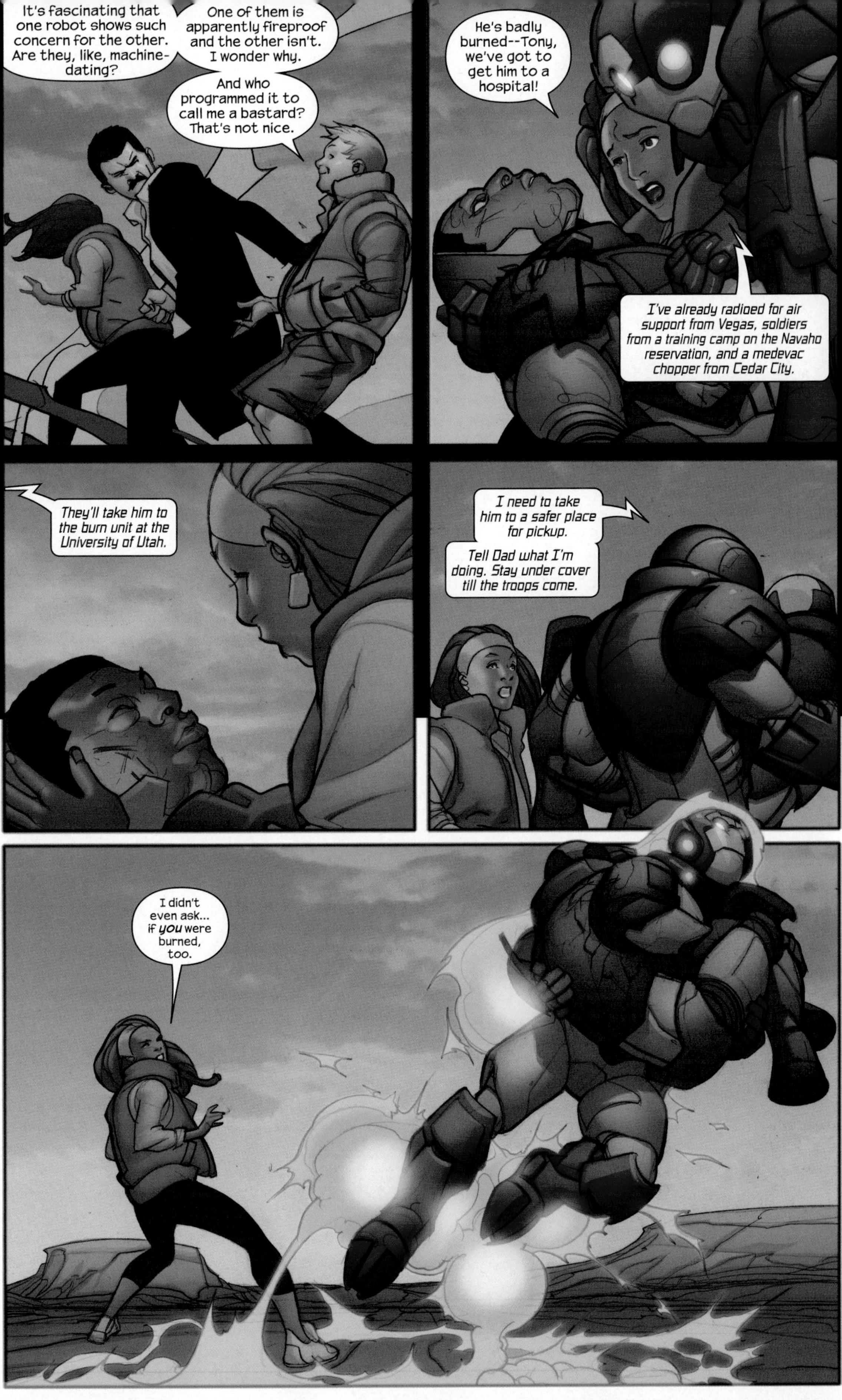
It's fascinating that one robot shows such concern for the other. Are they, like, machine-dating?
One of them is apparently fireproof and the other isn't. I wonder why.
And who programmed it to call me a bastard? That's not nice.
He's badly burned--Tony, we've got to get him to a hospital!
I've already radioed for air support from Vegas, soldiers from a training camp on the Navaho reservation, and a medevac chopper from Cedar City.
They'll take him to the burn unit at the University of Utah.
I need to take him to a safer place for pickup.
Tell Dad what I'm doing. Stay under cover till the troops come.
I didn't even ask... if *you* were burned, too.

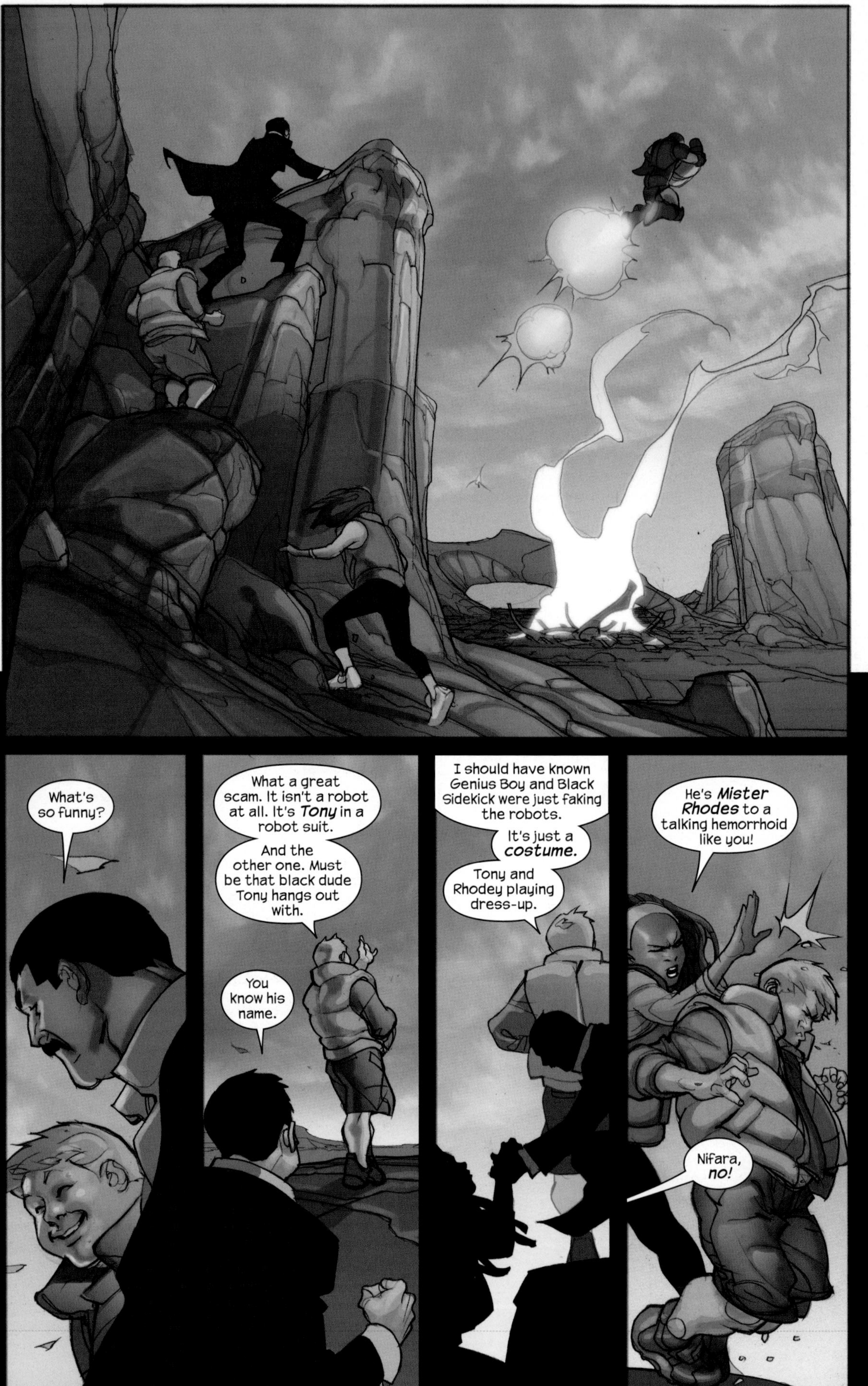

What's so funny?
What a great scam. It isn't a robot at all. It's *Tony* in a robot suit.
And the other one. Must be that black dude Tony hangs out with.
You know his name.
I should have known Genius Boy and Black Sidekick were just faking the robots.
It's just a ***costume.***
Tony and Rhodey playing dress-up.
He's ***Mister Rhodes*** to a talking hemorrhoid like you!
Nifara, ***no!***

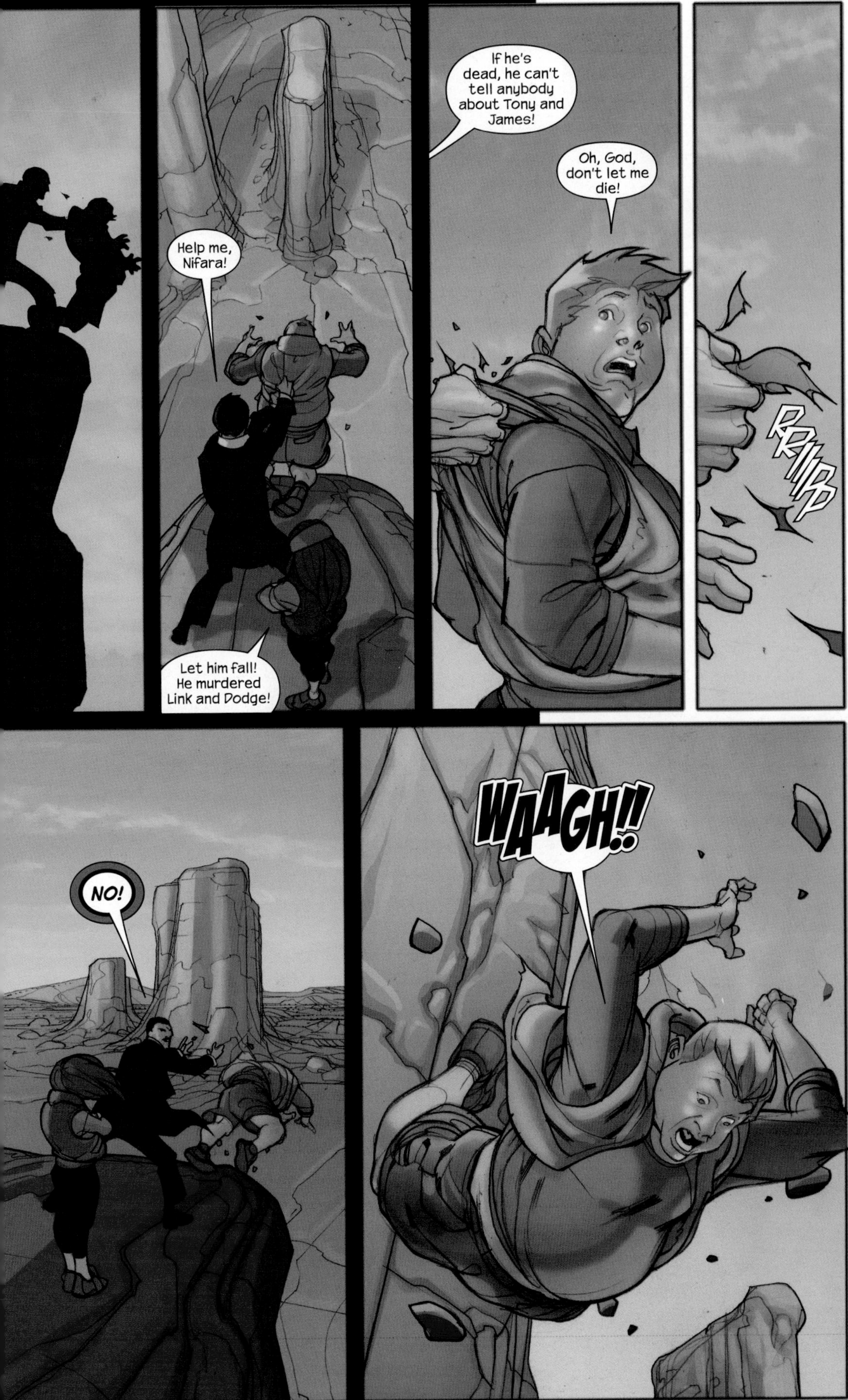
Help me, Nifara!
Let him fall! He murdered Link and Dodge!
If he's dead, he can't tell anybody about Tony and James!
Oh, God, don't let me die!
RRIIIP
NO!
WAAGH!!

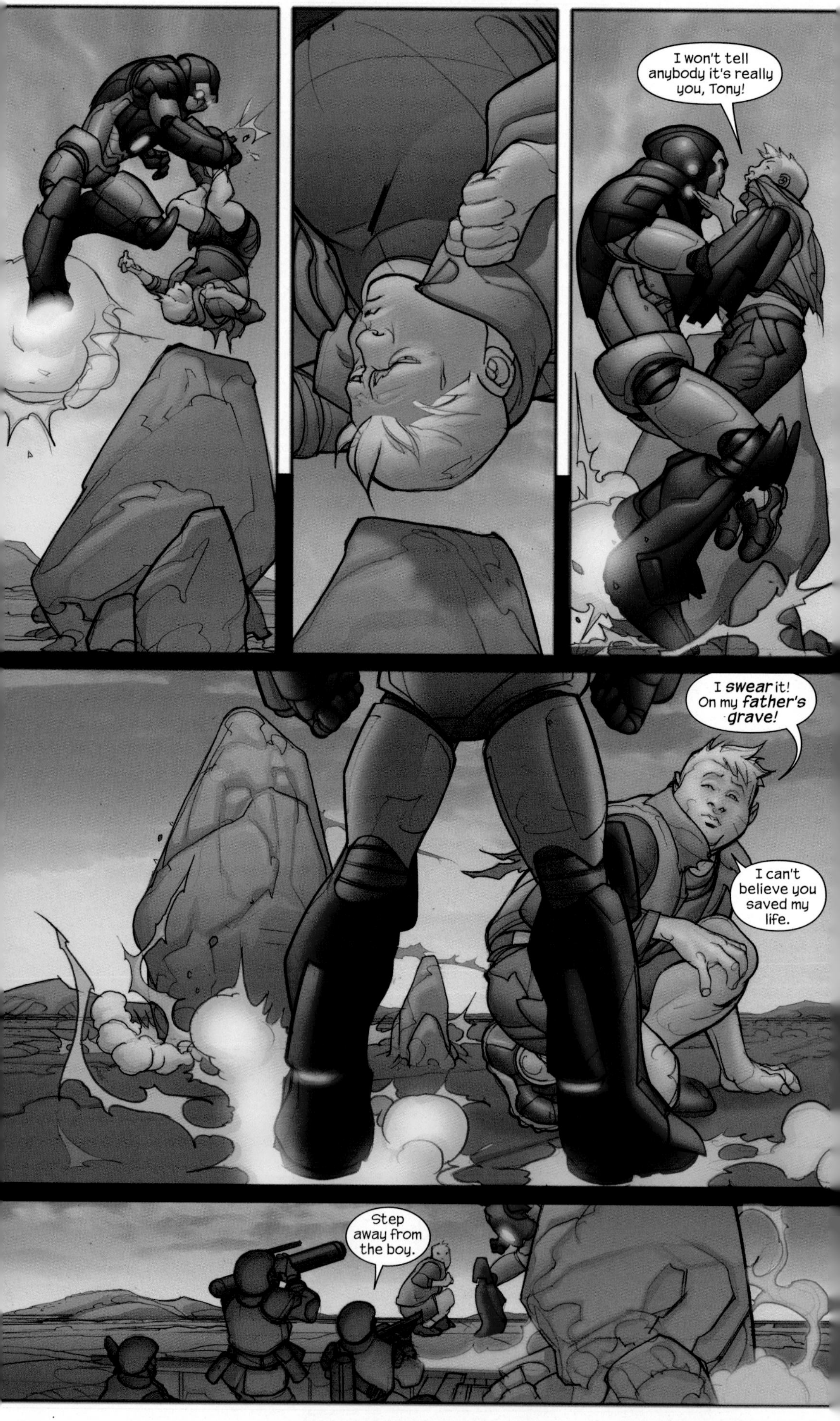
I won't tell anybody it's really you, Tony!
I *swear* it! On my *father's grave!*
I can't believe you saved my life.
Step away from the boy.

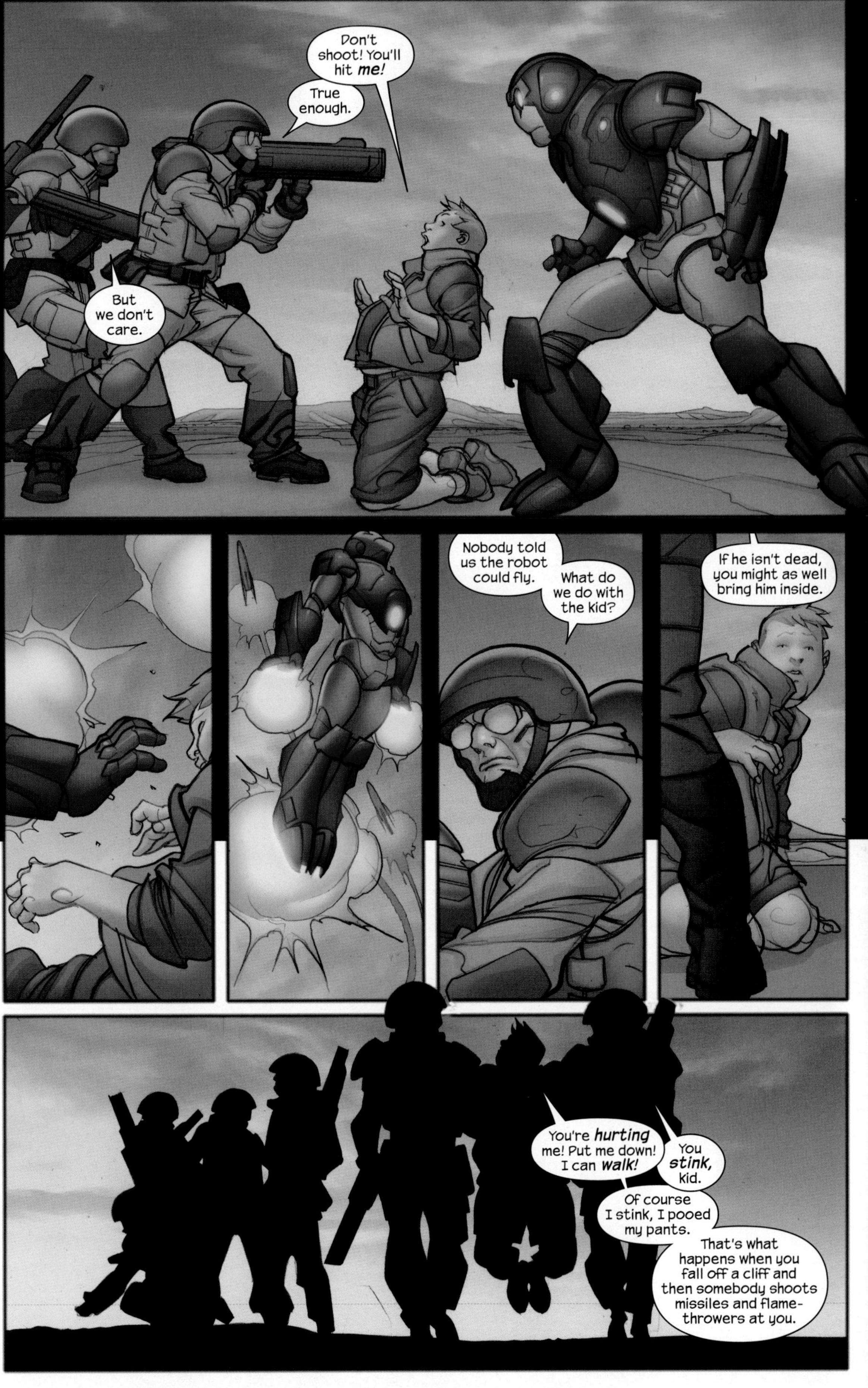
Don't shoot! You'll hit me!
True enough.
But we don't care.
Nobody told us the robot could fly.
What do we do with the kid?
If he isn't dead, you might as well bring him inside.
You're hurting me! Put me down! I can walk!
You stink, kid.
Of course I stink, I pooed my pants.
That's what happens when you fall off a cliff and then somebody shoots missiles and flame-throwers at you.

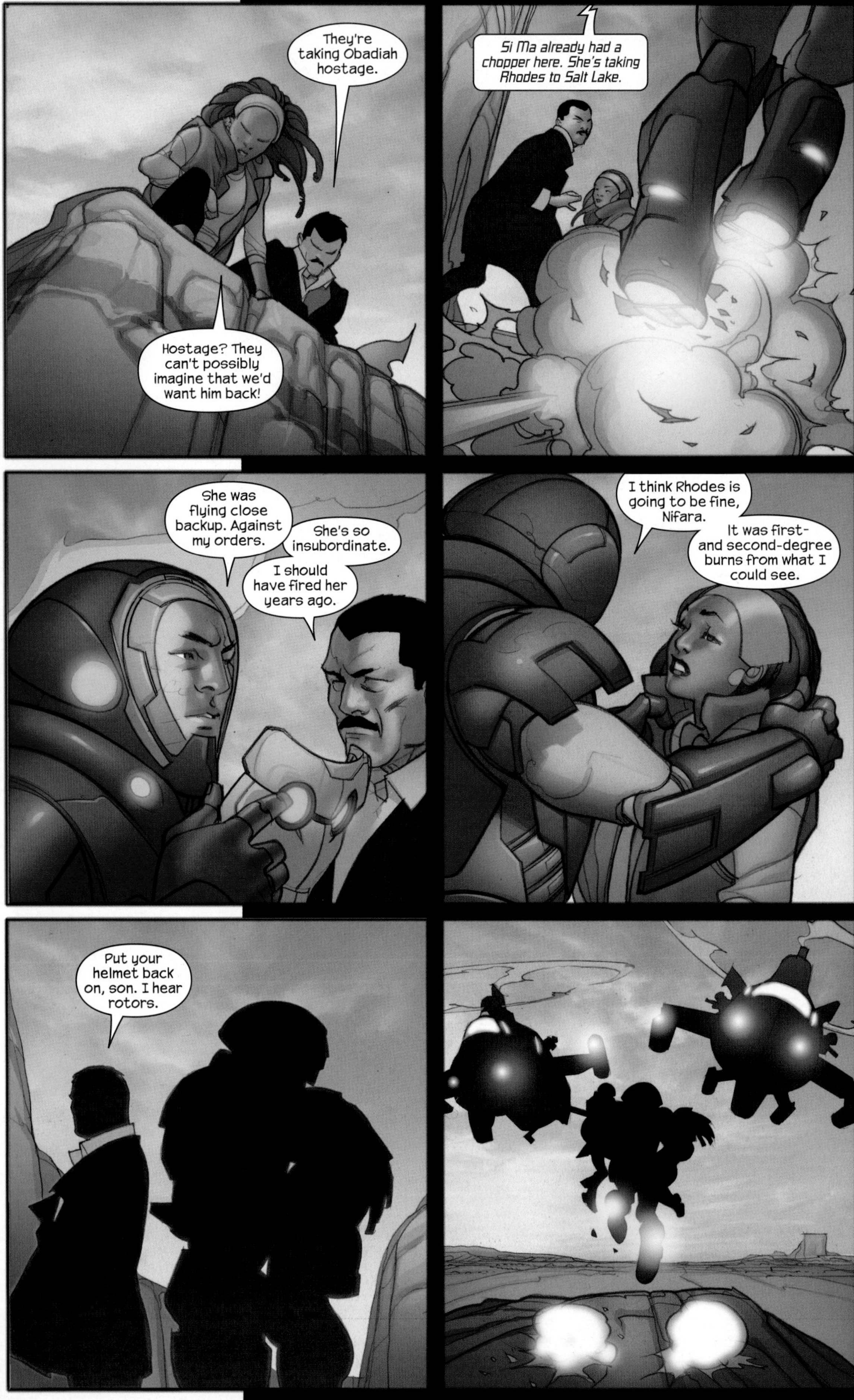

They're taking Obadiah hostage.
Hostage? They can't possibly imagine that we'd want him back!
Si Ma already had a chopper here. She's taking Rhodes to Salt Lake.
She was flying close backup. Against my orders.
She's so insubordinate.
I should have fired her years ago.
I think Rhodes is going to be fine, Nifara.
It was first- and second-degree burns from what I could see.
Put your helmet back on, son. I hear rotors.

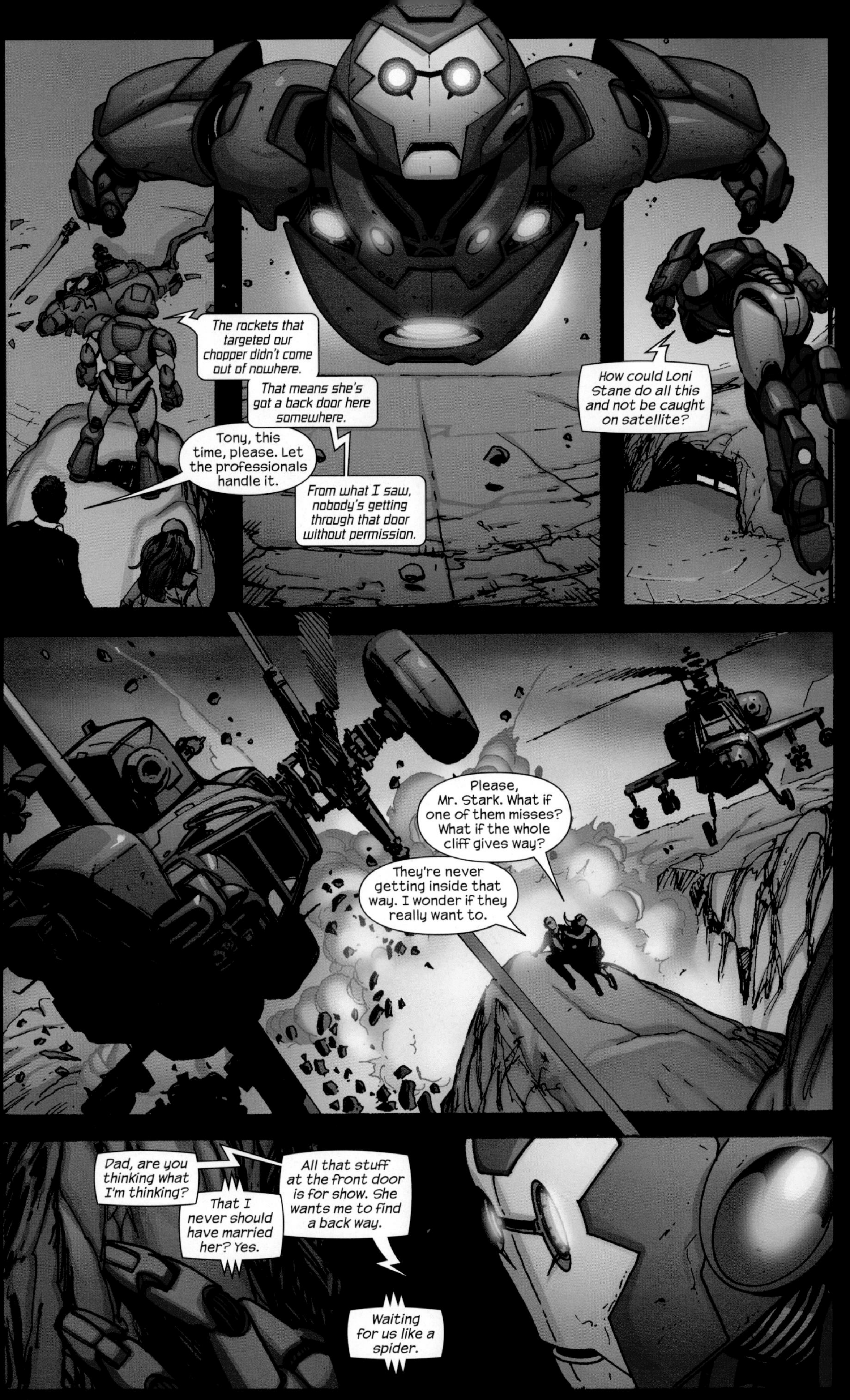
The rockets that targeted our chopper didn't come out of nowhere.
That means she's got a back door here somewhere.
Tony, this time, please. Let the professionals handle it.
From what I saw, nobody's getting through that door without permission.
How could Loni Stane do all this and not be caught on satellite?
Please, Mr. Stark. What if one of them misses? What if the whole cliff gives way?
They're never getting inside that way. I wonder if they really want to.
Dad, are you thinking what I'm thinking?
That I never should have married her? Yes.
All that stuff at the front door is for show. She wants me to find a back way.
Waiting for us like a spider.

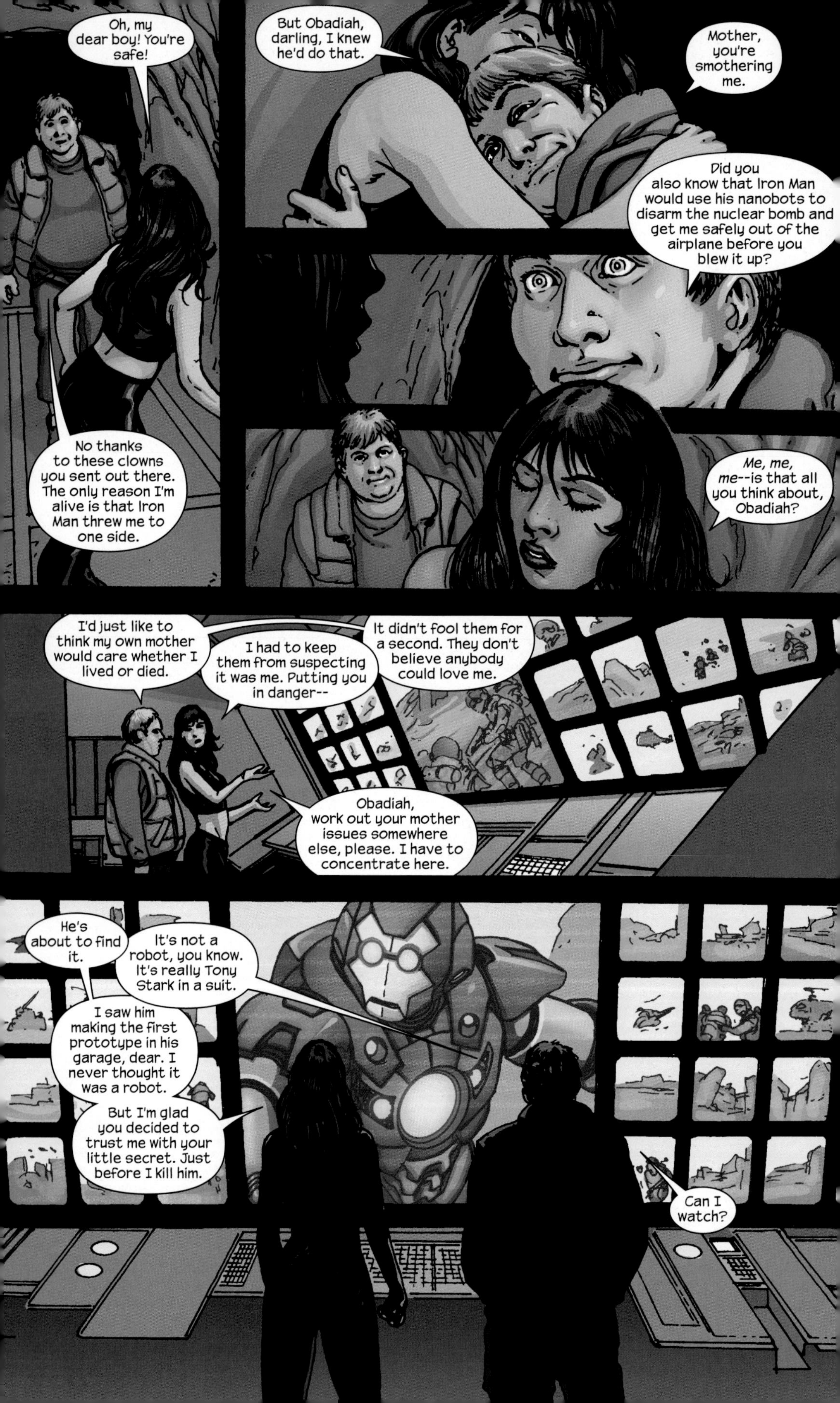

Oh, my dear boy! You're safe!
But Obadiah, darling, I knew he'd do that.
Mother, you're smothering me.
Did you also know that Iron Man would use his nanobots to disarm the nuclear bomb and get me safely out of the airplane before you blew it up?
No thanks to these clowns you sent out there. The only reason I'm alive is that Iron Man threw me to one side.
Me, me, me--is that all you think about, Obadiah?
I'd just like to think my own mother would care whether I lived or died.
I had to keep them from suspecting it was me. Putting you in danger--
It didn't fool them for a second. They don't believe anybody could love me.
Obadiah, work out your mother issues somewhere else, please. I have to concentrate here.
He's about to find it.
It's not a robot, you know. It's really Tony Stark in a suit.
I saw him making the first prototype in his garage, dear. I never thought it was a robot.
But I'm glad you decided to trust me with your little secret. Just before I kill him.
Can I watch?

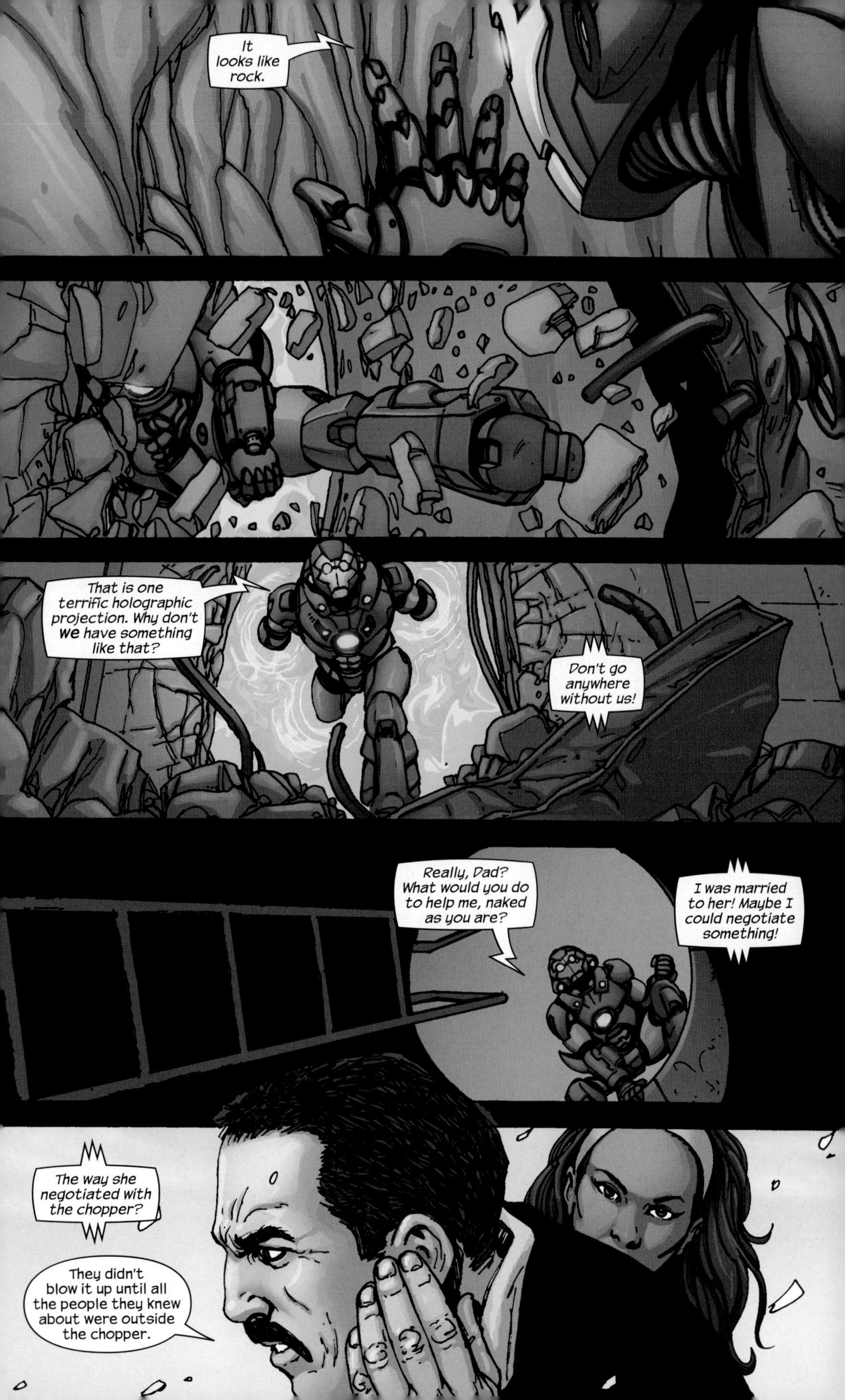
It looks like rock.
That is one terrific holographic projection. Why don't we have something like that?
Don't go anywhere without us!
Really, Dad? What would you do to help me, naked as you are?
I was married to her! Maybe I could negotiate something!
The way she negotiated with the chopper?
They didn't blow it up until all the people they knew about were outside the chopper.

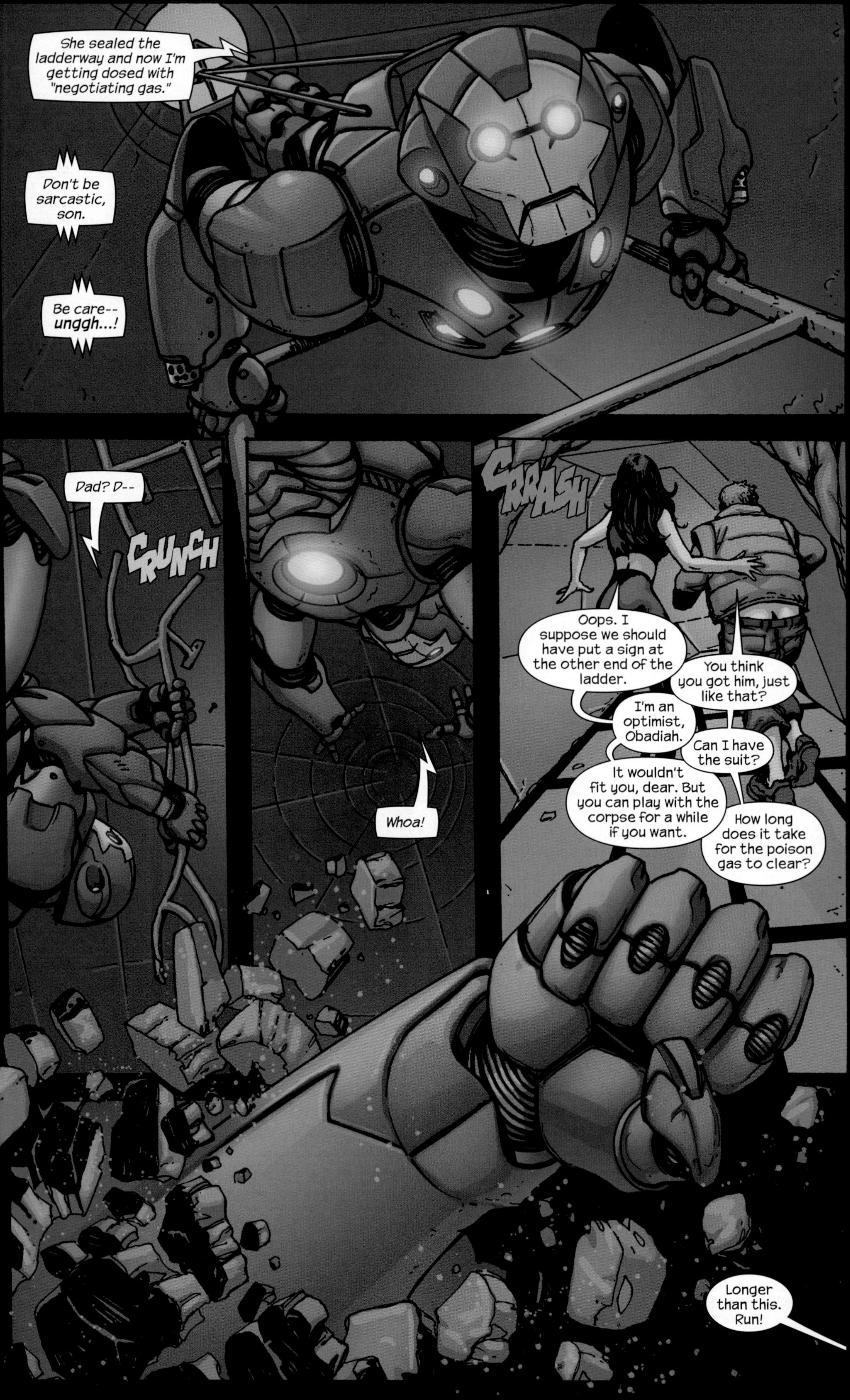
She sealed the ladderway and now I'm getting dosed with "negotiating gas."
Don't be sarcastic, son.
Be care-- unggh...!
Dad? D--
CRUNCH
Whoa!
CRRASH
Oops. I suppose we should have put a sign at the other end of the ladder.
You think you got him, just like that?
I'm an optimist, Obadiah.
Can I have the suit?
It wouldn't fit you, dear. But you can play with the corpse for a while if you want.
How long does it take for the poison gas to clear?
Longer than this. Run!

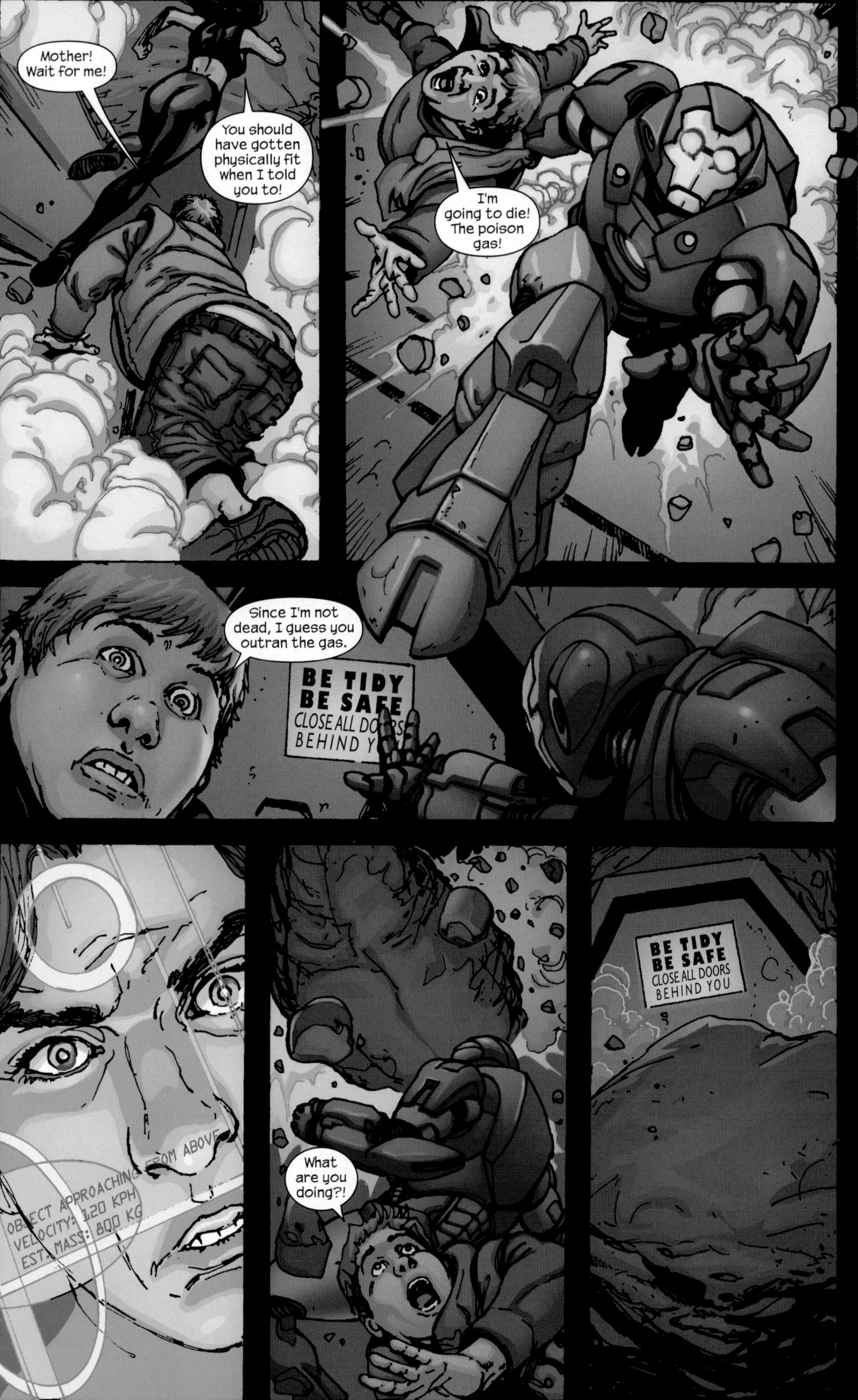
Mother! Wait for me!
You should have gotten physically fit when I told you to!
I'm going to die! The poison gas!
Since I'm not dead, I guess you outran the gas.
BE TIDY BE SAFE CLOSE ALL DOORS BEHIND YOU
OBJECT APPROACHING FROM ABOVE
VELOCITY: 120 KPH
EST. MASS: 800 KG
What are you doing?!
BE TIDY BE SAFE CLOSE ALL DOORS BEHIND YOU

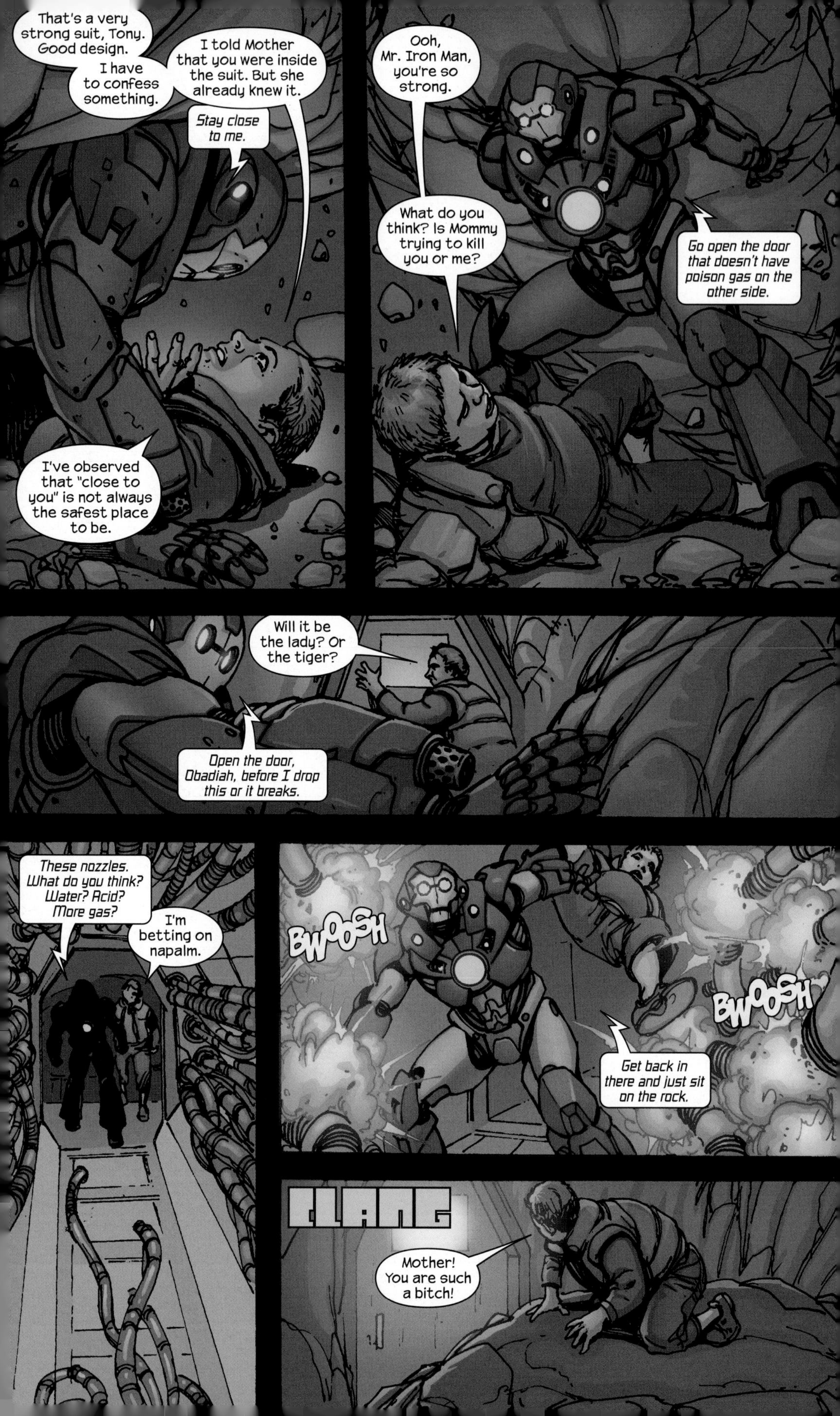
That's a very strong suit, Tony. Good design.
I have to confess something.
I told Mother that you were inside the suit. But she already knew it.
Stay close to me.
I've observed that "close to you" is not always the safest place to be.
Ooh, Mr. Iron Man, you're so strong.
What do you think? Is Mommy trying to kill you or me?
Go open the door that doesn't have poison gas on the other side.
Will it be the lady? Or the tiger?
Open the door, Obadiah, before I drop this or it breaks.
These nozzles. What do you think? Water? Acid? More gas?
I'm betting on napalm.
BWOOSH
BWOOSH
Get back in there and just sit on the rock.
CLANG
Mother! You are such a bitch!

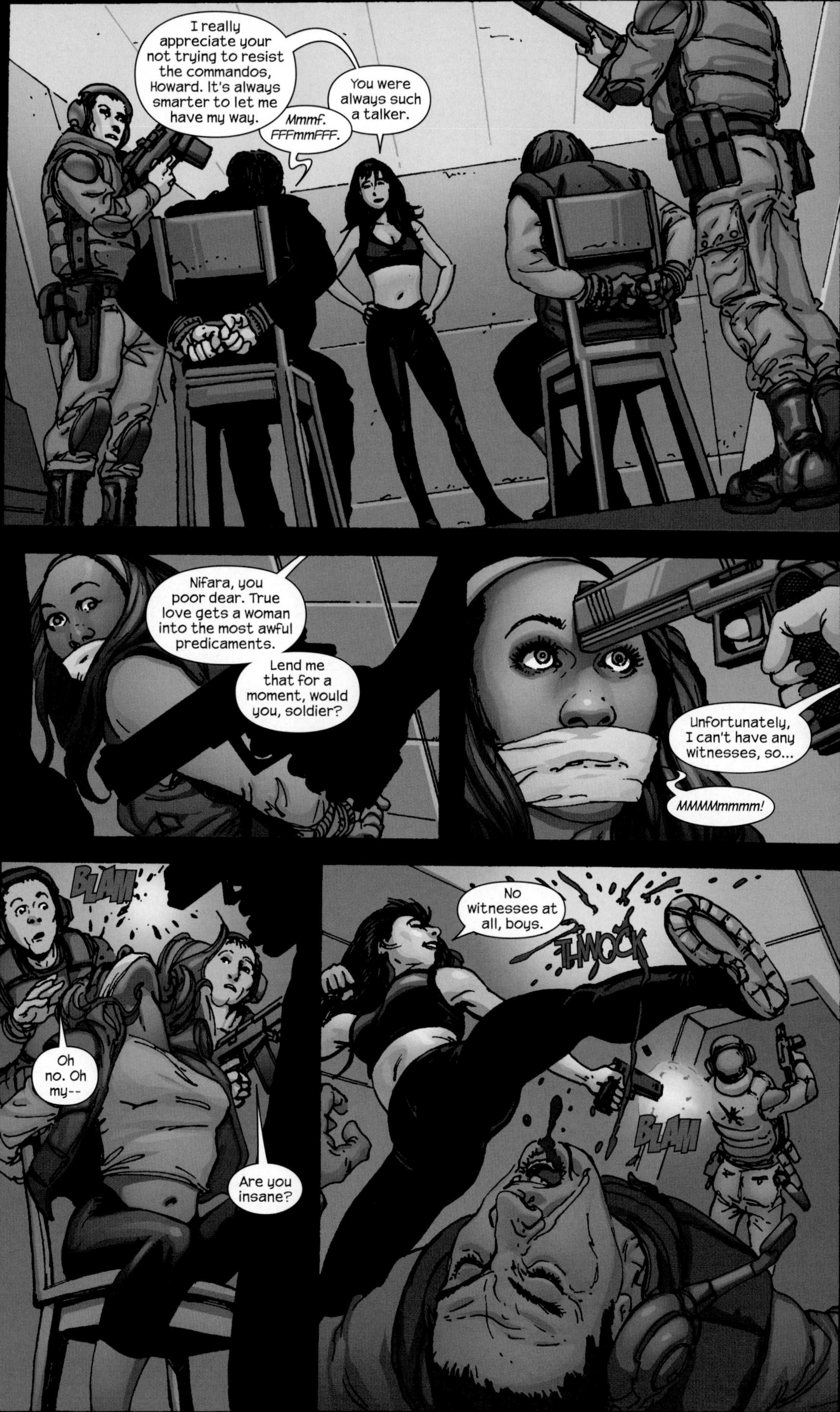
I really appreciate your not trying to resist the commandos, Howard. It's always smarter to let me have my way.
Mmmf. FFFmmFFF.
You were always such a talker.
Nifara, you poor dear. True love gets a woman into the most awful predicaments.
Lend me that for a moment, would you, soldier?
Unfortunately, I can't have any witnesses, so...
MMMMmmmm!
BLAM
Oh no. Oh my--
Are you insane?
No witnesses at all, boys.
THWOCK
BLAM

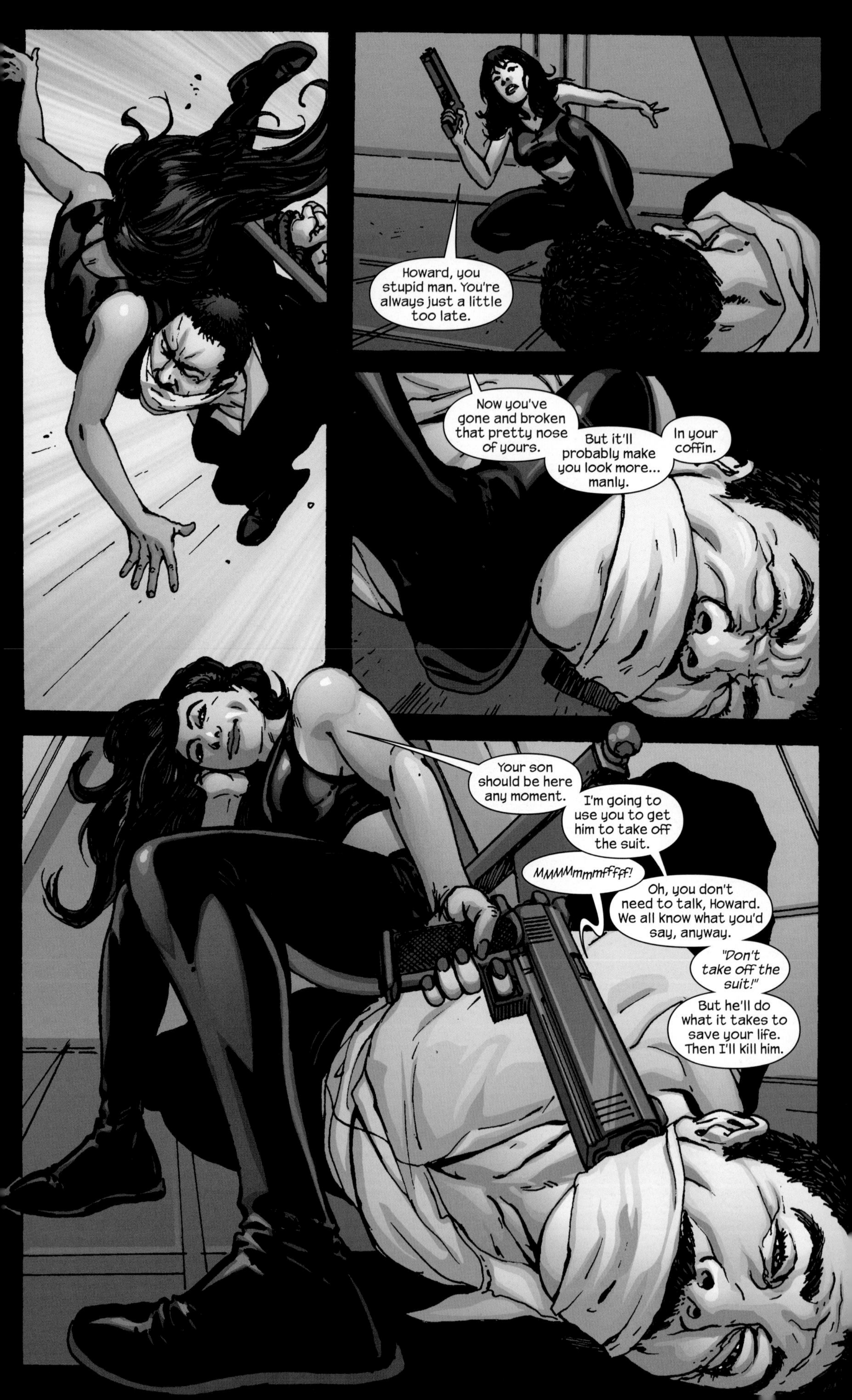
Howard, you stupid man. You're always just a little too late.
Now you've gone and broken that pretty nose of yours.
But it'll probably make you look more... manly.
In your coffin.
Your son should be here any moment.
I'm going to use you to get him to take off the suit.
MMMMmmmffff!
Oh, you don't need to talk, Howard. We all know what you'd say, anyway.
"Don't take off the suit!"
But he'll do what it takes to save your life. Then I'll kill him.

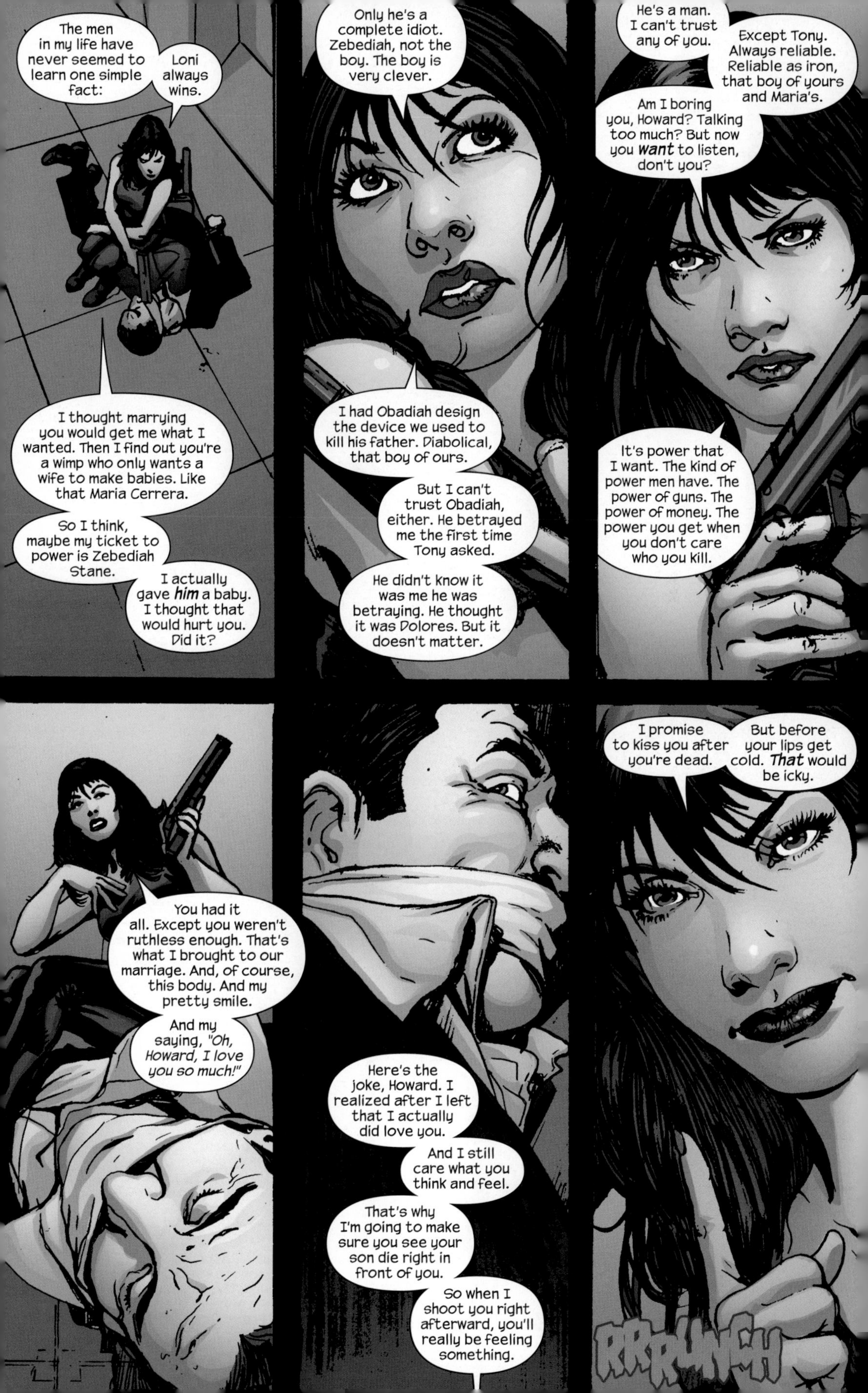
The men in my life have never seemed to learn one simple fact:
Loni always wins.
I thought marrying you would get me what I wanted. Then I find out you're a wimp who only wants a wife to make babies. Like that Maria Cerrera.
So I think, maybe my ticket to power is Zebediah Stane.
I actually gave *him* a baby. I thought that would hurt you. Did it?
Only he's a complete idiot. Zebediah, not the boy. The boy is very clever.
I had Obadiah design the device we used to kill his father. Diabolical, that boy of ours.
But I can't trust Obadiah, either. He betrayed me the first time Tony asked.
He didn't know it was me he was betraying. He thought it was Dolores. But it doesn't matter.
He's a man. I can't trust any of you.
Except Tony. Always reliable. Reliable as iron, that boy of yours and Maria's.
Am I boring you, Howard? Talking too much? But now you ***want*** to listen, don't you?
It's power that I want. The kind of power men have. The power of guns. The power of money. The power you get when you don't care who you kill.
You had it all. Except you weren't ruthless enough. That's what I brought to our marriage. And, of course, this body. And my pretty smile.
And my saying, *"Oh, Howard, I love you so much!"*
Here's the joke, Howard. I realized after I left that I actually did love you.
And I still care what you think and feel.
That's why I'm going to make sure you see your son die right in front of you.
So when I shoot you right afterward, you'll really be feeling something.
I promise to kiss you after you're dead.
But before your lips get cold. *That* would be icky.
RRRUNCH

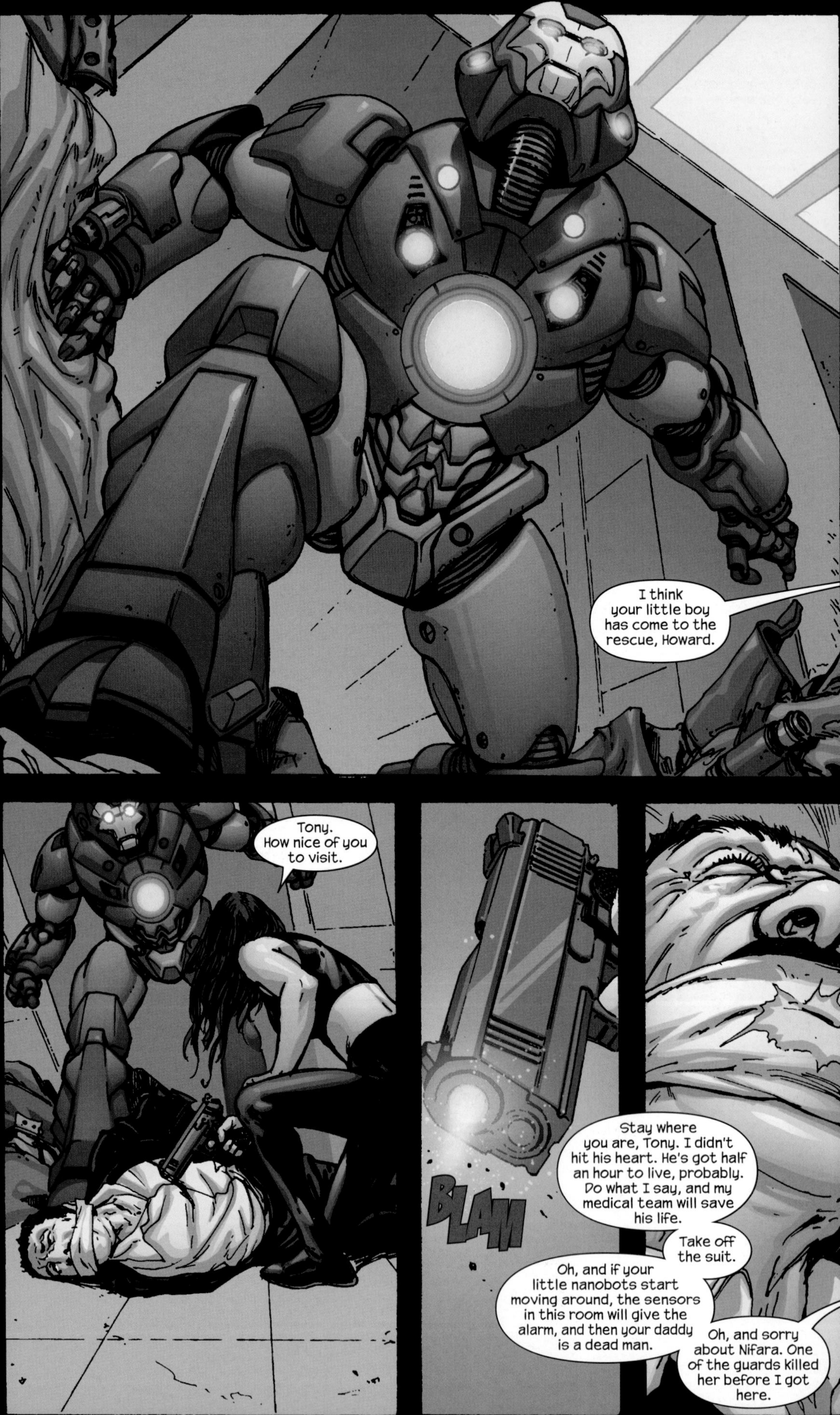
I think your little boy has come to the rescue, Howard.
Tony. How nice of you to visit.
BLAM
Stay where you are, Tony. I didn't hit his heart. He's got half an hour to live, probably. Do what I say, and my medical team will save his life.
Take off the suit.
Oh, and if your little nanobots start moving around, the sensors in this room will give the alarm, and then your daddy is a dead man.
Oh, and sorry about Nifara. One of the guards killed her before I got here.

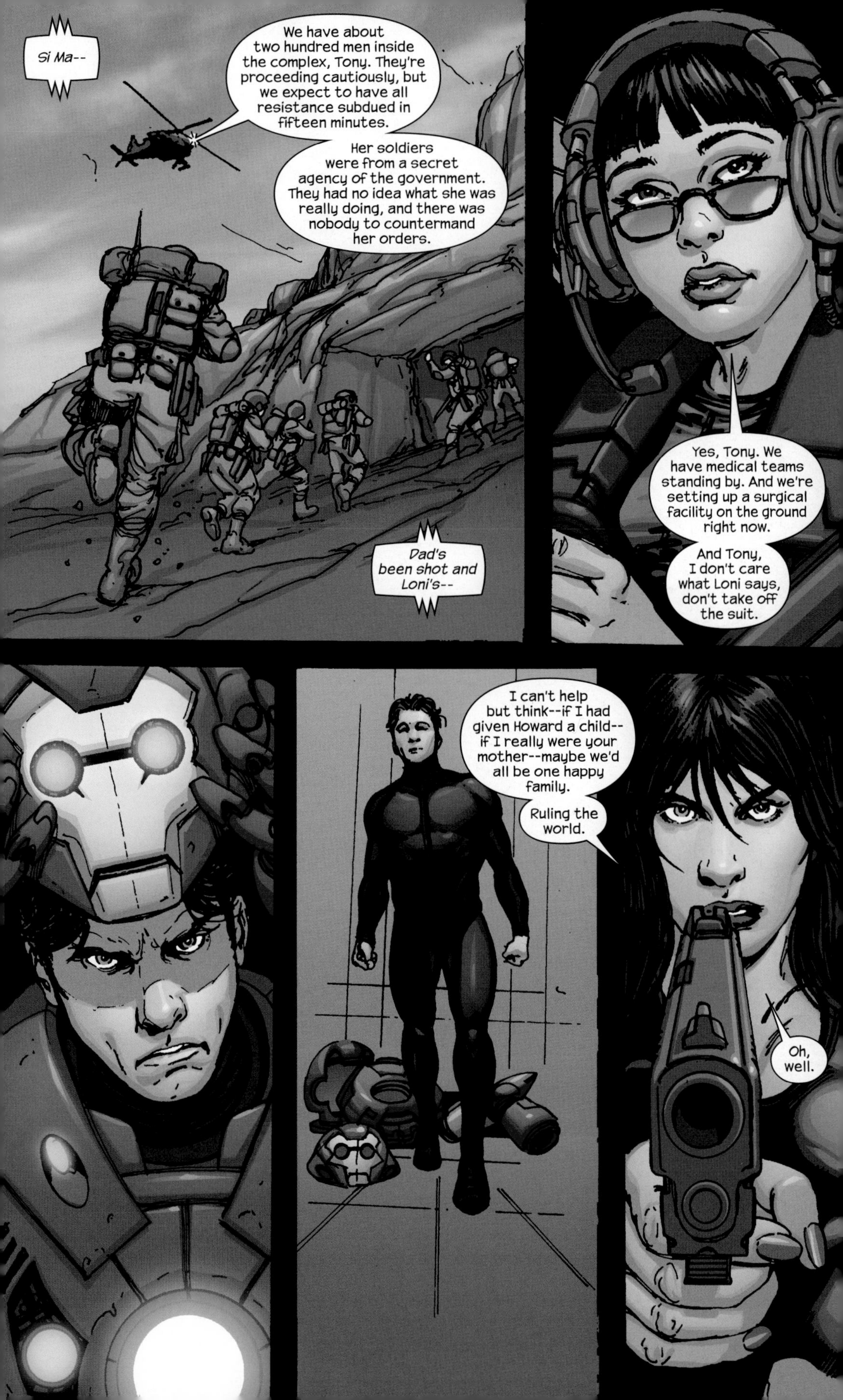
Si Ma--
We have about two hundred men inside the complex, Tony. They're proceeding cautiously, but we expect to have all resistance subdued in fifteen minutes.
Her soldiers were from a secret agency of the government. They had no idea what she was really doing, and there was nobody to countermand her orders.
Dad's been shot and Loni's--
Yes, Tony. We have medical teams standing by. And we're setting up a surgical facility on the ground right now.
And Tony, I don't care what Loni says, don't take off the suit.
I can't help but think--if I had given Howard a child--if I really were your mother--maybe we'd all be one happy family.
Ruling the world.
Oh, well.

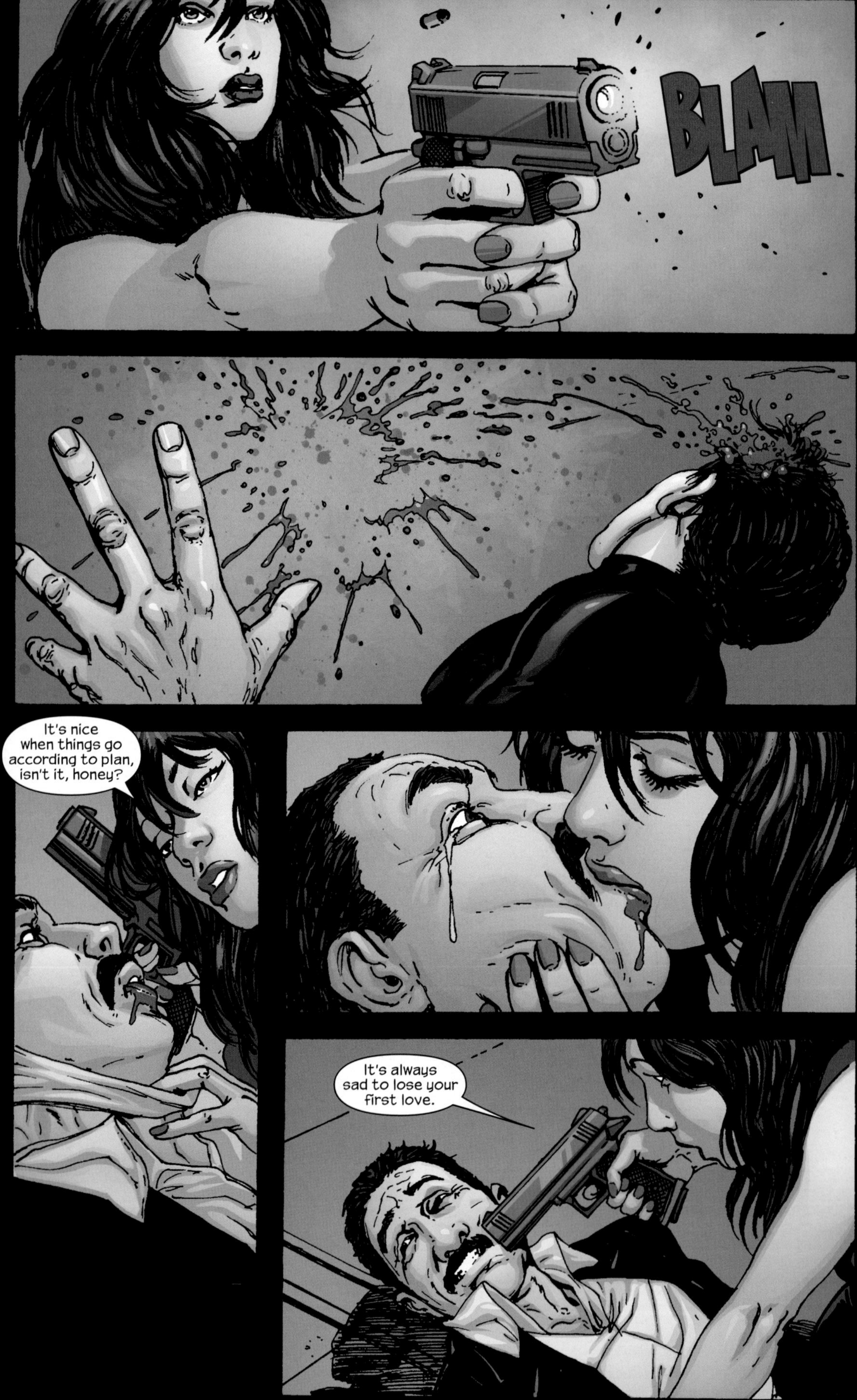
BLAM
It's nice when things go according to plan, isn't it, honey?
It's always sad to lose your first love.

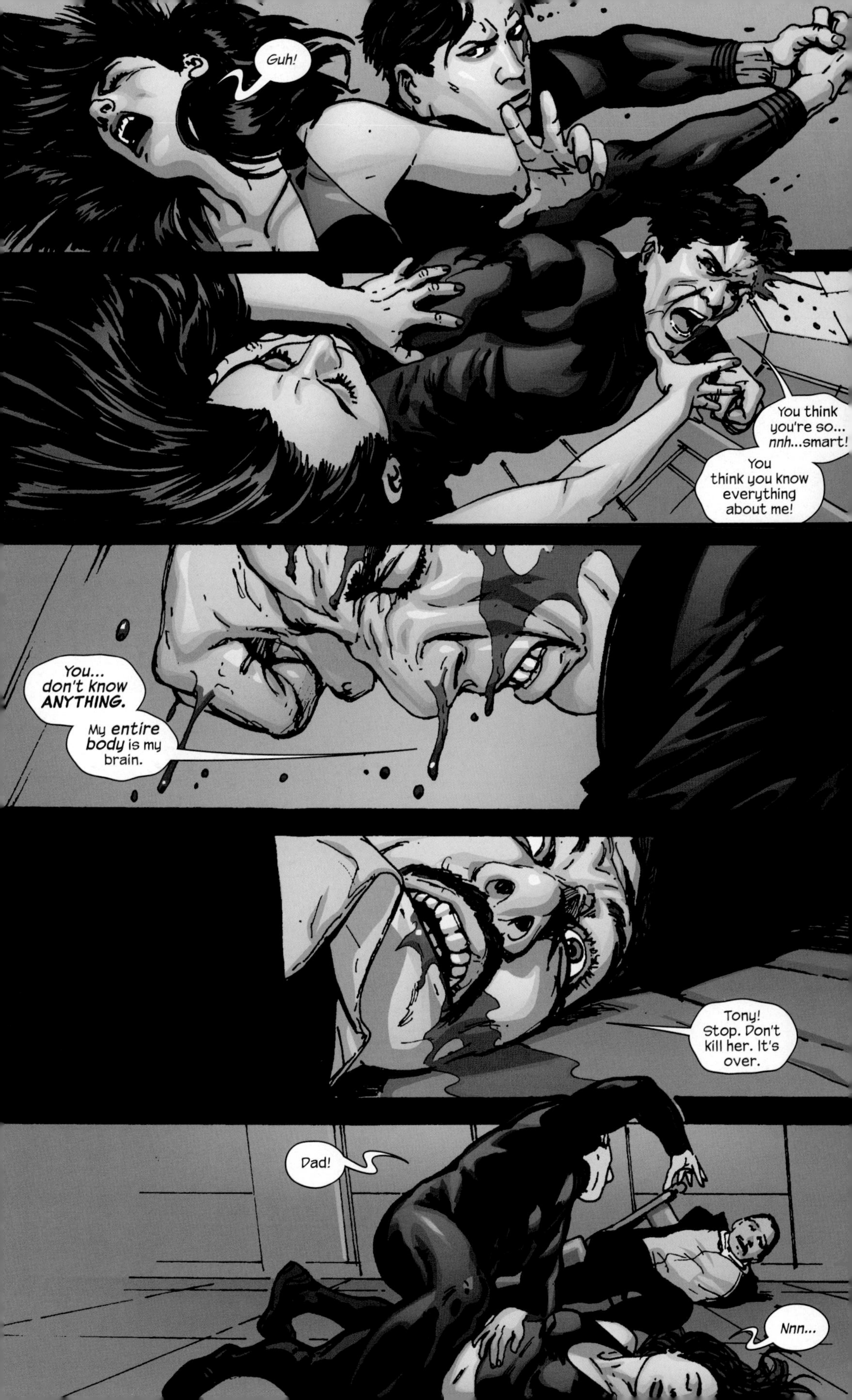
Guh!
You think you're so... nnh...smart!
You think you know everything about me!
You... don't know ANYTHING.
My entire body is my brain.
Tony! Stop. Don't kill her. It's over.
Dad!
Nnn...

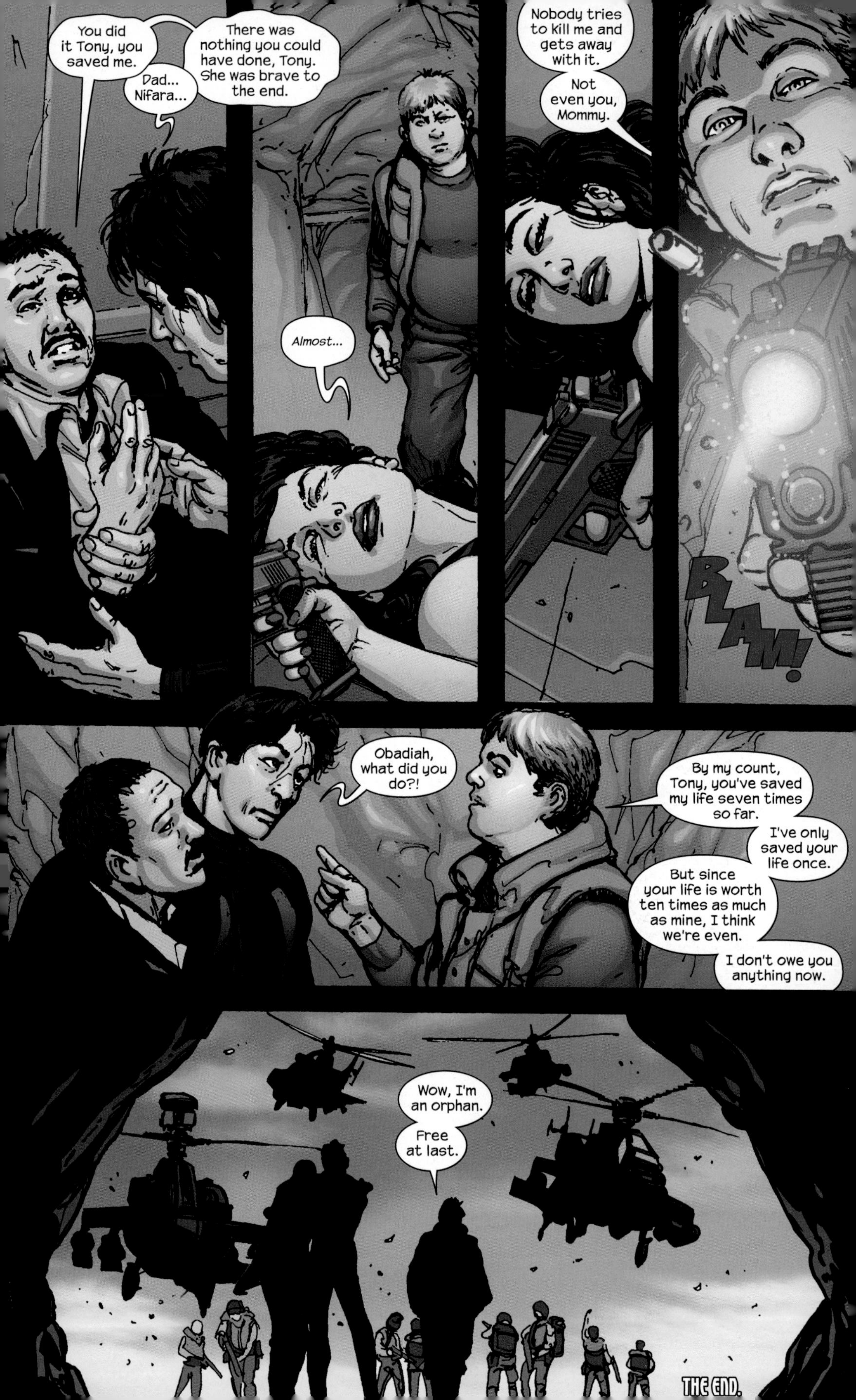

You did it Tony, you saved me.
Dad... Nifara...
There was nothing you could have done, Tony. She was brave to the end.
Almost...
Nobody tries to kill me and gets away with it.
Not even you, Mommy.
BLAM!
Obadiah, what did you do?!
By my count, Tony, you've saved my life seven times so far.
I've only saved your life once.
But since your life is worth ten times as much as mine, I think we're even.
I don't owe you anything now.
Wow, I'm an orphan.
Free at last.
THE END.

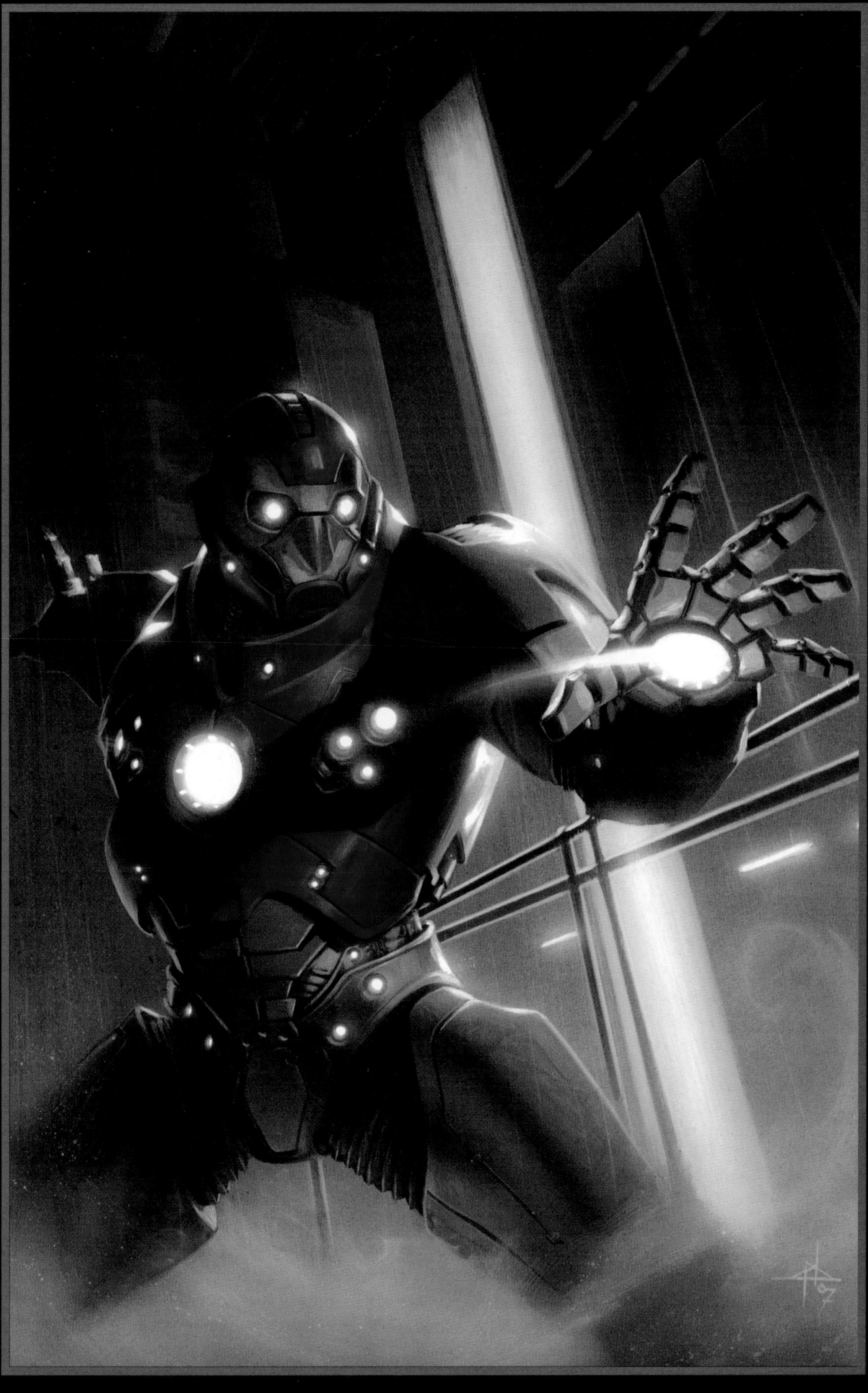

#1 Variant by Gabriele Dell'Otto

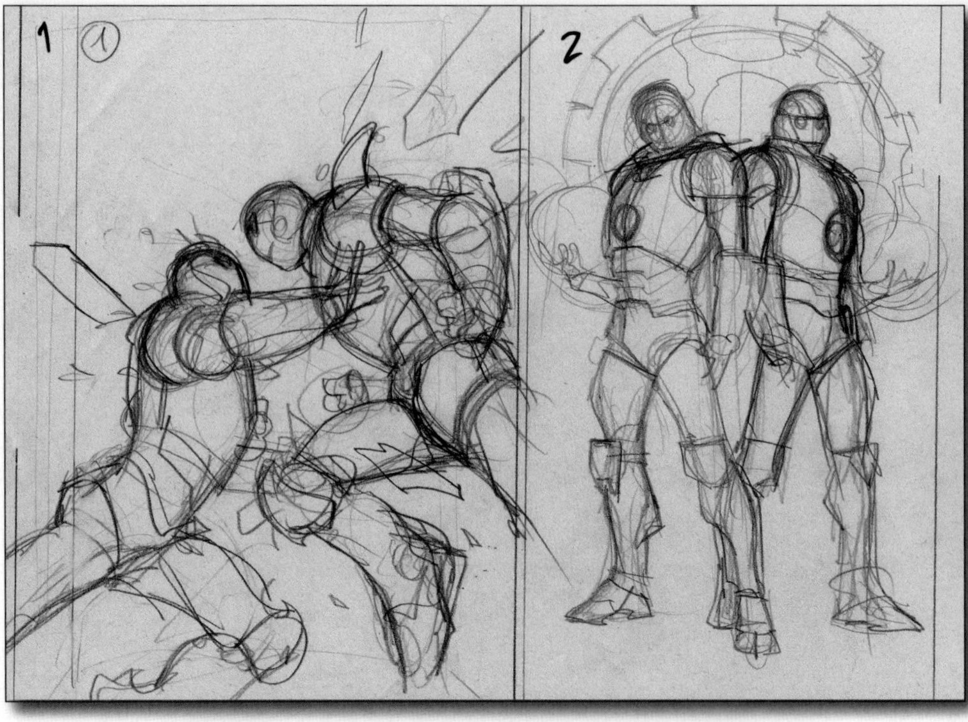
1
2

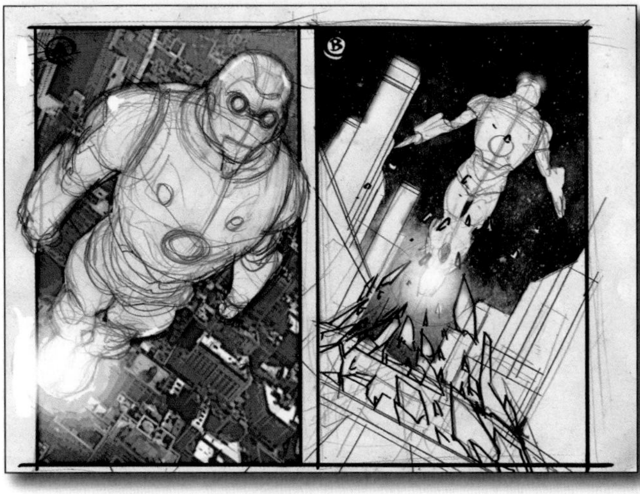

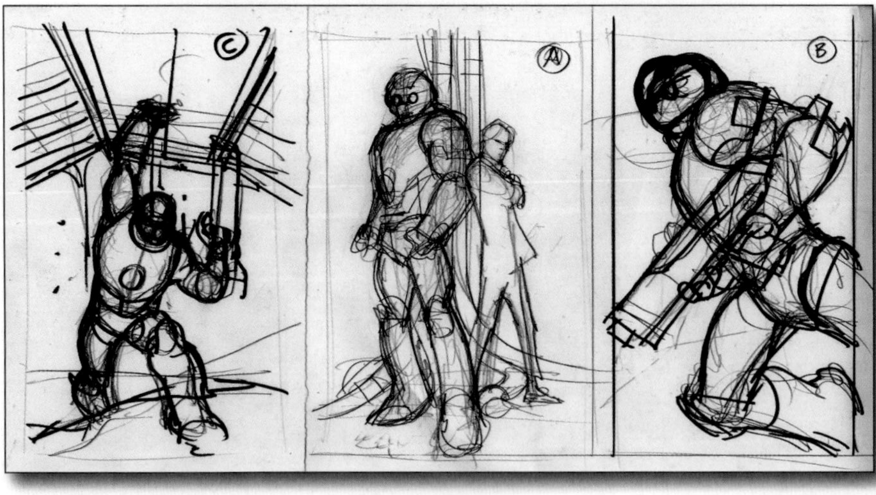

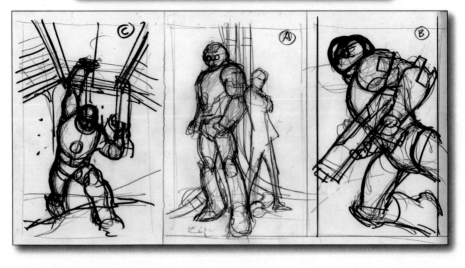

Cover Sketches by Pasqual Ferry

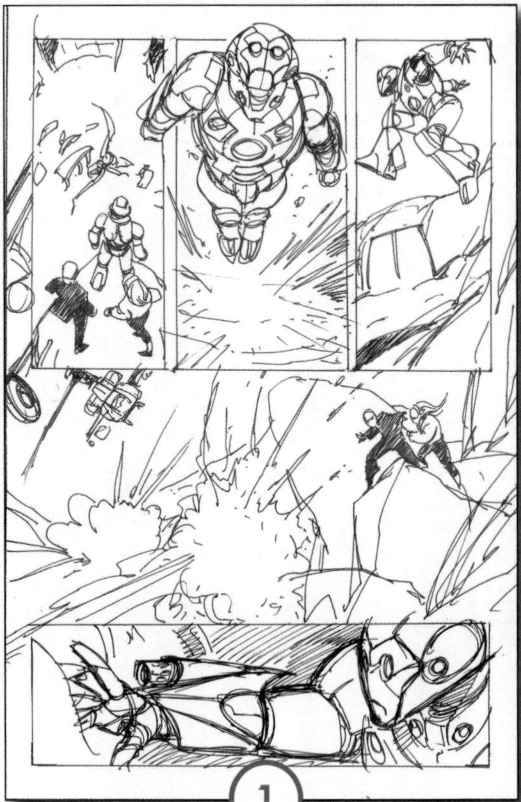

1

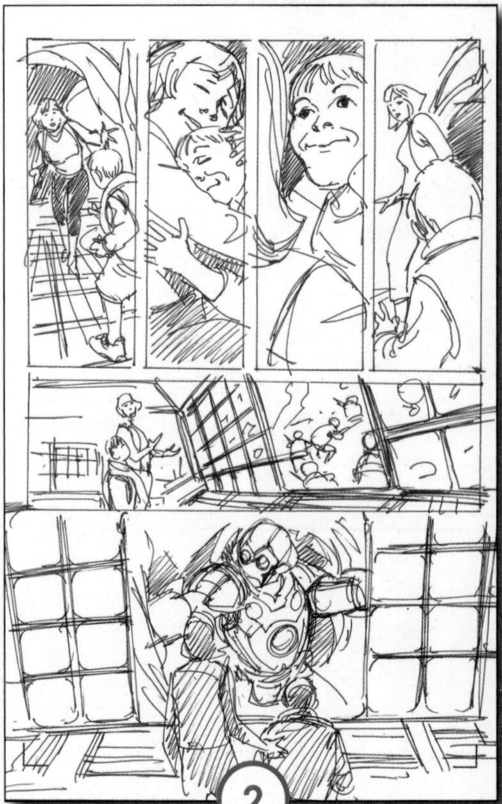

2

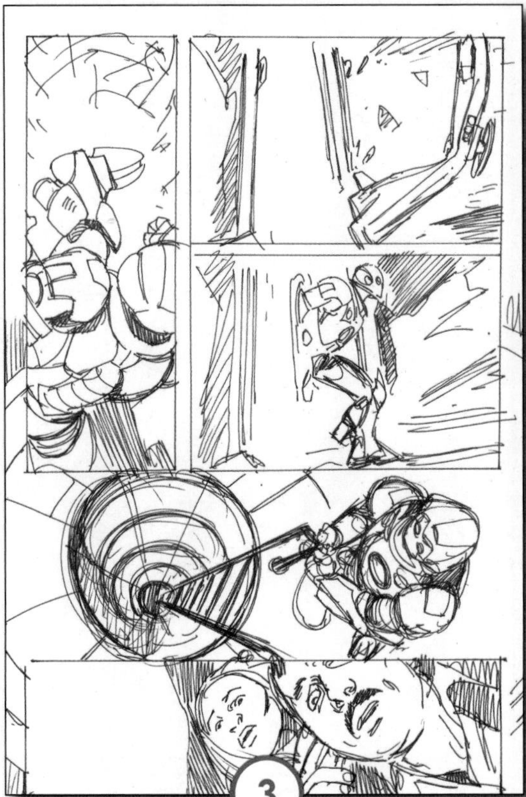

3

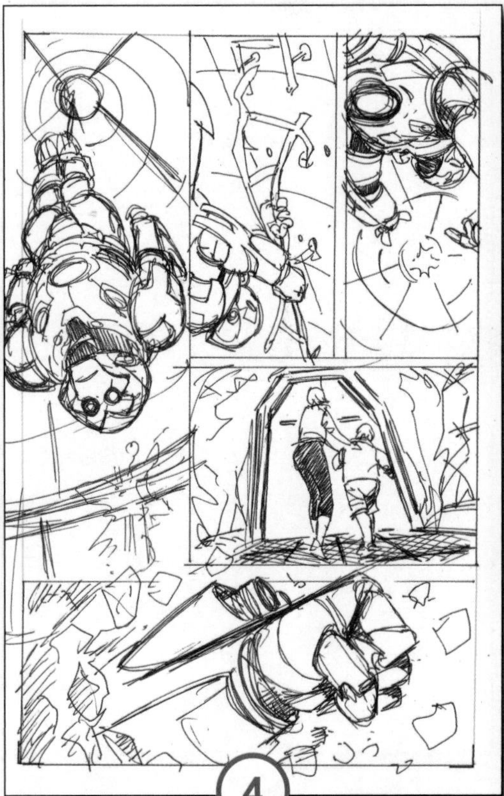

4

Issue #5 Layouts by Leonardo Manco

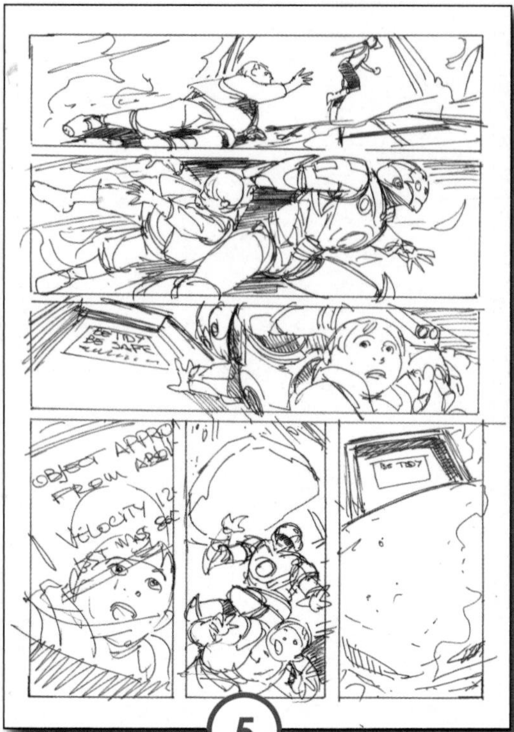
BE TIDY
BE SAFE
OBJECT APPRO
FROM ABO
VELOCITY 12
BE TIDY

5

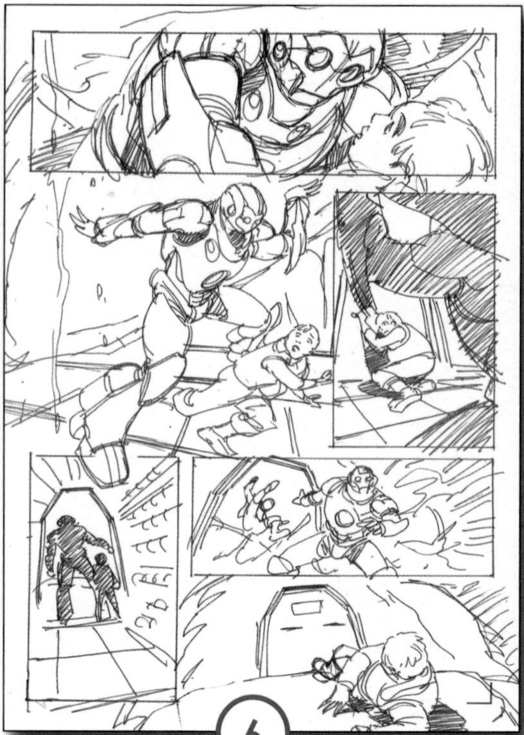

6

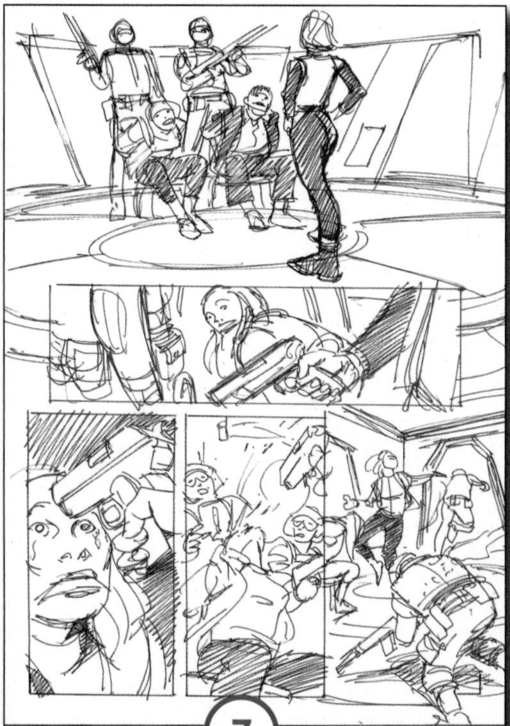

7

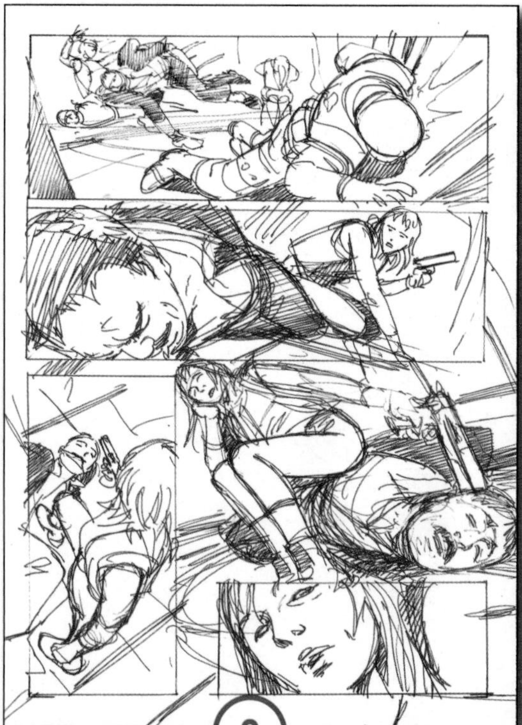

8

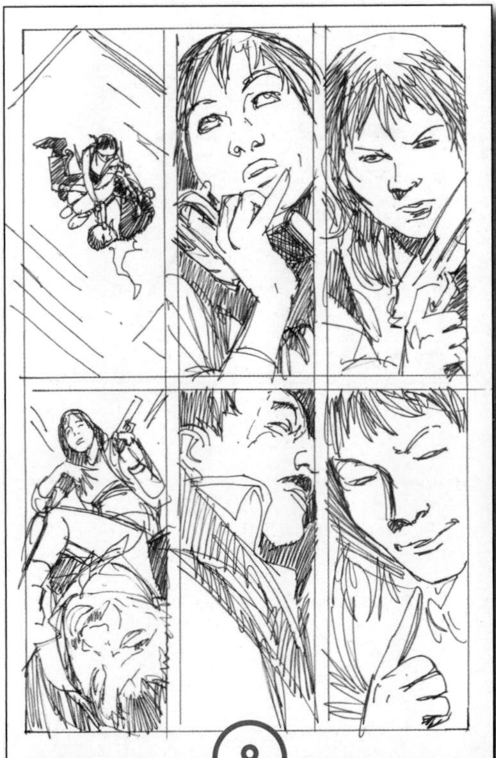

9

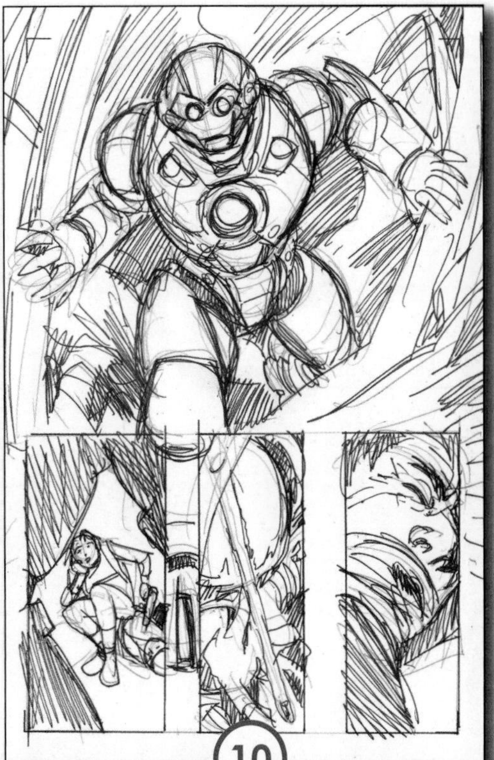

10

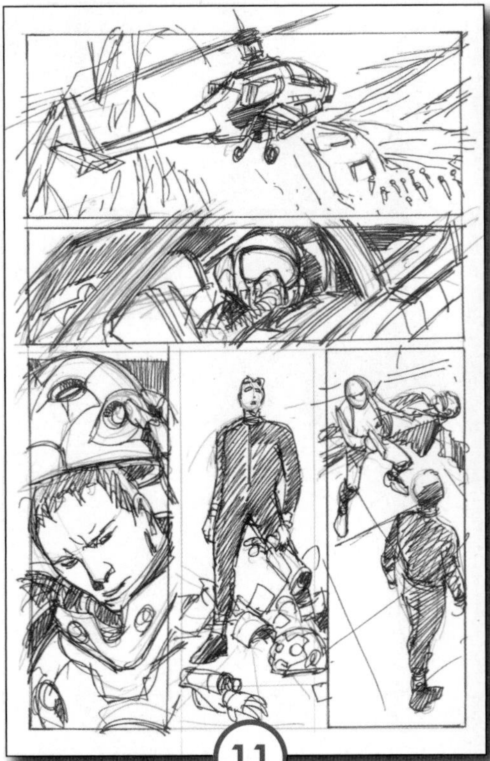

11

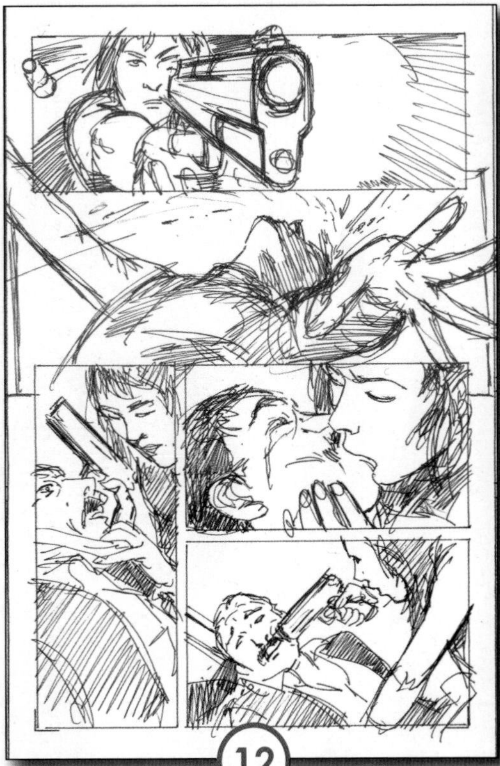

12

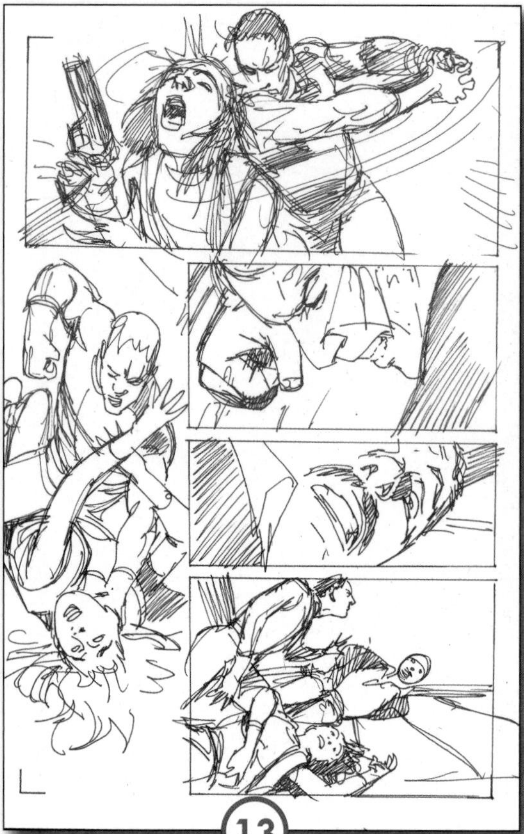

13

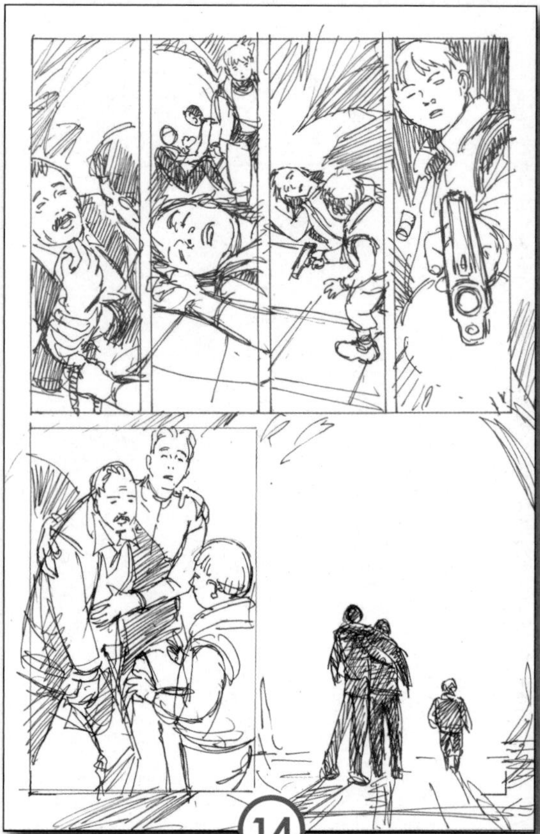

14

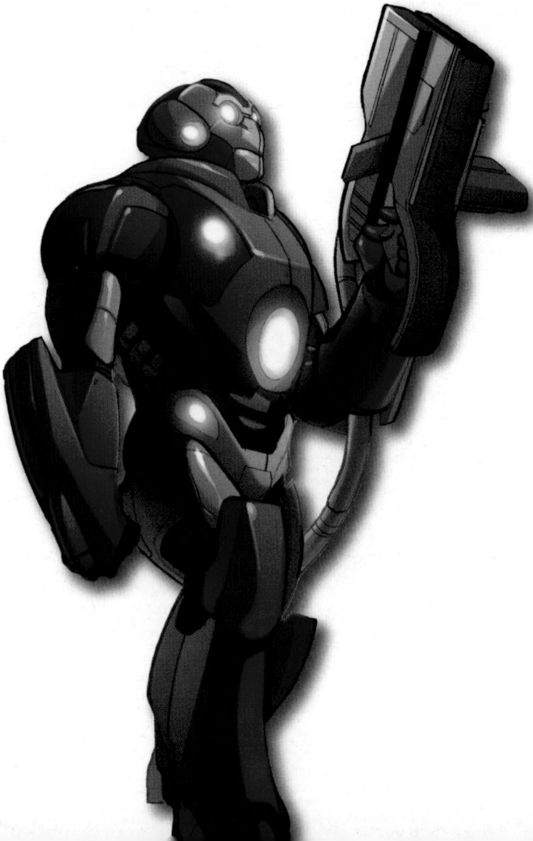